# A Medium Seldom Well Done

## *Critical Studies in Television*

**Second Edition**

**Patrick A. Trimble**

*Penn State University*

KENDALL/HUNT PUBLISHING COMPANY
4050 Westmark Drive    Dubuque, Iowa 52002

Cover image © 2003 PhotoDisc, Inc.

# Contents

# Introduction

The full quip from which the title of this text comes is "Television is a medium seldom well-done." It was spoken by a former vaudevillian and radio star named Fred Allen who was about to embark on a disastrous and brief television career in 1950. He was not photogenic enough for the medium and far too caustic to be coming into homes once a week. Most critics and scholars agreed with his statement in the 1950's because television was in its infancy and often crude and unsophisticated in its appearance. As television improved its technology, the product got slicker and more visually complex, but Allen's stinging remark continued to haunt the medium in the content it produced and recycled for home audiences. Television was now well-made but it was not worth watching.

Modern television has become even more lavish, but the question remains how well-done is it and to what purpose does all that expensive technology and sophistication serve? It has been easy to assume that television is a product for we viewers who watch an entertainment form free of charge except for those pesky commercials; and let's face it, often they are more entertaining than the programming. Most super bowls point that out. But what if the central purpose of television is not to amuse us; suppose we are not the major consumers of television but the product itself that the networks are delivering to advertisers? Allen's statement now takes on a dangerous and ironic tone; television is very well-done because it has so easily hidden its central purpose: to segment a mass audience into marketable groups of consumers that can be delivered fat and happy to a commercial where an advertiser can make his pitch.

The major problem with television is that we take it for granted. It is an appliance—a box if you will—that sits in our homes and in some subtle and not so subtle ways controls a great deal of the time and energy of our lives. That it does this with such incredible ease and our willing complicity only tends to make the process more invisible and naturalized. It happens so often in so many households that it is easy to accept as the normal way of doing things.

But the truth is that television may be the single most pervasive media influence in our lives. We wake to it in the morning, use it as a snooze alarm, and then lull ourselves to sleep with it at night; in between, we tell time by it and allow it to keep us company. It reflects our culture and yet takes us out of it, replacing day-to-day reality with a comforting and more controllable electronic version that suggests what we should wear, what we should eat, who we should socialize with, how we should solve our problems, and how we should go about attracting the opposite sex.

The purpose of this text is to examine, as thoroughly as possible, the conventions, formats and styles of television to understand its history and perhaps predict its future. More important it tries to give the reader an idea of television's effects on our society and the process by which it helps shape and control the ideological values of the individual watching it. All television, from the loftiest programming to the lowliest commercial, carries ideological meaning; **ideology** is the set of values, often subconscious, that a culture or individual lives by. Ideology can be as codified as a set of laws written in a text or it can be as informal and unspoken as people understanding how they are supposed to dress and act in certain social situations. Cultural ideologies are passed on from generation to generation through education, religion, social, familial, or peer systems, and, certainly not least important, through our mass media.

Media, i.e. television, reflects who and what we are, therefore, it reflects and reaffirms our basic social values. Many of those values are fine in the cultural order: love of family, nation, respect for individuality, belief in moral codes of conduct. But ideologies can also be problematic when they become a naturalized means of oppression. It seemed natural in the 1950's to believe that a woman's place was in the home, married, and mother to a family; this was showcased in media as the ideal goal of a young woman and any thoughts of a career or independent lifestyle was treated as social rebellion or as something laughable. Television, in programs like *I Love Lucy*, *Leave It to Beaver*, and *Father Knows Best* reaffirmed that belief so any young woman who preferred a career over marriage and a family was viewed with suspicion and scorn. While we may boast that our modern times are more enlightened, such ideologies have not completely disappeared and when they do, new conventions, equally oppressive, have risen to take their place. Today, a young woman wishing success in the business world must be, according to television, thin and attractive so that her appearance in a male world will not compromise her femininity and ability to attract a worthy male. Men may be recommended for their intellect and self-awareness, but women are still judged by appearance. The successful career women in modern television, like *Ally McBeal* and the young female doctor on a show like *Providence,* must be stylish, attractive, and nurturing, the same attributes that Lucy Ricardo, June Cleaver, and Margaret Anderson had to have.

In our historic past minorities were often depicted as second-class citizens or inferior in other ways. Modern television, on its surface, suggests that this problem no longer exist or that things have gotten noticeably better. A program like *Cosby* shows a world devoid of racial anger or hatred. Ideologies do change over time, but it would be a great mistake to think that oppressive beliefs simply go away or, because we ourselves do not believe them, that all other people think like we do. The values accepted and supported by the majority of the culture, or by those who are in the best positions of power to dictate and control media, is called the **dominant ideology**. Clearly, the ability of social groups or individuals to abuse these ideological concerns is great since controlling ideology is a certain means to maintain social control and power. Dominant ideologies are passed down through educational and organizational and familial processes but they may or may not be as direct and defined. As students sit in a classroom, they learn by watching and role-modeling what is the correct means to speak in class. Someone talking out of turn will be chastised or even dismissed while the student who raises their hand and speaks in an orderly, respectful manner will gain the approval of the teacher as well as the tacit acknowledgment of the rest of the class. A student who raises their hand but does not directly respond to the question or rambles on at length with little direction will, if they listen, soon hear the disapproval of the peer group and finally the teacher. To belong and win approval, we conform; not to do so becomes an act of social rebellion. This process of learning applies to all of our organizational and familial interactions and also ultimately media.

Television is happy to cater to the dominant ideologies but it does not seek social conformity but rather a consumer climate that guarantees profit. This means that the ideologies presented on television are there to reassure us with a comfortable vision of the world so that we will buy the advertised goods. Since profit is the bottom line, networks are happy to cater to the public needs even if this means that much of its images and messages are oppressive or exclusive of certain parts of our society. The cultural elite, who own most of the mass media in the nation, do not perceive themselves as purveyors of potentially damaging ideologies; they see the dominant values of the society as the norm and wish to maintain that normalcy since it in turn supports the social order. This also guarantees they continue to function at the top of the social ladder. Television, with its emphasis on consumerism, serves the capitalist system which is the basis of the society; so not only do media producers make large profits from television, they also, in their own minds, serve the social good. No one holds a gun to our heads to buy things; but television tells us that happy, well-adjusted families and individuals own appliances and cars and homes. It is not surprising then that when social unrest and public riots occur, citizens do not storm the halls of government or the courts but rather the local appliance stores to get their piece of the American Dream.

## THE PERVASIVENESS OF TELEVISION

The question is how pervasive is television? *The Statistical Abstracts for the United States* for 2000, published by the U.S. Census Bureau states that for 1998, 98.3% of all American households had television, more than had indoor toilets; this was 98 million households that contained approximately 235 million television sets or roughly 2.4 television sets per home. 84.6% have VCRs and 67.2% have cable. By the year 2003, the average number of hours an adult person is projected to watch television is over 1,610 hours per year. A normal high school student at the time of graduation would have spent 15,000 hours in the class room but over 18,000 hours in front a television.

What does all this mean to the producers of television? The gross domestic income for the television broadcasting industry for 1998 was an estimated $26, 551,000,000 with cable and pay television services contributing another estimated $35,231,000,000—huge potential profits are made from the medium. The fact is that television is present in most people's lives, and while it may not be the most powerful or singular influence in a person's day, it does have a real ideological and social impact. The problem is not just that people may watch too much television, but the way we watch television can also be a problem.

First, we need to ask why do people watch television. The first and probably foremost reason is **escapism**. Like any entertainment form, television takes us out of our mundane lives and allows us to enter into an idealistic world of fantasy where emotional and social problems have no immediate or profound effect on our lives. We can witness the trauma of *ER* and experience the stress and pain without putting ourselves at risk. Most television content gives us only a momentary catharsis or purging of emotions; we can watch a murder mystery, experience the effects of pity and fear, thrill to the chase and capture, and then a sense of satisfaction at the resolution. We risk nothing, and the ramifications of the story fade in moments as we move on to another program or something else in our lives. Our lives can be stressful, unpleasant, or sometimes just numbingly routine; television allows us to escape from ourselves, allowing us to laugh, cry, cheer, or boo without true emotional commitment. Nor do we have to work at this involvement since most television reduces experience to recognizable formulas and results we can all identify with. Thus, on television, the world is always a comfortable, happy place: the police always catch the bad guys, true love always finds a way, family always comes together to solve the emotional crisis; shows where this does not happen are not seen and seldom last long enough to reach a wide popular appeal.

Television is also a source of **information**. On a simple level, it supplements more traditional forms of education: children's educational programs, news and documentary shows, talk shows, etc. But television also gives us a **shared knowledge**—a common ground of understanding concerning ideologies and social behavior. So much of what we know in our daily lives is information gained and reinforced by the programming on television. A television sitcom might suggest what clothes we should wear if we want to fit in, how to act in specific situations, how to relate to other people in ways that are socially acceptable. This is the background information of all television content, the socialization factor that helps create and pass on the ideological content discussed early. We learn something of how the legal system works by watching mysteries, what foreign climates look like viewing travelogues and adventure shows, and commercials demonstrate a world of new products that will improve the quality of our lives. But is this information accurate? Not necessarily and we are bombarded with information every day and must learn selectivity if we are to remain afloat of the sea of misinformation that the media represents.

Television can then give us a sense of a **communal experience** even as it is destroying most conventional forms of community. Home entertainment has meant that people no longer go out as much for forms of entertainment which in turn means we do not have to interact with other people to any great degree. Instead of going to a movie or play where we have to become one of a larger audience, we can sit alone at home and be entertained. Town hall meetings, box socials, community dances have declined because to go out is more work than staying in and watching television. Still, television has also become an excuse to gather together to watch sports programs like the Super Bowl or World Series, special programming events like the Academy Awards or the last episode of a popular favorite, like *Seinfeld*. Really popular shows, like *Who Wants to Be A Millionaire* and *Survivor*, develop cult followings and people come together to share the viewing experience. Often the show itself is a common link among members of an outsider community that allows them to share a common experience; for example, Julie D'Acci wrote in her 1987 analysis of the show, *Cagney and Lacey*, how gay and lesbian groups gathered together to watch the program, reinterpreting its narratives about two female police partners/friends to fit their own visions of the world. But television can also bring individuals unknown to one another together to watch a common experience; people watching a game in a sports bar become a community while students will gather in a university's television room to watch soap operas with complete strangers.

Individually, television has also become a form of **companionship** for many people. It is a window on the outside world for invalids and shut-ins, for the lonely and disenfranchised. It is a voice or presence in an otherwise empty room; when asked in class, so many students claim they will often return home to an empty apartment or dormitory room and the first thing they do is turn on the television or radio. It is a connection to others even if they are not physically present. The television can become a part of our daily routine; some people tell time by it, others check the local weather, and still many more watch long running programs and think of the characters on them as long time friends.

A final reason people watch television has to do with all of the above. Television reaffirms our basic ideologies, suggesting again and again that what we should think, believe, and feel is okay. We watch television that we can identify with, meaning that we look for characters and shows that most reflect our own vision of the world. Therefore, a devout individual would see a program like *Touched By An Angel* and be comforted by its messages of divine guidance and spiritual caring. High school and college age viewers are attracted to shows *Dawson's Creek* and *Buffy the Vampire Slayer* because they resonate with a world vision teenagers and young adults want to identify with. The centrally ideological basis is, as stated before, almost always the values of the massive white, young, middle-class audience, so most of television reflects those particular values. And since men are the most prominent producers of television content, their tastes are reflected as well.

This means that a sitcom like *Friends* is a perfect example of this ideological mirror: the group of friends are all white, youthful, and singularly middle class; although the series takes place in New York, African-Americans or any other minorities, are rarely present. The friends have jobs that are delineated along strict gender lines: the males are Ross, a paleontologist, Chandler, a middle management corporate executive, and Joey, the most child-like of the men, a struggling actor. But the females have jobs more in keeping with the dominant ideological identities of women: Rachel is first a waitress then a shopper and lower management designer for Ralph Lauren, Monica is a chef, and Phoebe is a masseur. Despite a projected breezy sense of modern sexuality, the goal of all the women is to find Mr. Right and ultimately settle down to married life. In the course of the program, the men are allowed a great deal of latitude with their sexuality, often, as in the case of Joey, having multiple sexual partners with no social stigma attached; but when a female settles into an openly sexual relationship, she is shown to be neurotic, angst-ridden, or desperate, and the partnership is doomed to failure. The ideological messages are traditional despite the nod to modernity: women are unable to function well in the workplace, are poor at handling finances, and are emotionally dependent on the presence of men in their lives. The only kind of relationship allowed is the one where Chandler and Monica fall in love and move on a steady course towards marriage.

Television is filled with numerous examples like this. The narratives and ideological messages are built into the genre forms and production methods of the medium.

The producers of *Friends* understand television comedy is ultimately about failure; happy, well-adjusted lives do not lend themselves to humor so failed love lives are natural in the comedic formula. Also, you cannot develop multiple relationships in a half hour format—too many situations or characters will only confuse the audience and hurt ratings. Audience expectations must be satisfied. When Ross and Rachel break up and Ross has a brief affair with another woman, the audience accepts this as a male prerogative the character does not lose a great deal of audience sympathy. But if it were Rachel who had the affair (she even briefly flirts with another co-worker but rejects him out of loyalty to Ross), then the program risks bucking the double standard of sexuality in our culture, and Rachel becomes denoted as immoral.

This suggests that television is a tool for reaffirmation not enlightenment. Ideology can change over time, but the process is slow and often stagnant. Media critic Todd Gitlin labeled the process **inoculation**, meaning that like a medical inoculation, television allows small increments of new or radical thinking to get into the mainstream. If the programming survives this small injection, then more can be applied but only as long as the audiences do not find it moralizing or intrusive on their beliefs. Thus, in the 1950's and 1960's, it was almost unheard of to depict minorities or alternative lifestyles on television. Not only were producers afraid of offending their predominantly white, heterosexual audience, but they also assumed minority audiences were not a major purchasing power for advertising. As the diverse audience became perceived more and more as a purchasing power in the 1970's and beyond, more and more images of minority and alternative lifestyles appeared, but always with an understanding that the bulk of the viewing audience is still white middle class. Today we have programs that are predominantly African-American, but it is important to note that these shows are usually comedies and filled with comic stereotyping associated with the minority lifestyle. A show like *Cosby* can become an enormous success with cross-over audiences only as long as it displays a white middle class vision of Black America. Someone unfamiliar with American society and watching *Cosby* could only assume that racial assimilation was the norm; the show seldom grappled with racial or ethnic conflicts because white audiences did not want to be reminded that racial inequalities still exist within our society.

## THE DANGERS OF TELEVISION

The critical studies approach to media suggests that there are dangers inherent in the indiscriminate viewing of television. If you ask most people what these dangers are, they will answer too much sex and violence without fully understanding how the media work or how individuals perceive television. Quantitative clinical psychologists used to argue that indiscriminate television viewing habits promote negative role models which children especially can readily imitate. This emphasis on what was called **short-term effects** stated that impressionable minds will copy events and actions they witness on television. Children seeing violence in the media become prone to do violence; thus, after seeing a network premiere of a film entitled *Fuzz* in the early 1970's, teenagers in several major cities imitate a plot device where youths douse homeless people with kerosene and ignite them in a copycat manner; in the mid-

1990's, a five-year old boy watching *Beavis and Butthead* observes the characters building a fire and copies their actions inside his family's mobile home, igniting a blaze that kills his two-year-old sister.

At least that is how the media reported these items, but they were simplifying and confusing the real statistics concerning cultural violence. The young males caught in the 1970's dousing the homeless all had criminal records, histories of violence and abuse in their families, and poor social skills. The five-year old was left home alone with his sister while his single mother went with friends to a local bar for some drinks. The idea of copying and short-term effects is only true in a remarkably small percentage of people, those who already have a proclivity towards anti-social behavior to begin with. As stated before, we are products of a wide range of influences, the media being only one that includes families, educational systems, religious communities, peer groups, and all. Most viewers, watching television violence, do not imitate it because all these other social pressures concerning violence are in place. For years, researchers have pointed to Super Bowl Sunday as the day in America when domestic violence is most likely to occur; we must ask ourselves is it the violence of the televised game itself or the social context of the event, the incredible amount of liquor consumption, the large amount of betting that takes place, or some other factor not yet recognized? Short-term effects are speculative at best.

The real danger of television viewing is what scholars are beginning to understand as **long-term effects**. It is not a singular act of violence or sexual or racial stereotyping that causes the problem but an overarching constant exposure to such events over long periods of time. This does not mean that we wish to imitate violence, but rather than our perceptions and feelings towards violence can be shaped by overexposure to it in the media. The tendency in the modern world is to see violence as a necessary evil, or worse, that the people who are victimized by violence somehow deserve it. Watching the news, we witness street kids killing one another over drugs. Rather than analyze the causes of the violence—the breakdown of traditional family models, inner city poverty, easy assess to guns, racism—television displays the visual images with the purpose of horrifying and titillating us at the same time. We are curious about that world yet at the same time we are fearful as well; the medium allows us to distance ourselves from the acts; we are seeing it yet not experiencing it; therefore, we approach it with the idea that it could not happen to us because we would not allow ourselves to be put in such a position of danger. Either we blame the individuals caught in the violence or we blame modern society in general in what media scholar George Gerbner called **the mean world syndrome**. Here, the world as seen through television, is a dark and forbidden place where violence becomes the normal experience of everyday life. In such a world, especially as depicted on the six o'-clock news, the people we see victimized seem to deserve that victimization because they are not as cautious, intelligent, or moralistic as we are; we take a defensive comfort in assuming from our distance that somehow they deserve what they get. The tube then desensitizes us towards violence by the exposure of this dark world over and over again until we, as individuals and a culture, literally become indifferent to it.

Another problem with television is **mainstreaming**. Because television always seeks to maximize profits, the bulk of its content is aimed at the largest possible buying audience—the white middle class. Not wishing to offend that massive audience means eliminating radical or extreme cultural and political viewpoints. What gets on the air is comfortable and supportive of the consumers; diversity is replaced by homogenized content all designed to not offend the buying public. More to the point, this means that minority viewpoints are often ignored or misrepresented because they do not fit the norm. This exclusion is not because television producers are inherently racist, but because they seldom see minority markets as profitable to advertisers. Cable's concept of **narrowcasting**, gearing content to more restricted special interest audiences, might potentially change all this but so far has not done so. While the Black Entertainment Network exists to serve the needs of an African-American audience, compare it to the number of cooking, travel, and arts channels aimed at wealthy upper middle class viewers. It is less about race than economics but the results are the same. A segment of the viewing audience gets short-ended or ignored.

Worse, when minority or alternative images do appear in television, they tend to be, as already stated, negative images. This is especially problematic because of **underrepresentation**. If a white male is made fun of on a situation comedy, no one can complain because there are multiple images of white males—some good, some bad—on the tube. But because there are so few images of minorities on television, those that do appear tend to become representative of large parts of our culture. There are no counter-balancing images of black males to popular shows like *The Fresh Prince of Bel Air, Martin,* and *Living Single.* Black males are predominantly depicted as street-educated, sexually starved buffoons. On a show like *Family Matters*, the two young black males are divided into the jock mentality of the son, Eddie, and the intelligent but ultra-nerdy Steve Urkel, the latter being one of the most cartoonish and least human characters ever created for television. The same is true for other minorities as well: people watching the antics of the gay male characters on *Will & Grace* can only assume that they are representative of all gay males because they are very few contradictory images in the media.

This homogenization of ideology benefits what many critics feel is the most damaging of negative effects of television: the creation of **conspicous consumerism**. Scholars like Sut Jhally argue that the major product sold on television is not beer or automobiles but consumerism itself. Television creates a climate of consumerism, not just in its advertising but in all aspects of content. Television sells us an idealized vision of American life designed to best showcase all the best materialistic aspects of our culture. Situation comedies like *Friends* and prime-time soap operas like *Dawson's Creek* present lifestyles that equate happiness with material comforts. Each week, often while looking for work, the women of *Friends* still dress in the latest fashions complete with ever changing hairdos and make-up essentials. No one on *Dawson's Creek* ever drives anything less than the most recent makes of stylish cars, and their homes are never lacking for the want of a television, microwave, cuisinart blender, or the latest in stereo equipment. That these are beautiful people living exciting, often rewarding lives only makes the accumulation of these material things more desirable. Well-adjusted families own their own homes, have two-car garages, possess the latest technologies in their recreation rooms, their kitchens and bathrooms. Again, this is a long-term effects problem since constant exposure over a long period of time to this material world re-enforces the basic tenets of a capitalist society: the society only survives as long as products are produced and marketed to a mass audience. On the surface, the philosophy behind all this seems to benefit everyone. But some critics point to contemporary materialism as a cause of our culture's spiritual bankruptcy. As a culture, we too often equate financial success with personal satisfaction, an equation that too often leads to disenchantment and mid-life crises. This is very problematic for the poor who generally watch more television than the wealthy. On the tube they see a world of luxury and security they cannot attain, but even the middle class can feel a sense of frustration because our lives are not like those on television. We are constantly reminded that we are not those exciting and dramatically idealized families, and our own lives lack the glitter and glamour of that world. So we buy things to emulate that world and seek to better ourselves by the accumulation of wealth when in fact the spiritual and emotional needs of our lives go begging. For critics of television, this becomes a vicious cycle.

Perhaps the most-cited danger of television is its passivity. Unlike its predecessors, the movies and radio, television does not require imagination or any real kind of involvement. Radio demanded people listen to the programs and complete mental pictures of what they heard; the sheer act of going out to a movie and enjoying it with a crowd of other people demanded more active participation than television does. Like any true popular art, it was created as a disposable medium, meant to be consumed and then forgotten. It brings to our homes all the sound, color, dramatic cues and tensions we might want and asks little of us in return. Our only responsibilities are turning the set on and switching the channels when we get bored. It delivers an immediate impact that gives the viewer a vicarious thrill and maintains that rapid pace of entertainment for fear of losing the audience; the speed of storytelling and editing has greatly picked up over the last few decades because producers know how short attention spans can be, especially when audiences are expecting immediate satisfaction. Clinical studies demonstrate that the more children watch this kind of medium, the less likely they are to do other, more active things such as play sports or read or communicate with other people. Such children tend to be more overweight (they do not exercise) and will lag behind the others in school (lacking their communications skills) who do not spend as much time watching the tube.

All these perceived dangers are theoretical at best, but we do know that television is changing our social lives. Television loses all potential negative effects when we choose to view it critically. The purpose of this text, therefore, is to stimulate the reader into a more active, aggressive consumption of television, one that understands how the medium works, what its most basic intentions are, and what its impact can be on us as viewers. This critical studies approach is designed to teach the form and techniques of television so that if manipulation does occur, we the audience can be prepared for its intent and make up our own minds in terms of what ideologies and values we want to believe. More to the point, by being a better audience, we can hope to change the medium for the better, demanding more diversity and purpose, wanting better informational programming, and turning the watching experience into something positive and life-affirming.

# Introduction to Robert C. Toll's "The Entertainment Machine in the Home: The Phonograph, Radio, and Television as Media"

Robert Toll is one of America's foremost historians on mass media and the popular arts. His specialty has been nineteenth century popular art forms like vaudeville and the burlesque, but in *The Entertainment Machine*, he applied his skills to the emergence of new technology at the turn of the twentieth century and how popular culture becomes mass media. His focus is on three machines that change the way we live our lives: the phonograph, the radio, and the television.

Toll follows media scholar Marshal McLuhan's dictum that no new medium can appear spontaneously without benefit of earlier media. His approach is valid. Radio in the home was very much what the phonograph had been before it, and television, in its infancy, was little more than radio with pictures. Each new medium appropriates the structure, style, and content of the old so that quite literally, there is no form of television program today that did not first appear on radio. Toll's strength is as an historian so this chapter tends to focus on a great many dates and names. The fact is the chapter was assigned because the professor **does not want to encourage** students to memorize names and dates. This opening text is a handy source of historical background that can be referred to throughout the semester but names and dates are just that: background information to the far more important theories and concepts that this class will deal with. Because of this, and the fact that this is the first reading that comes so soon in the course, there will be no questions on this chapter.

# The Entertainment Machine in the Home: The Phonograph, Radio, and Television as Media

"The machine that talks—and laughs, sings, plays, and reproduces all sound," boasted advertisements for the Columbia Phonograph Company in 1896. The company bragged that its new entertainment machine was "so simple that even a child can make it pour forth the most enchanting selections of the world's greatest Musician, Singers, Actors, and Speakers." To illustrate the joys of the "entertainer of which one never tires," Columbia pictured three generations of a model American family enjoying music in their parlor. This was certainly nothing new in the 1890s. What *was* new was that the family was not gathered around a piano making its own music, but was seated quietly, its attention fixed on the horn of the phonograph that was providing the family's entertainment.[1]

For the first time an inexpensive, easy-to-operate entertainment machine was bringing professional performances into the average American home. This development signaled the beginning of changes in entertainment that were to be even more fundamental and profound than those caused by motion pictures. Late-nineteenth-century Americans had become accustomed to going to theaters for an incredibly rich variety of live entertainment. When movies replaced live performances, people continued to leave their homes to get their entertainment. Until the late 1890s only members of the upper class could afford to hire entertainers to perform in their homes. But at about the same time motion pictures were being developed, the phono-

graph began to bring the sound of show business into common people's living rooms. Ultimately, this had a great influence on American family life as well as on show business. But entertainment machines developed much more slowly in the home than they did in the theater. The story of entertainment can be divided into three roughly equal twenty-five-year periods, each dominated by a different medium—the phonograph, radio, and television.

Like the motion picture, the phonograph—using that word as a generic term for a machine that replays recorded sound—did not become a commercial product until twenty years after its invention. Thomas A. Edison had patented a "talking machine" in 1877, but it was not until the early 1890s that the phonograph was marketed for home entertainment, partially because Edison had originally conceived of it as a dictaphone-like tool for business. Early phonographs used wax cylinders that could both record and replay sound, but could do neither effectively. The range, quality, and diversity of early acoustic recording were severely limited by the period's crude technology. People had to perform directly into a phonograph horn which vibrated a stylus that mechanically cut grooves into a wax cylinder. The clarity and volume of the recording depended totally on the intensity and pitch of the performance. Though people could make their own recordings at home with blank cylinders, the public quickly showed its preference for listening to professional performers who had the strong, clear sounds needed to record effectively on the period's limited technology. John Philip Sousa and his military bands, May Irwin, the hard-belting "Coon Shouter," Russell Hinting with his "Casey" monologues, black whistler George W. Johnson, and Enrico Caruso, the great operatic tenor soon became popular recording stars. When permanently grooved, easily handled, and conveniently stored disc recording went on the market the public snapped them up even though discs could not be used to make recordings at home. By World War I discs marketed by Victor and Columbia were more popular than cylinders.

The popularity of records changed the popular music business. When the phonograph became a major source of music in the home, sales of sheet music plummeted, and popular songs became musically more complex but shorter to fit the three-minute playing time of records. Beginning in 1914 the record and phonograph businesses boomed as America was swept by new dance crazes such as the "Grizzly Bear," "Fox Trot," and "Tango," which were done to complicated ragtime and Latin rhythms. Although this music was difficult to play on a piano, it was easy to play on a phonograph. The public bought records and the new entertainment machines as quickly as they could be produced, and there was no lack of production. In 1912 only Victor, Columbia, and Edison made phonographs; by 1919 nearly 200 companies turned out some 2 million phonographs, a 200 percent increase in five years.

Business got even better after World War I when brassy Dixieland jazz, which recorded well, captured the public's fancy, and records provided the unfamiliar and difficult music for popular dances like the "Black Bottom" and the "Charleston." Besides serving the general, national market, record companies of the 1920s also discovered lucrative regional and ethnic markets in country music, which appealed primarily to white Southerners, and in blues and jazz, which appealed primarily to black people. Record sales exceeded 100 million in 1921 and

held up until the late 1920s. But in the early 1920s, the static-laden sounds of radio were growing clearer, stronger, more ominous for the phonograph and record businesses, and more promising for the public.

At the turn of the twentieth century the air had begun to come alive with the transmissions of Guglielmo Marconi's "Wireless Telegraph," which at first broadcast only Morse code. Before World War I amateur radio enthusiasts around the country broadcast voices and records, but the companies that invested in radio were interested in wireless communication with ships, not in entertainment. Until 1920 radio in America remained essentially a telegraph without wires, a business dominated by a few major companies—Radio Corporation of America (RCA), General Electric (GE), Westinghouse, and American Telephone and Telegraph (AT&T), which had entered the field in case a wireless telephone developed. The only entertainment machines in the average American home were phonographs and pianos, particularly player pianos, which become very popular after 1900. Radio only began to take its familiar form in 1920 when, besides the many amateur radio stations, Westinghouse started daily broadcasts in Pittsburgh to gain publicity and to create demand for simple-to-operate, self-contained radio sets similar to those the company had made for the military during World War. Professional broadcasting began when Westinghouse's KDKA took to the air. Envisioning "limitless opportunity" if it could interest the general public in radio, Westinghouse tried to attract the largest possible listening audiences. After a good initial response, the company expanded into other major metropolitan areas with powerful stations in Newark, Chicago, and Springfield, Massachusetts, where it manufactured its home crystal sets.

Radio became a popular fad in 1922. By the end of that year the federal government had licensed 670 stations, and sales of mass-produced radio sets and parts reached $60 million, a total that mushroomed to $358 million in 1924 and kept growing. The novelty of radio was probably its greatest initial appeal. Early stations broadcast almost anything they could get inexpensively. "The talent would come in to the office and tell us what they could do," a veteran of WWJ in Detroit recalled of the chaos of 1922. "We didn't rehearse them, we took their word for it."[2] Organizations of all sorts ran radio stations—newspapers, universities, churches, hotels, department stores, laundries, and even a poultry farm and a stockyard. But *none* of these stations directly earned *any* money for its owner. The owners paid the costs of broadcasting to gain the goodwill of listeners. The radio manufacturers—Westinghouse, RCA, and GE—opened powerful stations around the country to stimulate sales of their radio sets, which theoretically benefited all the companies by increasing general demand. But by then with listeners in many areas able to choose among programs, stations began to compete for audiences by offering more appealing shows. The competition rapidly drove up the costs of broadcasting.

Once the initial burst of radio sales began to level off, the manufacturers had to find a new method of paying for the rising expenses of broadcasting. Several solutions to this problem were discussed within the industry in 1922. None was adopted, but the idea of selling advertising to pay the bills seemed repugnant to many people, including Secretary of Commerce Herbert Hoover, whose department controlled radio licensing. "It is inconceivable," Hoover argued in 1922, "that we should allow so great a possibility for service, for news, for entertainment, for education to be drowned in advertising chatter."[3] Yet the chatter was already beginning.

AT&T which initially had invested in radio in case it became part of the telephone business decided to enter broadcasting in 1922. The company had no radio equipment to sell, so when it announced it was entering "public radiotelephone broadcasting," it had another product in mind. "We, the telephone company, were to provide no programs," recalled one of its executives. "The public was to come in. Any-

one who had a message for the world or wished to entertain was to come in and pay their money as they would upon coming into a telephone booth, address the world, and go out."[4] Just as AT&T provided the telephone facilities, not the phone calls, it would provide only the "toll-broadcasting" facilities, not the content of the broadcasts. AT&T's first station, WEAF in New York, went on the air in August 1992, and in its first two months sold $550 of broadcast time to businesses. It was $550 more than any other station had ever directly earned. The businesses—an apartment complex, an oil company, and American Express—used their time to talk to the audience. There was no other entertainment. But in its unsold time WEAF, using AT&T's long-distance telephone lines to pick up operas, concerts, stage shows, and football games from as far away as Chicago, provided programming that built a large listening audience and convinced more businesses to use radio to reach the public.

Concerned about the stigma of obvious advertising, AT&T insisted that its paying customers not mention their product's price or color or their store's location. No samples were to be offered, and nothing even potentially offensive was to be said. WEAF executives even postponed a talk by a toothpaste company while they decided whether anything as intimate as brushing teeth should be discussed on the air. But the station soon had to contend with professional pitchmen who bought radio time, resold segments to businesses, and used the purchased time to deliver their messages for them. Actor Bruce Reynolds made a lot of money doing this until WEAF found his pitches too blatant and urged him to "be more subtle so that the listeners won't realize it's advertising." WEAF finally refused to sell him time. When Reynolds suggested such sponsored talks to another station, its outraged executives replied, "We wouldn't prostitute our station by accepting outside advertising."[5] WEAF soon found a way to make money and to avoid objectionable sales pitches by persuading firms to buy air time and use it to broadcast entertainment that carried only the sponsor's name. There were no sales pitches. This discreet approach produced groups like the Clicquot Club Eskimos, Gold Dust Twins, A&P Gypsies, Best Food Boys, and Ipana Troubadours.

In December 1923 WEAF broadcast a new show that indicated the direction sponsored programs would take. The *Eveready Hour*, paid for by Eveready batteries, was a thoroughly professional, well-rehearsed program that evolved into a varied series of concerts, dramas, variety shows, and dance music. The show also had a major impact on the structure of broadcasting. Eveready got such favorable response to its programs on WEAF that the company sent the performers out to other stations to do additional broadcasts, which was like sending shows on tour and charging no admission fees. As the Eveready productions grew more elaborate and expensive this method of reaching more audiences proved impractical, especially when radio offered an inexpensive alternative. By linking stations with telephone lines, a single performance could be broadcast simultaneously on a network of stations with the sponsor buying time on each station. That is what Eveready did. By the end of 1923 AT&T had a six-station network in operation. This was a major step toward developing the unique capability of the new entertainment machine to blanket the nation with the same show at the same time. Unlike any previous entertainment medium, radio had the potential to be everywhere at once.

By 1925 at the end of the first stage of the development of entertainment machines in the home, phonographs and recordings had matured into a major popular medium while radio was still in an experimental phase, exploring the possibilities of selling advertising to businesses, broadcasting well-produced shows, and linking stations into networks. But it was on the eve of an explosion that would make radio a major force in popular entertainment.

The second major period in the development of entertainment machines in the home, a period dominated by radio, began in 1926 with the formation of the first national radio network. AT&T, which had created commercial broadcasting and the first radio network, left radio in 1925 when it sold WEAF to a new network, the National Broadcasting Company (NBC), which was owned by RCA, GE, and Westinghouse. In November 1926 NBC made a spectacular debut with a star-studded broadcast that showcased the unique potential of radio by originating parts of the show in New York, Chicago and Kansas City, among other locations. The debut was broadcast by twenty-six stations to as many as 12 million people. Within a year NBC had expanded to two separate networks, designated as red and blue, with over 100 stations, most of them independently owned and voluntarily affiliated with NBC. NBC paid its affiliates to broadcast nationally sponsored shows and charged its affiliates for unsponsored shows that the stations could sell locally. But NBC soon faced outside competition.

United Independent Broadcasters, Inc. (UIB) began as a financially wobbly network in 1926. Within a year, the Columbia Phonograph Company, pressured by radio's inroads into the record business, invested in debt-ridden UIB and formed the Columbia Phonograph Broadcasting System, which was reorganized and renamed the Columbia Broadcasting System (CBS). The new network barely survived until William S. Paley, the twenty-seven-year-old son of a wealthy family, bought it in 1928. After putting CBS on solid footing, Paley rapidly expanded the network. Unlike NBC, which charged its affiliates for unsponsored shows that they could sell to local sponsors, CBS *gave* these money-making programs to its affiliates in exchange for the right to preempt the affiliates' broadcast time which the network paid for. This system attracted stations and allowed Paley to guarantee sponsors national exposure on the entire CBS network, which NBC, unable to preempt affliates' local time, could not do. From 19 stations in 1928 CBS grew to 79 stations in 1931 and for the first time made more money than NBC. The competition changed advertising policies. NBC, priding itself on its decorum, maintained a long list of taboo words and would not let sponsors mention prices. CBS had no such qualms. George Washington Hill of the American Tobacco Company, who believed listeners remembered irritating commercials, could say what he wanted on CBS. What he wanted to say was that his Cremo cigars cost five cents and that "there is no spit in Cremo!" NBC began to adopt CBS's policies. Advertisers were taking control of radio away from broadcasters.

Radio was a unique entertainment medium that required a completely new method of financing, a method that was another major step in the destruction of the once intimate relationship between audiences and performers. Before radio, producers had created entertainment and tried to convince the public to buy tickets or records. The revenues paid the bills and provided the profits. This was as true for Adolph Zukor's Paramount Pictures as it was for Barnum and Bailey's Greatest Show on Earth. The public paid the piper and called the tune. In the first stage of the modern entertainment revolution, phonographs and motion picture projectors presented previously recorded and mass-produced entertainment, which eliminated interaction between patron and performer. But the success for these entertainment machines still required producers who understood show business and popular tastes. Radio was *totally* different. Businesses, which had nothing to do with entertainment, bought shows and paid to broadcast them to people who received the entertainment free of charge. Like medicine shows radio programs were given away to draw crowds so a pitchman could sell his wares. "The play is not the thing," observed veteran radio actress Mary Jane Higby. "The sponsor's message is the thing and no radio or television actor can ever forget it."[6]

By the early 1930s radio was controlled by a new breed of experts who specialized in meeting the needs of the people who paid radio's bills—the sponsors. Since the purpose of the radio program was to draw a large audience to hear the sponsor's commercials, there had to be a new way to judge the size of a show's audience. Obviously it was impossible to count heads or ticket stubs. In 1930 Archibald Crossley formed the first radio rating service. Using telephone interviews of a small population sample, Crossley projected the size of shows' audiences. Over the years rating systems grew increasingly refined and sophisticated and exerted a powerful influence on sponsors' decisions about what radio time and shows to buy. But even at their best, even if ratings experts could determine precisely how many people listened to each show, they could not tell how well the shows helped sell the sponsors' products. There certainly were some striking examples of what radio advertising could do. La Palina cigar sales jumped from 400,000 to a million a day after a 1928 radio advertising campaign, and Pepsodent toothpaste tripled in sales within weeks of Procter & Gamble's sponsoring of *Amos 'n' Andy*, radio's greatest early hit. Even though there was rarely such clear evidence of radio's sales effectiveness, many businesses found advertising on radio irresistible because the entertainment machine reached into the homes of millions of people across the nation. But radio advertising was also filled with uncertainty, insecurity, and anxiety for sponsors who turned for help to the experts—in this case advertising agencies.

Since the purpose of paying for the production of programs and for the time to broadcast them was to sell their products, businesses in the 1930s came to rely on advertising agencies not only to design the best commercials and select the right broadcast time, but also to *create* shows that would attract the right sorts of audiences. Advertising agencies produced almost all sponsored network radio shows. When an agency interested a client in radio, the agency, whose expertise was advertising not entertaining, began to produce a show. After it had chosen the show's concept, writers, and actors, a producer-director, often a member of the agency staff, developed a "pilot" show, while the agency secured an option on a broadcast time and prepared advertising copy. When the entire production was completed and rehearsed, it was auditioned for the sponsor, adjusted to his tastes, and, if accepted by the sponsor, was booked for thirteen weeks on a network. Although networks had to approve the programs the agencies created for the sponsors, that approval had become virtually automatic by 1932.

The commercial basis of radio did not seem to bother the public. In 1945 a public opinion poll asked Americans: "If your radio programs could be produced without advertising, would you prefer it that way?" An astounding 62 percent of the people interviewed, nearly two out of every three people, said *no*. They would *not* prefer programs without advertising. About half explained that commercials did not interfere with their enjoyment of the programs, and nearly a quarter of the people said they liked the advertising because "it tells me about the things I want to buy."[7] But perhaps the major reason that the public preferred radio programs with commercials was that most Americans first bought radios in the late 1920s and early 1930s when commercially sponsored, top-notch entertainment took over the airwaves. Many people probably felt that ads and good radio shows were inextricably linked and that removing one might remove the other.

In 1928 network radio was dominated by music, especially popular dance music, with a sprinkling of dramatic series. Then radio programming was permanently changed by the incredible popularity of *Amos 'n' Andy*, in which two white men acted out the comic exploits of two black men, their families, and their friends. Though using exaggerated black stereotypes, caricatures, and dialects that hearkened back to the minstrel show, the show also portrayed trusting, hard-working Amos and scheming, lazy Andy as appealing *people* with families and feeling, people fighting gamely to survive in the bleak despair of the Great Depression. The plots unfolded slowly through months of daily fifteen-minute episodes, a format that allowed far more time for characterization than was possible in self-contained single episode shows. The serial became an enduring pattern for radio, one that capitalized on the medium's intimate relationship with its regular listening audience by stressing the personalities of the characters rather than the action of the plots.

Between 7:00 and 7:15 every week night America stopped what it was doing to listen to *Amos 'n' Andy*. In the 1930s an estimated *40 million* people—about one out of every three living Americans—listened to *Amos 'n' Andy*, a figure that demonstrated the incredible reach of national broadcast entertainment as well as the unprecedented popularity of this show. To avoid losing customers, movie theaters played *Amos 'n' Andy* in their lobbies, and Atlantic City merchants piped it onto the boardwalk; utility companies reported a drop in water pressure as the program ended and people flushed their toilets; when the show asked listeners to name Amos's baby, nearly 2.5 million people offered their suggestions. "There are three things which I shall never forget about America," observed George Bernard Shaw, "the Rocky Mountains, Niagara Falls, and *Amos 'n' Andy*."[8]

Freeman F. Gosden (Amos) and Charles J. Correll (Andy), the creators and performers of the show, instinctively knew how to use the new medium. "Listening to them," observed critic Gilbert Seldes, "you never felt that they wished people could see them or were afraid their comedy was not getting across because they were invisible." Instead, they used that invisibility as an asset. Changing their inflection, tone, dialect, and phrasing, Gosden and Correll portrayed scores of distinct, easily recognizable characters—men, women, and children. Characterization was the key to the show's success. "Most (critics) did not realize that we were after the creation of character, not gags," Gosden explained on the twenty-first anniversary of the show. "We believed then and believe now that once you establish your characters, if they're likable, the public will become fond of them. All you have to do then is to put them into recognizable situations. You don't have to have a laugh in every line to be funny."[9] Following this pattern, *Amos 'n' Andy* defined and popularized situation comedy. After the show's astounding success, scores, then hundreds, of radio programs used *Amos 'n' Andy's* formula, making situation comedy a basic staple of broadcast entertainment.

As advertising agencies tried to reach the largest possible audiences with their sponsors' commercials, they developed different types of shows for different times of day. At night, shows that appealed to the whole family filled the radio dial—situation comedies like *Amos 'n' Andy*, music of all sorts, mysteries like *The Shadow*, drama like *First Nighter,* adventures like *Death Valley Days*, quiz shows like *Kay Kyser's Kollege of Musical Knowledge*, and variety shows starring big name vaudevillians Eddie Cantor, Ed Wynn, Al Jolson, and others who found new homes in radio when vaudeville collapsed during the Depression. The late afternoon and early evening hours were dominated by children's action and adventure serials, such as *Jack Armstrong, The Lone Ranger,* and *Little Orphan Annie*. Mornings and afternoons belonged to housewives for whom advertising agencies developed domestic serials popularly called "soap operas" because companies such as Procter & Gamble and Lever Brothers sponsored many of them. Focusing on the family and personal problems of perpetually plagued heroines, soap operas used the continuing story, characterization, and personal involvement that *Amos 'n' Andy* had pioneered, but put their characters into perplexing rather than humorous situations. Embroiling heroines in seemingly endless anguish, torment, and worry proved so popular that by the end of 1938 thirty-eight women's serials were broadcast every weekday, and their number was still growing. But daytime programming was not limited to soap operas. In 1934 Mary Margaret McBride created the "talk show" format later adopted by stars such as Arthur Godfrey. She informally interviewed famous guests and chatted casually with listeners about her opinions, tastes, experiences, and feelings. "You bring the world into my little kitchen—the people, the sights, the sounds," an ex-working woman wrote

to McBride.[10] That fan identified radio's single greatest appeal. It brought the world into kitchens, bedrooms, and living rooms throughout the country, making listeners feel that radio personalities and characters were people they knew.

As a unique entertainment medium, radio had to develop its own performance styles as well as its own shows. "Radio actors must achieve all their effects with their voices," explained radio veteran Joseph Julian. "They can't use gestures, expression, stances, or other visual nuances." Radio performances had to spark the imagination of listeners. "What was needed," explained radio star Mary Jane Higby, "was a quick impression, given with broad, sure strokes. It bore the relation to a stage performance that a pencil sketch has to to an oil painting."[11] Pencil sketches can have a directness, spontaneity, and immediacy that oil paintings lack, but they do not have depth, texture, and complexity. Neither did radio acting, because radio was one-dimensional, because there was little time to rehearse, and because there were no retakes or editing.

When Mary Jane Higby left the theater for radio, she quickly learned that she had to make major adjustments. After memorizing all her lines for her first radio role as she would have done for the stage, she arrived for the performance and was handed pages and pages of major revisions. Higby never memorized another radio script. But she did carefully study successful radio shows, especially *Amos 'n' Andy*, for techniques that worked in the new medium. She concluded that "intimacy was the keynote to radio acting" and that she could convey action and mood with her voice. "When I was supposed to be lifting a weight I learned to let the strain show in my voice. I would speak more loudly in an outdoor scene than I would in a fireside conversation at home."[12] These imaginative and subtle techniques, unnecessary in a visual medium, made Higby a great success in radio. She played in many shows and starred in *When a Girl Marries* for 19 years.

Many radio actors and actresses, in contrast to singers or comedians who appeared under their own names, were virtually unknown, even to the fans who absolutely would not miss the shows these performers starred in. Few listeners knew the names of the people who played Superman, Stella Dallas, Jack Armstrong, or Mr. District Attorney. The reasons lay in the nature of the medium. Radio audiences could identify actors only by their voices. But what listeners heard were the voices of the *characters*, not the natural voices of the performers. The actress who played a young boy at 9:00 a.m. might take the role of an old woman at 9:30, a lawyer at 10:00, and a seductress at 10:30. If she was good, listeners would have had no idea that one actress had played them all. This allowed skilled performers with adaptable voices to play an incredible range of parts. Actor Matt Crowley, for example, was the announcer for *Pretty Kitty Kelly*, John in *John's Other Wife*, Doctor Brent in *Road of Life*, and Jim in *Jungle Jim*. But the lack of public recognition for the actor also meant relatively low status and pay for radio stars compared with movie stars, which represented the great contrast between the two most popular entertainment machines of the period. Movie stars, working in a bigger-than-life, visual medium that commanded the audience's full attention, projected powerful personal images that overshadowed the roles they played. The personality of the movie star, not the character, held the central appeal. In contrast, radio actors, working in an intimate, aural medium that was part of the audience's home life, subordinated their personalities to the roles they played. The character, not the personality of the star, held the central appeal. People went to movies to see a Clark Gable or a Bette Davis picture, but they tuned in to radio shows to hear about the Lone Ranger or Helen Trent. Especially in radio's unique format, the daily serial, listeners believed in and cared about the characters as if they were real people, which further decreased interest in the actors and actresses.

Radio also developed its own unique specialist—the sound-effects man, who stimulated listeners' imagination with sounds. "This ability of the ear to convey a *picture* to the mind of a listener is one of the radio's most fortunate gifts," observed journalist John J. Floherty in describing how radio worked. Give listeners "the right sound effects and music," comedian Fred Allen explained, "and their imaginations will work for you. A man in his armchair can picture all kinds of fantastic scenes: a fly crawling up the Empire State Building, scenes in outer space or under the sea. These are things radio can do best—better than the movies."[13] The first problem the sound-effects man had was that he could not simply use recordings of actual sounds because microphones distorted them. On radio a record of a real automobile crash, for example, sounded like a battleship being torpedoed, so sound men had to find another way to re-create the familiar sound. They did it by dropping a stovepipe, a steel bar, and tin cans into a box of broken glass. As they mastered their new craft, sound-effects men stocked studios with the odd-looking tools of their trade—cellophane to crumple for a crackling fire, bird seed to spill onto stretched parchment for driving sleet, a shoe to tread in a box of gravel for footsteps on a path, a door to slam in a jamb, and coconut shells to thump for a horse galloping. Sound-effects men also faced some incredible challenges such as the scene in a *Lights Out* episode in which a man was turned inside out. After a great deal of experimentation, one sound-effects man slowly peeled off a tight-fitting rubber glove close to the microphone, while another crunched a strawberry box for the sound of breaking bones.

The same technological breakthroughs in electrical amplification that made possible radio's development also radically changed the record business. In the mid-1920s electrical microphones and amplifiers ended the era of direct acoustical recording. No longer was the quality of a record determined by a performer's volume, pitch, tone, and distance from a recording horn. With sensitive microphones to pick up all kinds of sound and amplifiers to boost their intensity, soft-voiced crooners like Rudy Vallee and Whispering Jack Smith and sweet sounding bands relying on strings and subtle arrangements could for the first time become recording stars. The new electrical equipment also allowed entertainers to perform naturally when recording. A full orchestra could now set up in its normal configuration, rather than being forced to eliminate instruments and to cram musicians together in front of the recording horn. A dynamic entertainer like Al Jolson could now prance around while he recorded rather than having two men hold him still so he would sing directly into the recording horn. The result of the new recording technology was a new diversity and quality of discs that the public loved.

But when the upbeat 1920s collapsed into the depressed 1930s, nonessentials became expensive luxuries just when radio began broadcasting top-notch, free entertainment. Like the stock market, record sales plummeted—from 100 million in 1927 to 6 million in 1932. As a result other entertainment media began to absorb the weakened recording industry. In 1929 the Radio Corporation of America took over Victor, forming RCA-Victor; in 1930, Warner Brothers, the pioneer of talkies, took over Brunswick's record and phonograph division; and in an ironic reversal that indicated the shift of power, CBS in 1938 bought Columbia Records, which originally had kept the fledgling radio network alive and had given it its name. By the late 1930s record sales had recovered, led by Jack Kapp's new Decca Record Company, which dropped prices from 75 cents to 35 cents, signed up top stars like Bing Crosby and Tommy and Jimmy Dorsey, and emphasized records' major advantage over radio. "Hear them *when* you want—as *often* as you want—right in your home," Decca advertised.[14] Unlike radio, phonographs put the home listener in charge of programming, which proved especially popular with music because people like hearing hits over and over. Record sales also got a boost from a new public entertainment machine—the jukebox, which provided inexpensive, popular dance music for Depression America in places like diners, taverns, and soda fountains. Hot new swing bands

which received little prime-time exposure on family-oriented network radio burned up records at the "juke joints." By 1939 there were some 225,000 jukeboxes using about 13 million records. Within three years, the number of jukeboxes nearly doubled. The record business was again thriving, having found a role which supplemented radio.

By the mid-1940s, as America emerged victorious from World War II and the second period in the development of entertainment machines in the home ended, show business was more varied and popular than ever before. Even in the worst economic depression in the nation's history the American people had found enough money and time to support entertainment machines in their theaters, their recreation centers, and their homes. The public's appetite for entertainment grew more voracious as technology produced an even more varied diet of enjoyable, inexpensive, or free entertainment. Once a major entertainment medium became popular it never disappeared, though innovations often forced major changes in the content, format, and audience of existing entertainment machined. The greatest example of this process came after World War II when a new machine revolutionized entertainment in the home.

The third major phase of home entertainment began in the late 1940s and was dominated by television, which brought the sights as well as the sound of show business into people's homes. Television technology had been developed by the 1930s. Regular, limited telecasting had begun at the New York World's Fair of 1939, and in 1940 there were twenty-three television stations and some 10,000 sets in operation. World War II postponed television's development, but in the upbeat, postwar economic boom when a great many working-class people were able to buy homes in the suburbs, new cars, and conveniences of all sorts, television spread quickly. For the new entertainment medium the years between 1946 and 1955 were years of expansion and experimentation, years in which television absorbed the structure, financing, and formats of radio and developed its own qualities. Like radio, early television broadcast live performances to audiences, but, unlike radio, television producers had to be concerned with visual as well as vocal impact. Centered in New York and totally boycotted by major motion picture studios, television, in this first phase, looked to radio and the theater for writers, directors, and performers.

By the late 1940s, drawing on radio, television began to develop a broad range of programming. In 1947 *Howdy Doody* and *Kukla, Fran and Ollie* established children's shows; *Charade Quiz* got viewers participating in game and quiz shows; and *Kraft Television Theater* introduced well-financed, well-produced drama. In 1948 Milton Berle proved that comedians would be superstars in the new medium, and Ed Sullivan began his influential variety show. In 1949 Arthur Godfrey popularized the personality talk show; *The Lone Ranger* staked the western's claim to the new territory; *Martin Kane, Private Eye* began the fight against urban crime; and *Mama* and *The Goldbergs* set up housekeeping for domestic, situation comedy. These and many other stars and shows made television into a major entertainment machine in American homes. The number of television sets in the nation grew from about 3 million in 1950 to 21 million in 1953, a 700 percent increase in three years.

Television contained elements of radio, film, and the stage, but it adds a distinctive new medium that required its own performance styles and techniques. Television producers used radio formats, programs, and stars and had to churn out shows at nearly the pace of radio producers. Like radio, early network television also broadcast its shows live, which was a far more formidable task for television than the radio directors. Television directors, like movie directors, had to worry about camera shots and angles, and, like stage directors, about live performances with no retakes and no editing. Early television's limited technology and resources made this a doubly difficult task. Cut off from Hollywood's film experts

who knew how to produce inexpensive, enjoyable pictures at a rapid pace, television's pioneers worked with the make-do, ad-lib approach of early film-makers.

Prior to 1952 television networks were not truly national. Until the first coast-to-coast telecasts in 1957, television producers could reach national audiences with their live shows only by making movies of the images on television sets and sending these murky, poor-quality kinescopes to other stations for rebroadcast. "Watching a kinescope," recalled television writer Max Wilk, "was like looking at a bowl of gray pea soup. Here and there you could barely make out the croutons." But in spite, or perhaps because, of the hectic pace, the limitations of the technology, and the lack of precedents, working in the experimental phase of this complex, new medium was an exhilarating experience. That was a very exciting period in my life," reminisced producer Mort Werner. "Television was such a brand-new medium. I don't really know how the Pilgrims felt when they landed in Massachusetts, but we were in somewhat the same position. We had to construct a whole new business, and we went ahead and did it, from the ground up."[15]

Getting a weekly show on the air was an enormous challenge. The Sid Caesar-Imogene Coca shows, which ran from 1949 to 1954, were live, ninety-minute revues, the kinds of shows that stage producers like Florenz Ziegfeld or Earl Carroll had worked months to create and then had refined on the road before opening night. But *Your Show of Shows* had to open a completely new show *every week* for five years. Working in this pressure cooker brought out the best in people, leaving them with a feeling of accomplishment and camaraderie that they never forgot. "I don't know whether there are any shows today in TV where producer, performers and writers were as tuned to each other's talents as we were then," observed Lucille Kallin about the staff of *Your Show of Shows* which included writers Mel Brooks, Carl Reiner, and Neil Simon. "Coming up with an idea in that group was like throwing a magnetized piece of a jigsaw puzzle into the middle of a room. All the other pieces would come racing toward it, each one adding another necessary part. Suddenly there was the whole picture!" There was no time for discord. In early television, the need to produce show after show, week after week meant abundant opportunities for creative talents and no long, drawn-out process for filtering and modifying them. "Television was brand new," observed Charlie Andrews, who wrote for Dave Garroway, "you could do any damn thing you wanted to, and nobody could tell you, 'No, don't do that, it won't work,' because nobody knew anything. So there was this burst of creativity around NBC because there was so much room to burst."[16]

The type of show that best represented the distinctive problems and achievements of live television was the weekly dramatic anthology, a series of independent productions presented under a common name, which began on television in 1947 with *Kraft Television Theater*. Unlike other series, dramatic anthologies had no continuing characters, stars, or themes to carry the shows and sustain audience interest. Each production was a totally self-contained play that attracted and held viewers on its own. To accomplish these goals, producers of television drama turned to the American stage for help. Major Hollywood studios not only denied early television their films and expertise but also their stars and properties, which included most past and present Broadway hits and most popular novels. With few guaranteed attractions and little money to spend on scripts, producers of live television drama of necessity turned to classics, like Shakespeare, which were in the public domain, and to original plays by unknown writers, like Paddy Chayevsky and Rod Serling who wrote major television plays such as *Marty* and *Patterns*. With early television's hectic production pace, young actors, directors, and writers had a chance to learn their craft on the job and quickly evaluate the results, just as D. W. Griffith had done with his early films. "You could get an idea and write it, and a couple of weeks later,

you could see it performed," explained Chayefsky. Between 1953 and 1955 there were as many as a dozen original dramatic productions on network television *every week*. The great number of scripts needed for these shows meant that writers did not have time to produce blockbuster scripts, but had to write "small stories about people," which Chayefsky astutely argued was just what television did best. "Movies need much broader scope—but as far as I'm concerned," he explained, "on the home screen you work best on a small canvas. You create character, and that becomes your plot."[17]

Creators of live television drama had to learn to work within the restrictions of the new medium's "small canvas," which was best suited to mid-range shots and closeups. Live television drama was largely confined to interior settings with few scene changes, few characters, and lots of dialogue. Early television camera work did little to enliven productions because studios generally used only one fixed-lens camera for long shots and another for closeups. The cumbersome cameras made fast takes, dolly shots, and quick cross-cutting virtually impossible. As a result television drama had a far slower pace and much less visual variety than contemporary movies had. In this sense early television reverted to the limited camera work of pre-Griffith, silent one-reelers. And there could, of course, be no editing of live telecasts to pick up the pace or add tension and excitement. With limited settings, movement, and camera work, directors focused on people, dialogue, psychological tension, and characterization. Live television drama was like live theater with closeups.

Early television was an actor's medium. Since the stories centered on characterization, not action, the performers had to create the mood, feelings, and intensity of the shows. Their problem was to develop the right acting style for the new medium. Television's heavy reliance on closeups magnified actors' gestures and movements and forced actors to move slowly and to use a wide range of subtle visual gestures, as well as subtle gradations in intonation and phrasing. The television actor had to have the theatrical performer's command of dialogue, the movie performer's mastery of closeups, and the radio performer's intimacy. These broad requirements, plus the absence of established movie stars, perhaps explains why early television produced so many new stars, many of them trained in theater but not yet experienced enough to have to unlearn the styles of other performing media, people such as Paul Newman, Estelle Parsons, Steve McQueen, Kim Stanley, Lee Marvin, Lee Remick, Rod Steiger, and Joanne Woodward.

Although live telecasts dominated network television programming prior to 1952, some television series were filmed. Frederick W. Ziv, a radio producer who had syndicated his shows directly to individual stations instead of to sponsors or networks, did the same thing in the new medium in the late-1940s with modestly produced filmed adventure series such as the *Cisco Kid*. In 1951 Lucille Ball and Desi Arnaz greatly influenced television programming with their situation comedy *I Love Lucy*, which was filmed by three cameras before a live audience. The three films were than edited like a movie before being broadcast which gave the programs the variety of camera angles and the rapid pace of films along with the spontaneity and immediacy of live performances. Because *I Love Lucy* quickly dominated the ratings, there were soon many other short, filmed television series, comedies like *The Life of Riley* or *Make Room for Daddy*. By 1954 film had just about replaced short, live episodic series.

ABC Television, with few top dramatic anthologies, few top comedians, and no shows in the top fifteen, decided to gamble on new programming in 1954. Its telecast of the U.S. Senate hearings investigating Senator Joseph McCarthy's charges of Communist infiltration of the army won high ratings and demonstrated the power of television to bring news events into people's homes and to influence politics and politicians. But since live events with such high tension and drama were rare, ABC had to look elsewhere for programming to improve the

dismal rating of the network. Using the movie studio contacts of ABC corporate president Leonard H. Goldenson, who had headed United Paramount Theaters before it merged with ABC, the network looked to Hollywood, not to Broadway.

Robert Kinter, then responsible for ABC programming, went to Hollywood in 1954 to persuade major movie studios, which had not yet sold their old pictures to television, to film programs for ABC's regular schedule. At first he got an even colder and more antagonistic response than he feared. "You dumb young son of a bitch, you won't get any of my stars, you won't get any people—*you* can't make films!" bellowed Harry Cohn of Columbia. "People…want their movies the way they *are*—not on TV!"[18] But Jack Warner, the man who in the 1920s gambled successfully on the new sound technology, again took a major initiative by agreeing to film forty hour-long action-adventure episodes for the network. ABC paid $3.5 million for the programs and the right to rebroadcast twelve of them. Of the three alternating programs—two of them based on the hit movies *King's Row* and *Casablanca*— only the television original, *Chyenne*, became a hit television series. It ran from 1955 to 1963 with its filmed western action and made a star of Clint Walker. Kintner also convinced Walt Disney to film television shows, which proved tremendously popular. By 1956 most major studios were filming episodic series for television and had sold the rights to telecast nearly two thousand pre-1948 feature films.

"Starting with Jack Warner and his film shows," television veteran Perry Lafferty observed, "the live TV shows were doomed." Lafferty felt that dramatic anthologies, which were basically limited to four-walled studios, simply could not compete with "guys running up and down the streets, in cars, with guns, shooting at each other, and chases."[19] Without action stories to fill program schedules and provide basic plots, the 11 or 12 live network anthologies needed 450 or so good dramatic scripts every season, enough material to last years on the stage, where shows played to new audiences every night, and even in Hollywood where major movie studios in 1955 made only about 250 films. Besides demanding so many plays, television drama anthologies also had to satisfy the tastes of a changing audience. When the price of sets dropped and television reached a mass audience, the appeal of live drama's talky, introspective scripts declined. "Our total audience then was about 20 percent of today's audience," observed Worthington Miner of *Studio One*. "There's a law of diminishing return when you increase an audience. That 20 percent is now the expendable part of the audience."[20] The new, broader audience had more of a taste for movie action and adventure than for the best drama that live theater could produce. Live drama was also at a decided economic disadvantage. While inexperienced television producers fought a losing battle with cost control, movie studios adeptly turned out entertaining, low-budget programs. The series that Hollywood made for television took the place, the form, and much of the audience of "B" movies. Another major advantage of filmed shows over live shows was that after the broadcast the film could be rerun, which decreased the demand for new material. The filmed shows could also be sold to other stations, or dubbed and marketed abroad, which increased the profit per show. In the late 1950s Hollywood replaced Broadway as a major influence on television.

As films were replacing live performances on television, Ampex, in 1956, introduced videotape, a system of recording and reproducing high-quality pictures and sound magnetically on tape, which offered television many advantages over film. With videotape, stations could record network telecasts and with no loss of clarity rebroadcast them locally in better time slots. Using this technique networks overcame the three-hour time difference between East and West and could schedule programs for the some hour throughout the country. Videotape, which was cheap, reusable, and could be replayed instantly, also cut production time and costs. Mobile videotape cameras revolutionized television

news by allowing cameras to range freely and to bring breaking stories quickly into people's homes. The instant replay, stop-action, slow motion, and quick cutting from long shots to close-ups that videotape made possible enabled football, with twenty-two people exploding in short spurts of violent action, to surpass baseball, with its slower, more easily followed action, as television's most popular sport. Videotape even influenced entertainment formats. Quick electronic editing made possible rapid-fire, kaleidoscopic barrages of disjointed images in such distinctive *television* programs as *Rowan and Martin's Laugh-In* and *Sesame Street*.

Just as it did with programming, television adopted radio's system of commercial sponsorship. But the uneven distribution of early television stations made national advertisers reluctant to shift their major budgets from radio. As late as 1952 the nation had only 108 television stations in operation. Cities such as Austin, Denver, Little Rock, and Portland had none. In late 1951 AT&T cables and microwave relays made coast-to-coast television networks a reality, and the number of stations and sets increased every year, which lured big advertisers to the tube. Sponsors were also attracted by the response some television ads received. In 1950 Hazel Bishop lipstick, with sales of $50,000 began advertising exclusively on television. In 1953 it had sales of $4.5 million. By the 1956–57 season television was truly national. America had over 500 stations, three major networks, and some 40 million homes with television sets, which people watched about five hours a day, making television an irresistible way for advertisers to reach national audiences. Following radio patterns, sponsors usually bought show and the time to broadcast them. In October 1955 the networks controlled only half of the 844 hours of weekly shows and produced only half of the 20 new shows scheduled for 1957–58. Advertisers, rather than networks, were determining television schedules in the late 1950s.

Network executives, long unhappy that sponsors' control often left networks with poorly designed, non-competitive schedules, used a 1959 scandal about sponsors' rigging major quiz shows to seize control of scheduling. Network control of programs and schedules fundamentally changed television as a business. Instead of selling blocks of time to sponsors or advertising agencies to fill as they chose, *networks* selected and scheduled the shows and then gave businesses a chance to sponsor them. In the 1960s sponsor influence on programming was further weakened when high production costs made it virtually impossible for one company to sponsor an entire program. By 1971 ninety-three out of every hundred network shows had more than one sponsor. No longer did networks sell time at flat rates for given time periods. Instead, they sold thirty-second or one-minute "spots" to sponsors at prices that varied with the show's rating and demographic analysis. Ratings took on a new meaning. In radio and early television, the *sponsor* used ratings to judge the size of the audience. After 1960, the *network* used ratings to decide how much to charge the sponsor for a spot; ratings determined network income. For *The Flip Wilson Show*, for instance, NBC began in September 1970 with a rate of $46,000 per commercial minute, but as the show's popularity climbed, so did the price, which reached $80,000 per minute only four months after the show's debut.

The selection and scheduling of shows, obviously, became a central concern of the television networks. By 1969–70, program proposals had to go through at least five major steps, each reviewed and scrutinized by network committees until a pilot was finally produced—at a cost of about $600,000 for a one-hour show. This slow process of decision-by-committee stood in great contrast to the early days of television when ideas were virtually tried out on the air. The stakes had become so high that risk-taking had to be minimized, which was done by putting the responsibility on committees, not on individuals. Like other large modern institutions, television networks suffered the problems of bureaucratic thinking and decision-making. Inse-

cure executives tended to choose tried and true formats and formulas rather than risky innovations that might be either great successes or disastrous failures. "We don't pick the shows we think will have the best chance of becoming popular," a network executive admitted in 1970. "To be honest, we're attracted to those that seem to have the least chance of failing." A frustrated agent complained that whatever he proposed to the networks ended up as "something very reminiscent of one or two shows that have been seen before. Everything on television becomes a composition of stale ideas that once worked."[21]

By the early 1970s ABC, dead last in the ratings, was in a position to gamble. When it found a man who ignored the committee system and relied on the same personal sense of audience moods and tastes that had always characterized top showmen, the network rose to the top. That man was Fred Silverman, who at age twenty-five had become director of daytime programming for CBS in 1964, and who in 1970 had taken over all its programming. In 1975 he moved to ABC as chief of programming. ABC did not have a single show in the top ten in 1974–75, but the following season it had five of the top ten shows, and the year after that it could boast seven of the top ten. What thrust ABC from last to first was Silverman's blend of youth-oriented, situation comedies such as *Happy Days* and *Laverne & Shirley*, sexy shows such as *Rich Man, Poor Man* and *Charlie's Angels*, and violent action such as *The Six Million Dollar Man* and *Baretta*, a lineup promoted extensively during the ABC telecasts of the 1976 Olympic Games, which drew many new viewers to the network. In 1978 Silverman reached the top of the business when he moved to NBC as president of the entire network operation at a salary reported at a million dollars a year. Yet, in 1981 Silverman, who proved a better programmer than he did a network president, resigned from NBC.

For networks the race for ratings was a race for profits. Even when the rating spreads seemed relatively slight, the stakes were incredibly high. In 1977–78, when first place ABC was watched by only an estimated 2.7 percent more homes than third place NBC, ABC reportedly outgrossed NBC by something like $65,000,000. Advertising revenues, not entertainment for its own sake, remained the basic goal of broadcasters. Shows did not just have to draw large audiences, they had to draw the *right* large audiences as determined by demographic analysis of viewers. In 1969–70 even though CBS shows starring Red Skelton and Jackie Gleason were the most popular programs in their time slots, sponsors shied away from them because their audiences were too old. As a result CBS made only a slight profit on Skelton and lost money on Gleason. Despite top ratings, both shows were cancelled. "Television is a medium not so much for entertainment as for selling products," reminded Screen Actors' Guild executive John L. Dales. "Actors and actresses are the frosting on the cake mix, the medicine show that comes with cough syrup."[22]

Television advertising began as basically radio with pictures, what people in news reporting called "the talking head"—Arthur Godfrey raving about the pleasures of Lipton tea or Bill the Bartender boasting about Pabst Blue Ribbon beer. Then advertising agencies began to make fuller use of television's visual dimension with eye-catching advertising symbols, like the Old Gold dancing cigarette pack, and appetite-whetting shots, like a beautiful slice of white meat rolling off a Swift Butterball turkey—a shot that required two days of production time, sixty-one turkeys, and the services of a professional slicer. In the 1960s commercials became much more sophisticated as the price of advertising time mounted and as advertising agencies turned to complex technology to make commercials appealing enough to "stop the lady with the full bladder for one full minute."[23] Advertisers caught people's attention with spectacular scenes, like the beautiful woman in a chiffon dress and a shiny new convertible on a Colorado pinnacle 2000 feet above the desert; with special effects, like giant arms coming out of washing machines or carless drivers steering down the street; or with lavish production numbers

such as a thirty-second canned soup ad featuring tap-dancer Ann Miller and a large cast directed by Busby Berkeley, which reportedly cost $250,000, or some $8300 a second.

Television viewers, like radio listeners, gladly accepted commercials. In a 1960 national poll designed by Gary A. Steiner, people were asked if they would "rather pay a small amount yearly if they could have television without commercials," and only one out of every four said yes, which was the same attitude expressed about radio commercials in the 1940s. The poll also asked if the people sampled would agree that "I would prefer TV without commercials," which was loaded in the affirmative since people are more inclined to agree than disagree. But only 43 percent agreed! Well over half the people sampled said they preferred TV *with* commercials.[24] Besides the unconscious association people probably made between commercials and entertaining programs, many people felt the commercials were informative and entertaining. Since television commercials were the most expensive and most carefully planned, researched, written, produced, and edited shows on television, it is no wonder people vividly and affectionately recalled masterful commercials.

The American public lived television. Extensive surveying in the 1960s revealed that over 60 percent of the public considered television the invention in the last 25 years that had done the most to make life more enjoyable. Steiner's 1960 poll showed more than three-quarters of the people happy with what was on television and unable to think of anything else they wanted. Even the 25 percent of the public that criticized television programming watched essentially the same escapist shows as the general pro-television public.[25] Still, many of the criticisms of programming were well founded. Television does seem to have detrimental effects on children who are virtually raised and socialized by it. But even though television may contribute to deeply disturbing modern problems—parental irresponsibility, hedonism, low levels of literacy and culture, and increasing violence and inhumanity—it can not fairly be charged with creating these problems. If television fare often resembles cafeteria food, it should be no surprise. It is doing the equivalent of delivering meals every hour of every day and night to tens of millions of homes. For all its weaknesses and shortcomings, television has brought more entertainment to more people than ever before in history.

Television's enormous popularity forced radical changes in other entertainment media. Although movies changed markedly in the age of television, it was radio that underwent the most profound and pervasive changes. Radio emerged from World War II at the height of its popularity and with its form and content intact. In 1950 network radio broadcast over one hundred series that had been on the air at least ten years, and dozen others, led by *Amos 'n' Andy*, that were nearly as old as network radio. The major impact of television on radio did not come until after 1954, when the new medium became truly national and siphoned off radio's national advertisers, forcing radio to make its most basic changes since the late 1920s. From national networks broadcasting a wide range of entertainment designed for the general public, radio increasingly specialized in attracting narrow, local audiences by broadcasting one particular style of recorded music, such as jazz, rock and roll, classical, rhythm and blues, traditional pop, Latin, or country and western. This approach attracted sponsors who wanted to target their commercials at specific groups, and radio prospered. For most people, radio became a supplement to television, by providing the music and news people wanted when they wanted them, at home, in cars, or almost anywhere else. Transistorized portable radios even allowed people to carry music with them wherever they went. For some groups, such as teenagers, minorities, and intellectuals, radio became kind of in-group communication, a central part of group identity.

When radio switched to local programming and recorded music, radio and the record business dovetailed as never before. This relationship was symbolized by radio's new star, the disc jockey, the man who introduced and played the records. By the early 1950s the power of disc jockeys to make hits out of the records they played and plugged was clearly evident. Deejays, as they were often called, could even create new markets, as Alan Freed did when he got white teenagers to buy rhythm and blues records originally intended for black listeners. Even though radio stations were local, or at most regional, broadcasters, the key disc jockeys, like Alan Freed, became national hit-makers. Every week the major trade publication printed charts of the records big-city deejays played most often, charts that stations all over the country then used to decide what record to play. In the lucrative youth market, radio stations evolved a simple, reliable format—Top 40. Using national pop charts and local sales figures, the station drew up a list of only forty records, which it played over and over for a week, with the Top 10 being broadcast as many as thirty or forty times a day. For records on the play list, sales were almost assured. But in the highly competitive record business getting on the lists was as difficult as it was essential.

To get exposure for their new releases with important deejays record companies used the tried and true American way. They bought it. Payola, giving money or valuables to disc jockeys to play records, became widespread in radio. "Nobody will admit to paying off, and nobody will admit to getting paid," a music business executive explained off-the-record in 1957. "But trying to plug a tune without putting your hand in your pocket would be like trying to bail out a leaky rowboat with a pair of chopsticks."[26] In 1959 the lid blew off undercover payola, exposing disc jockeys throughout the nation who took money, gifts, trips, and even part ownership of record companies or distributorships, in exchange for plugging records. Payola became a federal crime, but it did not disappear because the stakes and the competition were high and the number of major outlets was low.

The post-World War II explosion of modern technology that produced television and transformed radio also radically changed every facet of the phonograph and record businesses. In the late 1940s, the perfection of tape recording, converting sound into electrical impulses, magnetically encoding them on tape, and then decoding the impulses to reproduce sound, revolutionized recording. Besides providing excellent fidelity, tape—which could be cut and spliced back together—made it possible to record several versions of the same music and then combine the best segments of each into a final product that was better than any of the takes. Tape recording also made entry into the record business much easier by greatly reducing the equipment needed. Between 1949 and 1954 the number of recording companies exploded from eleven to two hundred. Records themselves also changed. In 1948 Columbia introduced a new 33 1/3 rpm long-playing record (LP) by unveiling two stacks of records, each containing 325 selections. The pile of LPs stood about fifteen inches high, while the conventional 78 rpm records towered well over a man's head to a height of eight feet! RCA Victor responded with 45 rpm records that held no more music than 78s, but were lighter, smaller, more durable, easier to store, and more quickly and cheaply shipped. The 45s replaced 78s in the single song, pop record market, while LPs dominated the classical and traditional popular music markets. For the first time average Americans were also able to buy high fidelity phonographs and recordings.

In the late 1950s, with these technological developments, record sales grew rapidly—from $277 million in 1955 to $460 million in 1957. These were the years when radio converted to recorded music, and when huge sales of rhythm and blues and rock and roll records established that there were large markets for 45 rpm singles produced for minority groups and teenagers. With a few notable exceptions like RCA Victor, which had Elvis Presley, and Decca, which had Bill Haley and the Comets and Buddy Holly, major record companies tended to leave the rock and roll, 45 rpm market to new, independent companies specializing in this music. The

major companies could afford to downplay the youth singles market because long-playing albums of traditional music—pop, classical, and musicals—were selling so well. In 1955 LPs accounted for over half the dollar value of record sales in America. By 1960 that figure was about 80 percent. Original cast albums of stage and screen musicals led the way, *The Sound of Music* topping the list with sales of 15 million albums.

But in the late 1960s youth music invaded the LP field in a big way, beginning with the Beatles' *Sgt. Pepper's Lonely Hearts Club Band* (1967), an LP which sold more than seven million copies. After that, major record companies moved into youth music. "When we saw the numbers that those records could sell in, we said 'Wow, there's something here,'" explained an executive of Warner Brothers Records. "You'd struggle with a middle-of-the-road artist to sell maybe 300,000 albums when you could sell two million Jimi Hendrix albums. Frank Sinatra never sold two million albums. Dean Martin never sold two million albums."[27] The reason for the great rise in sales of rock LPs was not just that young people had money to spend on records. That had been true for decades. In the late-1960s a new youth "counter-culture" emerged—the world of hippies, love-ins, and psychedelic drugs—with rock music at its core, music which was made possible by major technological innovations, especially stereophonic sound and complex recording techniques.

Stereophonic sound, put very simply, reproduces the way people actually hear, with fine distinctions made between the sound reaching each ear which gives depth and complexity to recorded music. By the early 1960s stereo was widely accepted. By the mid-1960s youth music had grown very complex—rhythmically, melodically, and instrumentally—and could no longer be captured on short, monaural 45s as early rock and roll had been. Rock albums also grew increasingly dependent on studio engineers whose highly sophisticated electronic and taping equipment could isolate every instrument and voice, control its quality, add or delete elements of all sorts, and mix the sounds into any form or structure. The resulting music, in many cases, was not only impossible to reproduce in live performance, but could not have been produced at all without studio technology and technicians. *Sgt. Pepper's Lonely Hearts Club Band* reportedly took hundreds of hours to produce, blending the Beatles' instrumentals and voices with crowd noises, barking dogs, kazoos, calliopes, barnyard animals, and a full symphony orchestra. In one of the songs, "A Day in the Life," the music of a full orchestra was built up by laying track over track on the tape to achieve a feeling of waves of shining, soaring sound that climaxed in a crashing crescendo. This stunning effect was entirely the product of the modern recording industry's sophisticated technology.

In the late-1960s the structure of the recording industry changed in ways that paralleled the decline of major movie studios as production units and the rise of independent movie producers. Head-strong popular rock groups frequently clashed with major record companies over work schedules, life styles, and the large amount of time and money the groups spent perfecting their albums. As a result it became common for independent record producers, sometimes for the groups themselves, to create the albums and for major companies to market and distribute them. By the end of the 1960s as many as 80 percent of all records may have been the work of independent producers.

The final change in the record and phonograph industry in this period was the development of tape equipment and recordings with broad, mass appeal. Tape previously had been important only to the recording industry and to a relatively small number of "hifinatics" who used reel-to-reel tapes and equipment too costly and cumbersome for the general public. But in the late 1960s the industry introduced self-contained, stereo tape cartridges which just had to be popped into playback equipment and turned on. Though these eight-track cartridges

were unable to record or to replay selections without going through the whole tape, they proved very popular, especially for cars. By 1975, sales of cartridges, used primarily in automobiles, reached nearly $600 million, a quarter of all recorded music sales. In 1969 the industry produced small, self-contained tape cassettes that could run backward or forward, record or replay, skip to specific selections, and hold as much as an LP. These mass-produced cassettes made all the advantages of tape—high-quality sound, long wear, and ease of storage—available, affordable, easy to use, and very popular. By 1970 cassettes accounted for nearly a third of recorded music sales, and in 1971 the value of tape players sold exceeded that of phonographs.

By the mid-1970s, the end of the third major period of entertainment machines in the home, average Americans took for granted an astonishing number and variety of entertainment machines—television, phonographs, radios, and tape machines. In the early years of the twentieth century, only dreamers or lunatics thought there were disembodied voices, music, and specters whirling about in the air. Now the overwhelming majority of Americans get their entertainment from voices, music, and specters whirling about in the air, which remain unseen and unheard until people turn on wonder-working machines that transform this cacophony into entertainment.

In the late 1970s a new phase in entertainment in the home seemed to be beginning. Television, the most popular entertainment machine, faced major new challenges. Videotape and equipment that previously had been the preserve of technicians within the industry was becoming available and affordable for the general public, just as audiotape had become in the late 1960s. Using videotape equipment, the public could record and replay free telecasts and could purchase or rent video recordings of major movies and other attractions. Pay television offered people a wide range of films, sports, and other attractions that they might otherwise have gone out to see. Telecasting via satellite made it possible to diversify broadcasting and to reach the entire nation inexpensively, so television channels began to specialize in one type of programming and to appeal to specific, not general, audiences, as radio had done in the 1950s. Even as the sociological, psychological, and spiritual costs of having technology do more and more things for more and more people become evident, there is no evidence that the American people want to rid themselves of their entertainment machines or to reverse the revolution that has made even the most modest American home an amusement palace.

# Notes

1. Roland Gelatt, *The Fabulous Phonograph*, 2nd revised edition (New York, 1977), pp 69–70).

2. Erik Barnouw, A Tower in Babel: *A History of Broadcasting in the United States*, Volume I–to 1933 (New York, 1966), p101.

3. Ben Gross, *I Looked and Listened: Informal Recollections of Radio and TV* (New York, 1954), p. 64.

4. Barnouw. p. 106.

5. Gross, pp. 66–67.

6. Mary Jane Higby, *Tune in Tomorrow*, paperback edition (New York, 1968), p. 151.

7. Paul F. Lazarfeld. *The People Look at Radio* (Chapel Hill, N.C., 1946), p. 110.

8. Arthur Frank Wertheim, *Radio Comedy* (New York, 1979), pp. 48–49.

9. Gilbert Seldes, *The Public Arts*, paperback edition (New York, 1956), p. 63; Freeman Gosden quoted in Gross, p. 154.

10. Mary Margaret McBride, *Out of the Air* (New York, 1960), pp. 26–27.

11. Joseph Julian, *This Was Radio: A Personal Memoir* (New York, 1975), p. 47; Higby, p. 12.

12. Higby, p. 36.

13. John J. Floherty, *Behind the Microphone* (New York, 1944), p. 60; Fred Allen quoted in Wertheim, p. 162.

14. Gelatt, p. 268.

15. Max Wilk, *The Golden Age of Television: Notes from the Survivors*, paperback edition (New York, 1977), pp. 85, 221.

16. Wilk, pp. 168–70, 194.

17. Wilk, pp. 130, 134.

18. Wilk, p. 258.

19. Wilk, pp. 259–61.

20. Wilk, p. 40.

21. Les Brown, *Television: The Business Behind the Box* (New York, 1971), pp. 125–26.

22. Terry Galoney, *Down the Tube, Or Making Television Commercials Is Such a Dog-Eat-Dog Business It's No Wonder They're Called Spots* (Chicago, 1970), p. 114.

23. Galoney, p. 3.

24. Gary A. Steiner, *The People Look at Television* (New York, 1963), p. 219.

25. Steiner, pp. 203, 234.

26. Hazel Meyer, *w* (Philadelphia, 1958), pp. 154–55.

27. Gelatt, p. 332.

# Introduction to Muriel G. Cantor's "Organizational Context and Control"

Muriel G. Cantor has been writing about the organizational elements of network television for the past thirty years. She was a media consultant for the Corporation for Public Broadcasting, the National Organization of Women, the federal Office of Education and the National Institute for Mental Health. All this while she contributed to the influential Report to the Surgeon General on Television and Social Behavior and sat as Chair of the Department and Professor of Sociology at American University in Washington, D. C. As a Ph. D. in sociology at the University of California, she did her doctoral dissertation on the sociology of television producers which turned into this research now in your hands.

Her interests in this work is in how the institutional aspects of network television as a cultural organization impacts on media content. What she presents has long been the traditional view of network hierarchy and how network executives relate to other social organizations such as advertisers, the federal government, and local broadcasters. We use it in this class because it is an excellent overview of how the production formula in network programming works, how organizations and institutions relate to one another, and how all concerned produce profits.

# Organizational Context and Control

Network power and control. How drama is produced and created. Description and analysis of the present system of production and dissemination. Television networks and their relationship to program suppliers, advertisers, local stations, and rating services.

Although television is a regulated industry in the United States, the organizations responsible for both the transmission and the creation of content have as their primary goal *profit*. There are, of course, other social functions associated with television: Television serves as a means of supplying entertainment and information to almost every household in the United States. However, entertainment and information are provided by organizations directed primarily by the profit motive, rather than to enlighten or educate viewers.[1]

Because the product of television is culture, its creation is different from other profit-making activities, such as the manufacture of material goods. The production of any commercial film drama, whether it is meant for theater distribution or for dissemination over television, can analytically be divided into two functions: those concerned with profit and those concerned with the craft aspects of creation. (Moor, 1961). The craft aspects of production will be considered in the next chapter. Here the major focus will be on the business functions associated with production. However, because profit is the major determinant of the content of television drama, the profit motive is influential on craft decisions as well. Those who control access to

the airways—the networks and the advertisers—set the stage for the creators, limiting their autonomy in many ways. To make a film, financial support is necessary. To have a film disseminated the filmmaker must find those who control the means of distribution. The financiers and distributors can be conceptualized as primary audiences for a film. If creators do not receive financial support, they cannot make a film. In addition, if the creators do not please the distributor, access to the ultimate audience is impossible.

Nowhere is the relationship between the creation of art (or culture) and the market economy more apparent than in the way the broadcast industry operates. Program suppliers or producers of film hire writers, directors, actors, and technicians to make films. These films are purchased by the television networks. The networks transmit the drama along with commercial advertisements through local broadcast stations which are either owned and operated by them or affiliated with them through contractual agreement. To judge whether the programs and commercials are reaching the target audience, rating services are employed who, through polling and sampling homes with mechanical devices and diary-type records, find the approximate size and composition of the audience. If a program does not reach the desired number and type of viewers, it is dropped from the schedule and another program is broadcast in its place. Production companies therefore are dependent on the networks to purchase the programs they produce and to continue to show these programs throughout a season. The networks provide the subsidies necessary to make a film and also provide the means of distributing the film. For a theater film, these two functions are separate. Because the networks finance the creation and distribution of films, they have extraordinary power in the complex processes associated with the creation of drama. Of course, the networks are dependent on the producers, the advertisers, and the local stations for their profits. Control shifts as various groups and individuals gain or lose power in the ongoing struggle over the content of television drama (Cantor, 1979b). The power of the networks was at its height in the late 1960s. Events such as government antitrust actions and citizen group pressure have contributed to a slight erosion of network power and to an increase in control from program suppliers.

Although the three networks at the present time are the most powerful influence on television drama, they too exist in a social and political context where they depend on others for profits and where outside groups want access to the airwaves. In Chapter 3 some of the legal and regulatory constraints were discussed. The legal system essentially supports the market operations of the networks at the present time. In this chapter the relationship among the networks, program suppliers, advertisers, and the local stations will be examined. The chapter will be divided as follows: (1) A description of the present system; (2) networks-advertisers in historic context; (3) networks and program suppliers; (4) networks, advertisers, and the ratings; and (5) the local stations and the networks.

# THE PRESENT SYSTEM

A commercial television network is part of a national broadcasting system characterized by (1) competitive free advertising, (2) distribution of programs by means of a national network of stations, and (3) government regulation (as a compromise between public and private interests). The three major networks in the United States function in a similar function. A network sells advertising spots and programs to national advertisers and distributes programs which are either produced directly or licensed from other producers. A network has been described briefly as "a group of connected stations broadcasting the same television programs" (Spilbeck, 1960).

Due to the nature of the medium (distribution of program material and the repetitive pattern of broadcasting), the major local television stations find it desirable to affiliate with a major network. The network-affiliation relationship is contractual and controlled by government regulation (see Chapter 3). Networks can also own and operate stations, but they are limited to seven (five if VHF) by the FCC. Such stations provide income as well as production facilities for the network. Most stations are affiliated by contract, not ownership. A local affiliated station, if it is not network-owned, legally controls what actually appears on the air.

Although there is some variation among the networks, the organization of all three is similar: (1) *sales division* with departments for research, advertising, and promotion; (2) *distribution division* with departments of engineering, station relations, and traffic (communications networks among the stations); (3) *program division* with departments for production, production services, continuity acceptance, news, public affairs, and general programming; (4) *business division* with departments for administration, finance and accounting, labor relations, personnel, and legal matters. Headquarters for the three major networks are in New York City, and each of the networks also maintains major production and programming centers in the Los Angeles area.

The departments in the program division concerned with programming and continuity acceptance are of major interest in this book. All three networks subscribe to the Television Code of the NAB. The code has been revised several times since its adoption in 1952, but its essential character and functions are to keep governmental regulations minimal by avoiding program practices that would offend pressure groups and advertisers. Also, within the programming department there are officials who make decisions on financing and scheduling matters. Because the networks' primary function is to provide programming which will attract audiences, they presently control the production process of drama in a variety of ways: (1) The networks finance the development of story concepts, scripts, and pilot films. (2) The networks decide what drama will be broadcast each season. (3) They decide when a particular show will appear during the prime-time hours. (4) The networks decide whether an episodic series once on the air will be discontinued (cancelled) or whether it will continue. (5) In the name of self-regulation they apply censorship to all scripts. (6) Finally, the networks decide how much air time will be devoted to drama, variety shows, public affairs programs, specials, documentaries, and sport events. The power of the scheduling and production of drama has ramifications in Hollywood because if the networks decide to devalue drama, less work is available for the creative people.

The structure of the network system of broadcasting has changed very little since its beginnings in radio over 50 years ago (Barnouw, 1977). However, the control the networks have had over programming has changed substantially. To repeat, a television network is simply an organization which transmits programs (historically over telephone lines) to local broadcasting stations which in turn broadcast the programs to those homes reached by their assigned frequencies. Although all three networks have produced (and still are producing) some of the programs which they then transmit, their primary purpose is to supply programs to those stations they own or are affiliated with through contractual agreements. NBC, ABC, and CBS each have about 200 affiliated local stations across the United States to which they feed 12 to 14 hours of programming and commercial advertisements daily. Three of the 12 to 14 hours each day are considered prime time. These evening hours from 8:00 to 11:00 on the east and west coasts and 7:00 to 10:00 in the midwest and Rocky Mountain states attract the largest numbers of steady viewers. Thus, they are the most profitable hours for the networks. A large proportion of the prime-time hours each week is devoted to drama.

The networks pay program suppliers to produce the drama they disseminate. In addition, they pay affiliated local stations a small fee for running the shows. The networks make their profits from selling air time to the advertisers (sponsors). The sponsors in turn produce the commercial advertisements and pay the networks huge fees to show these commercials during the broadcast day. The costs to the advertisers vary according to the size of the audience. Therefore, the fees generated during the prime-time hours are greater than at any other time.

The local stations are not obligated to carry network programs, but most of their revenues also come from selling their own commercials which are aired alongside those supplied by the networks (especially during the station breaks). The popularity of a network-sponsored show will also determine the fee a local station can charge for a commercial. The local stations do not have the financial resources to produce shows which will attract large audiences; therefore, they are dependent on the networks for programming. Because the advertising rates charged at both the national and local levels are determined by the ratings, both the networks and the local stations want to maximize the number of viewers. Most of the time local stations and networks have the same objectives, and both rely heavily on the rating services to help them determine the popularity of the shows and the fees charged to advertisers.

## NETWORKS—ADVERTISERS— HISTORICAL CONTEXT

Prime-time drama had its antecedents in network radio (see Chapter 2). In the 1930s, the sponsor decided on radio dramatic programming. If a sponsor decided to change a program, network assent was considered pro forma. The sponsor was assumed to hold a "franchise" on the time periods purchased directly from the networks. Many programs were created by advertising agencies and were designed to fulfill specific sponsor objectives. The director was likely to be an advertising agency staff employee. During dress rehearsal, an official of the sponsoring company was often on hand in the sponsor's booth, prepared to order last-minute changes. In NBC's headquarters and studios—Radio City in New York City, completed in 1933—every studio had a sponsor's booth (Barnouw, 1978:33).

During the decade 1945–1955, television drama was almost wholly produced live with strong theater influence. By the end of the decade network dramatic programs were almost exclusively filmed in Hollywood. Advertising agencies provided the subsidies needed to produce both live and film drama. However, the power of the sponsor in relationship to the networks was changing. The networks were not pleased with the degree of control wielded by the advertising agencies and the sponsors. William Paley, President of CBS, was determined that television should evolve differently from radio; and Sylvester L. Weaver, Jr., who became President of NBC in 1953, argued for a "magazine concept" of placing commercials. Under the magazine system, a program would not be under the control of a single sponsor, but rather sponsors would buy inserts in programs produced by the networks or by independent producers under network control. The magazine concept was not well received by the advertisers.[2]

Most sponsors continued to control programs. However, producing television drama was far more costly than radio drama, and segment sponsorship or alternate sponsorship became common during the 1950s. For example, *Philco Television Playhouse* and *Goodyear Television Playhouse* were the same series, with Philco and Goodyear alternating sponsorship each week. These arrangements involved some diffusion of control, but until the quiz scandals of 1959, sponsors essentially retained control over dramatic production. Independent producers sold their films directly to the sponsors, who in turn purchased prime airtime from the networks. *I Love Lucy*, an early film series, was sponsored entirely by the Phillip Morris cigarette company and was under its direct control. U.S. Steel sponsored a live dramatic series produced by the Theater Guild under the supervision of Batten, Barton, Durstine, and Osborn, an advertising agency. Although the live productions were considered by many to be artistically superior to the film series, the advertising agencies exercised editorial control over both. Many topics were considered taboo and were censored, especially those considered to be "liberal" or "anti-American" by the right-wing groups them pressuring the networks and advertising agencies.

The sponsor control of all prime-time programming did cause concern in the FCC. In 1959 it authorized a staff study of "television network program procurement" in which advertising agencies and others were questioned about program decision-making (Barnouw, 1978:53–54). Almost concurrently with the FCC investigation, Charles Van Doren, who had won $129,000 as a contestant on the quiz show *Twenty-One*, finally admitted after repeatedly denying any misconduct that all answers to quiz questions had been given to him in advance. His admission of perjured testimony brought forth some 100 other contestants who had appeared on several quiz shows then popular. Contestants and producers of the shows admitted they had lied to a grand jury investigating the irregularities of the quiz shows. This scandal led to congressional hearings, more FCC probes, and lawsuits. A most important consequence of these quiz show scandals was the reorganization of network operations regarding sponsorship.

This reorganization had two major effects on prime-time drama. Instead of the sponsors acting as primary censors, the networks became the only censors for the dramatic series. All scripts had to pass censor approval, and network officials often sat in on story conferences and watched series and other dramatic productions. Before 1959 the networks had offices called "broadcast standards" or "standards and practices" which applied the NAB code to programs (see Winick, 1959), but after the quiz scandals these offices became much more powerful than they had been in the past. In addition to applying the NAB code, the censors also applied standards concerning the use of hidden commercial advertisements within the program content. Often these commercials were accidental. In outdoor street scenes a sign advertising a particular company might inadvertently be captured on film. Since 1960 great care has been taking in seeing that such advertisements do not appear in drama. A more serious problem is displaying a commercial product during a drama, such as a bottle of whiskey on a table. These kinds of hidden commercials were the result of an agreement between producers and advertisers. In return for mentioning or showing the product, the producer was rewarded with money or a gift (often the product) in lieu of money. Network control stopped this practice. After 1959, there were incidents when the sponsor objected to some material on a show, and rarely an actual film segment for a series was made but not shown on the air because the advertiser did not approve (Cantor, 1971:64). However, because of network practices, the power of the sponsor remained, but became less direct.

The most important change came in 1960. That year four out of five dramatic shows in prime time were licensed (sold) to the networks which carried them, and in turn segments or spots were sold to the advertisers for commercials. This essentially reversed previous practice. Up until 1967, a few of the more prominent sponsors (such as Proctor and Gamble) were still making an occasional pilot film, but after 1960 these pilots often were not purchased by the networks although they had a guaranteed sponsor. By the mid-1960s the networks had gained firm control of the selection and scheduling of shows.

# The Production Companies

Although prime-time drama is broadcast on television, its production represents a marriage between the Hollywood movie and radio drama. The episodic series were originally radio with pictures (see Chapter 2). The format for television drama is partially determined by the 15-minute station break, partially by the themes and stories which were popular with radio and movie audiences, and partially by the nature of the movie industry in the United States. Decisions concerning the selection and placing of shows within the prime-time schedule are made in New York by network executives; the idea for the shows usually come from the production houses in Los Angeles. When drama moved to Los Angeles in the 1950s, independent producers rented space in the empty Hollywood studios which had once hummed with feature film activities. Because film production companies in Hollywood were suffering financially, independent agencies were able to rent studio space and develop and package low-budget series, usually 13 weeks long (Seldes, 1964). However, because such programs had to attract a large audience, more money was put into their production by the larger studios. These studios (and during the 1960s the networks themselves) captured film production for television. After the Justice Department brought its antitrust suit in 1972, the networks divested themselves of much of their production facilities. Now most drama is made by producers and production companies which are independent of the television industry.

Making any kind of film for wide distribution involves a number of large-scale organizations as well as outside financial backing. The systems that have evolved in the United States and elsewhere are similar. Amateur and semiprofessional films can be and are being made by small groups or individuals with relatively little money. However, most of the films shown on prime-time commercial television and in the commercial movie theaters are rarely, if ever, made by a lone entrepreneur with his or her own money. The independent producers of television drama and the large movie studios in the United States must find financial support before a project can be started. Theater movie production usually is supported by banks or through corporate enterprises from which investors buy stock. Each film made represents a gamble on the part of investors who are not guaranteed a profit from their investment. When a film is profitable, the rewards are so great as to make risk-taking worthwhile. The stars, the director, and the script enhance both the chance for financial support and the chances of success.

Movies made for television, the episodic series, and children's animated cartoons are rarely made without support from sources outside the production companies who make the films. An essential difference between a movie made for theater distribution and a television film is that most television dramas receive the outside support from one of the three networks instead of a bank, individual, or corporate structure. Although there are over 20 production companies in Los Angeles making or trying to make television films, only four or five produce most of the drama seen on prime-time television. While the number of networks has remained constant, the number and power of these program suppliers vary from year to year. For example, when I did my study of program suppliers and on-the-line producers who worked for them, the major suppliers were Universal Studios (MCA), Desilu, Quinn-Martin, and one or two others. Now, in 1980, there are several new names among the producers, and a few of the former suppliers are no longer producing for television.[3]

Essentially, there are only three primary buyers for all television drama, the networks. Program suppliers occasionally sell original drama to syndication companies which supply the few independent local stations throughout the country. This practice has increased in the last few years. Norman Lear (T.A.T./Tandem Productions) has done so with some success (*Mary Hartman, Mary Hartman*) and some failure (*All That Glitters*). Also, several stations have formed a cooperative to buy drama directly. However, the program suppliers prefer selling to the networks because the profit is higher and because a successful network show has greater possibility for multiple showings than an originally syndicated show. Most of the successful episodic series (those on air for two or more seasons) are syndicated for one or more additional runs. Every program suppliers desires to produce a series that is successful enough to be syndicated in the United States through the independent stations and through network television during the daytime or late evening hours. A very successful series may be shown through syndication by releasing old programs previously on the air during prime time while still showing new programs of the same series during the evening hours. Two examples are *M\*A\*S\*H* and *Charlie's Angels*, which were both seen during the 1979 season in prime time as well as through syndication at other times of the broadcast day.

## The Pilot Film

In former years most of the episodic series that appeared on the air were presented to the networks for purchase in the form of a pilot film. The pilot film is still used as a primary source for selection of new series. However, because the investment in a pilot film is so great, many are also seen as films which can have wider distribution than simply a vehicle to show off a program idea. Often a pilot film will also be seen as a movie made for television. As such it will be shown on the air several times during a season or repeated in several seasons. In addition, it will be sold to a syndication company for showings abroad, either in the theaters or on television (or both). Thus, the investment in the pilot is profitable to both the program supplier and the network. In addition to their initial wages, actors, writers, and directors receive residual payments (royalties) from repeated broadcasts.

Not all pilot films are purchased as series. The networks are involved in every step of the creative and production process from story concept to a successful series. Before a script can be written, the story idea is presented to one of the network's executives, usually a person in charge of programming. This is done by conversation, because under the rules of the Writer's Guild nothing should be presented in writing without a formal contract. Even after a script is written and purchased by the networks there is no guarantee that the network will finance the pilot film. When a script is completed, it is the property of the network. However, contracts are usually written so that the program suppliers are free to try to sell the script elsewhere should the original contracting network reject it. If not satisfied with the script, the network has the option of asking for rewrites either from the original author of from someone else. If and when the network is satisfied, a contract for a pilot film is negotiated with the program supplier.

## The Series

Most pilots do not become episodic series. The network along with the advertisers decide whether or not to place an order with the program supplier for a certain number of additional scripts and films to be produced if they think the pilot will make a successful series. This order may be for as few as four or six but the usual minimum order is 12 or 13 (to be shown for half a season). After a show is on the air for three or four weeks and there is some indication of audience approval, a decision is made whether to order more scripts and films. If ratings are low and advertising support is no longer forthcoming, the series will be cancelled. In reality, this means that no further shows will be ordered. A series which is on the air for 13 weeks or less

usually disappears from the air, never to be seen again by any audience.

Many shows that finish a season are renewed for a second season. There are examples of successful series which remain on the air for five, six, seven, or more years. Such shows are very profitable to the networks, program suppliers, the creative people working for the production houses, and the local broadcaster. As mentioned earlier, these shows are usually syndicated and often shown repeatedly on independent stations throughout the program day and on the network stations during the late evening and during the day. Also, they are often seen abroad, in both developing and developed nations.

Because of the potential profit associated with the episodic series, their initial costs are very high. According to *Broadcasting* magazine, neither the networks nor the program suppliers are anxious to divulge the specific costs of a prime-time series. Producer Grant Tinker, head of MTM productions, a very successful program supplier who had five series on the air during the 1974–1975 season, contends that because costs are so high producers are underpaid by the networks for first-run dramas. According to Tinker, it is impossible for a show to pay for itself from the original sale (*Broadcasting*, 1974). Most of those I interviewed as far back as 1968 agreed that it is unlikely for a show to recover costs while in its first run (before syndication) even if it were on the air for several years. This means that the real profit from the production of prime-time drama must come from reruns and syndication.

The networks at the present time are dependent on the program suppliers for ideas, scripts, and actual production. In the late 1960s the suppliers' power was even more pronounced than it is at the present time because each network also operated as a program supplier producing drama directly. *Bonanza*, for instance, was produced by NBC. In 1972 the Justice Department brought antitrust actions against ABC, CBS, and NBC for alleged monopoly practices. Although the suit has not been settled, the result of bringing the action is that the networks produce fewer of their own programs than they did in the recent past. At this writing, the Justice Department has reached an out-of-court settlement with NBC. The agreement imposes a number of restrictions on NBC in the programming area, but those restrictions are not effective unless ABC and CBS agree. Since the Justice Department suit was filed, the Federal Trade Commission (FTC) also began preliminary inquiry into broadcasting antitrust questions. The allegations being considered by the FTC, the Justice Department, and the FCC are that the networks have monopolized and restrained trade in prime-time programming. The Justice Department agreement with NBC will prevent the network from producing any television entertainment programs or feature films, but the network will still control scheduling including choice of programs and time. This agreement does not prevent the networks from financing the production of pilots; it simply prevents the networks from producing the films directly.

The program production companies hire the creative people, actors, writers, directors, on-the-line producers, and other personnel who actually create the films. Thus, the producers function as the liaison between the networks and the creators of drama. The networks deal with the production companies (program suppliers) for a flat fee plus a share of the syndication rights. The networks claim they are as dependent on the program suppliers as the suppliers are on them. The mutual dependence that has evolved between the networks and program suppliers is clear. In reality, although production companies provide new ideas for the shows and the actual films, the networks decide whether these ideas are accepted. The networks sometimes accept new ideas. Both the content and form of television drama have changed since television first became a national mass medium. However, no matter how creative a program supplier is, most television drama seen each season

is a direct result of network policy and decision-making.

## NETWORKS, RATINGS, AND ADVERTISING

Network profits come from advertising revenue. Network advertising rates climbed 30 percent in 1977 and have been going up ever since. In 1973, the advertiser paid $125,000 a minute for a spot on a show rated in the top ten. In order to attract advertisers, the number of viewers becomes the important consideration for program selection. The cost of a commercial spot is calculated to the all-important cost per thousand viewers (CPM). Thus, if a program attracts more viewers than another show, the profit to the network increases.

It is almost impossible for the networks or anyone else to predict with any certainty whether a new dramatic show will attract a large enough audience (measured by the ratings) to be profitable. Decisions on what to show appear to be made on the previous track record of the program supplier, what has been popular during a previous season, and often on "instinct." Although some kinds of audience pretesting surveys are made on certain shows before they are added to the schedule, these measures have proved unreliable (although they are still used). The two ways shows are pretested, either by presenting the plot idea verbally or on paper to a sample of viewers or by pretesting the pilot film with a captive audience, have not guaranteed more successful shows.

Martin Seiden (1974) has suggested that television drama is not under the control of the networks, but rather under the control of the A.C. Nielsen Company, whose rating services are treated as gospel by the networks and advertisers. I agree that after a show is developed and scheduled, the ratings obtained from Nielsen are very important. The networks have the most power in deciding what will be broadcast. They select the shows for their first run on the air. The ratings determine what will stay on the air. An episodic series is considered a success when there are two or more seasons of episodes available for syndication. For a series to stay on the air for more than its initial run, it must secure high ratings. The ratings of a miniseries and a movie made for television are also important to profits. For all kinds of drama, the ratings determine both the cost of the commercials to the advertisers and the profits to the networks and program suppliers.

## Ratings—A Definition and Explanation

Ratings are estimates, mostly projections, obtained from sampling techniques. They are expressed most often in the following ways: (1) the percentage of sets in use or homes watching television in the area being sampled at a given time (ratings), and (2) the percentage of the audience a particular program is drawing in comparison with those programs being television at the same time (share). Over 200 broadcast-rating services or audience-research films exist in the United States. The largest and most powerful is the A. C. Nielsen Company.

Advertisers and advertising agencies rely on Nielsen ratings in buying more than $900 million worth of network television time and programs each year. Along with the national television networks, they have invested over $20 million annually in Nielsen contracts. Each of the major networks alone spends over $300,000 for various audience-research reports and relies on Nielsen for 90 percent of its information.

The basic component of the Nielsen broadcast research operation is an automatic recording device called an audimeter. The device is wired, out of sight, to the television set in each of some 1,160 participating sample homes which make up Nielsen's fixed panel. When the set is in operation, the audimeter records minute-to-minute set tuning on 16mm film in the cartridge that is changed every two weeks by

the set owner. From the data gathered from the audimeter cartridge and from diaries, the Nielsen Company computes both local and national data for the television industry and issues information to subscribers through a variety of reports released at various intervals. Of all the reports, the Nielsen Television Index is perhaps the most influential in the industry. It includes (1) estimates of the number of U.S. television households using television at various times (*rating*); (2) average audience (homes viewing during an average minute of a program); (3) total audience (homes viewing the program in excess of five minutes); (4) the *share* of the audience during the average program minute, according to the number of sets actually in use at the time; (5) the average audience by programs' time segments; and (6) the number of stations and programs covered. Also included are sponsor and program indices, audience estimates by sponsorship, program-type audiences, television audience trends, and a national ranking of top programs.

There is little controversy that the Nielsen ratings are a powerful force in American broadcasting. The Nielsen ratings are considered to be official by the advertisers for the national market. Les Brown (1971) asserts that the Nielsen ratings are the real product of American television. They are what the networks sell to the advertisers and what the programs are designed for. For example, if a show has a 20 rating at 8:30 p.m., it supposedly reaches 25 million people. The rating can be broken down to "demographics," that is, the ages, sex composition, regions of the country, and income categories. The advertisers buy numbers and particular demographic subsamples. Brown contends that a sponsor who places his commercial in a time spot may not even know the name of the program he is sponsoring.

The two sets of numbers which are prime indicators of success or failure of a show are the rating and the share. In network television, a national rating of 17 or more is generally satisfactory in prime time. This indicates that 17 percent of American homes are tuned in to the particular program. The share, as noted above, is a competitive evaluation, denoting how a given program is performing opposite others on the air at the same time. A show usually does not survive unless it receives a share of 30.

Before 1970, the commercial value of a network television program was judged simply in terms of the percentage of households and the share a particular program attracted. Since that time demographics (especially age, income, and sex) of each program's audience has become crucial. According to Barnouw (1978), when the magazine concept of placing commercials was widely adopted, slot-buying became highly scientific. Nielsen data can tell a sponsor the male/female composition of the audience and can break the audience into age groups. In addition, because Nielsen conducts marketing research for products as well as audiences, sponsors can get matching demographic information on their retail customers for any of their products. Thus, sponsorship became a matching exercise—the demographics of the audience against the demographics of the buyers of the products.

## Program Survival

Network programs and especially dramatic series tend to survive, not if the content pleases the advertisers or the networks, but on other criteria. One necessary requirement for survival is the size of the audience. The other is if the audience meets the demographic requirements of the sponsors. Many sponsors are mainly trying to reach women, especially those between the ages of 18 and 49, because the products most commonly advertised are drugs, cosmetics, soaps, and other household products. Thus, survival of a program depends on high ratings as well as an audience with the necessary demographic requirements. High ratings alone are not enough to ensure survival. Some contend that the ratings, because they are scientific, are a democratic means of determining audience demand (Seiden, 1974). Others disagree on the

basis that certain groups are not included in the consideration of what is meant by demand. It is clear that programs are not designed for everyone, but rather for specific audiences. For the most part, minority audiences and those with less money for consuming, such as intellectuals, and the aged, who in particular make up a large segment of viewers, are rarely considered by the program suppliers and the networks. This will be further discussed in Chapter 6.

# THE LOCAL STATIONS

According to the Communications Act of 1934, individual stations, not the networks, are licensed and held accountable for what is broadcast. Many citizen groups and critics have argued that a local station, by affiliating with a network, actually forfeits its local responsibility. They contend that because the networks have complete control over programming (especially in prime time), they are not merely suppliers but virtual dictators.

Although there has always been some concern over the relationship of the networks and the affiliates, this concern increased during the late 1960s and 1970s. Pressure from one chain of local affiliates (Westinghouse) led to the Prime Time Access Rule discussed in Chapter 3 (Howard, 1979). The dissension between networks and affiliates has grown because of a major shift in the economics of television. In 1976, many major companies sharply increased their national budgets for television advertising. This resulted in increased demand for television commercial time, a shortage of commercial time available, and increased rates by the networks for this time. Under agreement with the affiliates, network commercial time is traditionally limed to three minutes per prime-time half-hour. A half-hour dramatic show is approximately 20 minutes long. This leaves approximately seven minutes for promotions, station breaks, and commercials to be sold at the local level. This three-minute limitation on the networks only applied to shows made for television. Movies made for theater distribution (and sports events) were exempt from the limit. In 1976 the networks redefined what qualified as a movie to include movies made for television, miniseries, and extra-length versions of regular programs. According to a study by Howard (1979), during the 1976–1977 television season 25 percent of all prime-time half-hour segments contained three and one-half minutes of network commercials instead of the acceptable three minutes. The result of this increase meant that local stations were denied the time to sell two or more commercials (a commercial spot is usually 30 seconds long).

Affiliates have argued that network control of programming limits diversity as well as their profits. In June 1978, the FCC started the first investigation into network operations since 1955. The final report from the investigation will not be submitted until the middle of 1980. As with all such investigations, no major changes in broadcasting operations are expected.

Nonetheless, most local stations are not necessarily committed to diversity or higher-quality programs, but to higher profits, as are the networks. Although the differences among the three networks may be minimal when it comes to overall programming, differences exist in terms of ratings that vary from year to year. For many years, CBS shows received the highest ratings, followed by NBC and ABC. In the last few years ABC's ratings have been the highest. This has changed the network affiliate structure somewhat. During the years 1977 and 1978, one station a month left either CBS or NBC to join ABC. At the same time, affiliates have shown an increased tendency to resist network pressure and look elsewhere for programming. Several years ago, a group of stations joined Tel Rep, a national advertising sales company, to form Operations Prime-Time for the purpose of producing alternatives to network dramatic programming. The first production (miniseries), Taylor Caldwell's *Testimony of Two Men*, was very successful. The stations carrying the program were able to bring enough advertising revenue to pay for the program and still make a larger profit than if they had used a network program. This cooperative, which some are calling a fourth network, includes approximately 65 stations which are network affiliates plus 25 independent stations.

Out of the more than 600 affiliated television stations in the United States, 65 might not be considered a great exodus. Most stations want to retain their affiliation with the networks because network affiliation is virtual assurance of station profit. One reason network programming assures profit is that network owned and operated stations reach at least 25 percent of the television viewers in the United States because these stations are in the major market areas. Networks have a strong audience base even without the affiliate stations.

## CONCLUSION

The possible future of network control is uncertain, not only because of some affiliate discontent, but because of the technologies available that could bring greater diversity in programming. However, as of now, the three networks decide on most of the dramatic programs televised in the United States. The history of dramatic production since the invention of the moving picture should alert those who are antinetwork that monopoly over filmmaking has always concerned critics , the courts, and Congress. There seems little reason to suppose that the adoption of greater diversity in dissemination will result in a more open system. This will be discussed in the concluding chapter.

The following chapter will discuss how network control influences the craft aspects of film and tape production. Those who create television drama—the writers, actors, directors, and on-the-line producers—are dependent on both the networks and the production companies in order to work. Problems of control as well as problems of employment and unemployment depend on the organizational and industrial structures that finance and disseminate drama.

# NOTES

1.  In the United States most television is provided by commercial enterprises. There is an alternative system of broadcasting established by the Public Broadcasting Act of 1967, commonly known as public television and radio. Public television is partially supported by the United States government, partially by contributors at the local level, and partially by grants from foundations and business enterprises at both local and national levels. The public system, although national, does not have the financial resources that are available through the networks and advertisers. The number of public stations are fewer than the number of commercial stations, and the audience is smaller as well (Lyle, 1974).

2.  The magazine concept of television advertising is similar to buying ads that are interspersed among stories and articles in a magazine. The system adopted in the United States is different from that adopted in England and other countries, where the broadcaster decides where to place commercials, rather than having the sponsor decide.

3.  Every Friday, *Daily Variety Western Edition* reports on the television shows in production in the Los Angeles movie and television studios. If a show is on location but made by an L.A. program supplier, that show also will be listed. Similar but not as detailed information is available in *Weekly Variety* for the New York area.

## Questions for the Cantor reading:

1. What is the relationship between networks, production companies, and local broadcasters? How are they tied together legally and economically? Who, in your opinion, stands to gain the most power from the relationship between them?

2. Briefly what is the relationship between networks and advertisers? According to Cantor, who controls most of the media content and why?

# Introduction to Todd Gitlin's "Making Schedules" and "The Triumph of the Synthetic: Spinoffs, Copies, Recombinant Culture"

Todd Gitlin was an associate professor of sociology and the director of the mass communications programs at the California, Berkeley when he wrote this seminal ethnographic look at the middle management aspects of network television. It was based on an extensive series of interviews and on-site observations with television producers and examines how they make the decisions they do to be successful in television programming. Like Cantor (see elsewhere), he is interested in the structures and social orders—the power hierarchy—of television management, but his approach is more personal and psychological than Cantor's organizational examination.

The chapters here deal with scheduling and marketing and how networks select the content that they believe will best succeed on the tube. Like the other readings, the suggestion here is that the television audience is not a homogenized, singular mass but a diverse body that must be segmented if programming and advertising is to have its maximum effect. And the targeting of that audience is what scheduling and programming is all about. The chapter on the recombinant culture is interesting because it reveals what television producers think in terms of their viewing audiences. All of this is designed to show how the thinking at network programming occurs and how personal tastes and values have less impact on content than we might originally think.

This work is also designed to reveal how the system itself and its needs for maximizing profits pressures individual creative people into shaping television to the lowest possible denomination; like so many of our readings, the bottom line when dealing with television content is that it is much more a business than a creative art form.

# Making Schedules

If prime time TV seems senseless, that may be because we view it through the prism of old-fashioned standards. We may expect loveliness of language, expressive acting, shadings of performance, and intimations of depths rumbling beneath the surface. We import ideals of craft and quality from ages of artisanship, even from the teleplays of the fifties. And indeed craft and quality do survive, at least as ideals, among Hollywood's craftsmen and -women. The networks, though, have a prior objective. Although executives may not be allergic to what they deem quality, the networks as a whole aim to create not purposeful or coherent or true or beautiful shows, but audiences. Any other purpose is subordinated to the larger design of keeping a sufficient number of people tuned in. That is, after all, what advertisers pay for. That is why the shows so often look concocted, forced, to critics trained to spot internal niceties. The sophistication goes not so much into shows as into calculations about audience "flow" and composition.

The networks are not only seeking aggregate eyeballs, they also aim to reach and hold particular target audiences—since inertia keeps many viewers tuned to the same network for hours on end unless they are driven away. Different histories, first of all, have furnished each network a different core of relatively reliable viewers. As a whole, CBS's audience is disproportionately older and more rural because CBS signed up more affiliates first and has always had relatively more affiliates in the smaller markets. ABC countered younger and more urban, for it was the third network to emerge, and therefore, at least until recently, has had fewer affiliates in the small markets (many of which had only one or

two stations before cable came along) and proportionately more in big cities. Having started that way, ABC reasoned that older viewers were creatures of habit, harder to woo from CBS and NBC, whereas the younger viewers would be easier to attract and keep, even as children and adolescents.* They proved right and stayed younger. NBC, in its dog years, can count on little, having even lost some affiliates to the more successful networks. With less market to take for granted, less "flow" from show to show on a given evening, NBC has to attract its audience from program to program. This leaves it, in the eyes of competitors, hopelessly floundering; or, in the hopeful words of NBC Entertainment president Brandon Tartikoff, "the most experimental of the three," aiming to "urbanize" its audience and lower its age.

So audience differences originated in CBS's small-town monopoly; CBS programmed to suit and ABC countered, which in turn solidified some expectations about what a CBS- or ABC-style show was—not in the whole audience, of course, but in enough of it to make a difference. "The three networks are department stores," says the bronzed, thirty-one-year-old Tartikoff, all California informality. "I'll go to Korvette's for a vacuum cleaner; I wouldn't think to go to them for a suit. I wouldn't go to Saks for a vacuum cleaner."

"We always look for programming that appeals to everybody," says CBS's avuncular programmer Herman Keld, "but that kind of program doesn't exist, really." So the networks tend to program for their core audiences. "When-

---

*There is evidence to support this ABC reasoning. According to a Nielsen study, adults over forty-nine are more likely to prefer long-running programs than are younger viewers.

ever we would put on programs that are what we might call the ABC-type programs," says Keld, "the more sophisticated, slick, big-city-type programs like *Three's Company, Charlie's Angels, Vega$, Hart to Hart,* we're not too successful." *Paper Chase* was a show that failed on CBS, Keld argues, because it was aiming for ABC-type demographics. ABC did well with teenage shows like *Happy Days, Laverne and Shirley, Mork and Mindy*; but at NBC, Tartikoff told me early in 1981, "the last real bubblegum show we did was *Brothers and Sisters*," a failed 1979 *Animal House* copy. At NBC such demographic reasoning is ad hoc and transitory, like so much network lore; a year later, NBC was running the teen-conscious *Fame.*

Not only do the networks set their sights on slightly different masses, but scheduling and even development take into account the shifting demographics of time-slots. The evening starts with an audience that averages about 17 percent children under twelve, with some 23 percent adults over fifty-five. By the ten-to-eleven time period, children are only 6.5 percent of the audience, and adults over fifty-five are now 26 percent. (The percentage of teenagers falls only slightly, form 10.6 percent to 8.3 percent.) Accordingly, the networks develop shows tailor-made for particular slots: *Happy Days, The Greatest American Hero, Mork and Mindy, Little House on the Prairie* were predestined to be eight-o'clock shows; *Lou Grant, Dynasty,* and *Strike Force,* ten-o'clock shows. At the last minute, a show might fail to sell because the network doesn't have the "right" slot open for it. Demographics likewise dictate different thresholds for censorship; *Hill Street Blues* can get away with language at ten that NBC would never permit in the child-laden eight-o'clock spot.

Precise demographic calculation became appealing to advertisers and the networks in the late sixties. Advertisers wanted to be sure they were buying their money's worth of women eighteen to forty-nine, or teenagers, or whatever their target of choice happened to be. For all the sophistication in data gathering, though,

CBS's Arnold Becker, for one, thinks sales departments have come to exaggerate the importance of audience composition. Suppose, for the sake of argument, CBS and ABC each has an audience of ten, he says; CBS with four young and six old, ABC six young and four old.* ABC goes to advertisers and argues that ABC is 50 percent better because it has six of the desirable young against CBS's four. But actually 80 percent of their viewers (four young and four old) are demographically the same. If advertisers and agencies also exaggerate the difference, to make themselves look more scientific, they are mistaken, too, because they fail to take into account the number of products they can sell to young and old. Suppose further, then, that the young buy twice as many units of Product X as do the old. Then CBS can sell one unit to each of its six old, and two to each of its four young, for a total of fourteen, while ABC can sell one unit to each of its four old and two units to each of its six young, for a total of sixteen. This makes ABC's spots not 50 percent more valuable than CBS's, but only 14 percent more.

Moreover, Becker doubts whether hit programs can even be targeted so specifically to age. He puts it this way: "I have a nice group of highly skilled professional people sitting over there, whose job is to make successful programs. And I say to them, 'Fellas, go out and make me a successful show. I want big numbers.' And they knock themselves out, and most of the time they fail. Now I say to them, 'Fellas, I got a new assignment for you. I want a hit program, big numbers, but I've got a little extra twist. Nothing much. I want it to be peculiarly popular with young people.' That's cruel and unusual punishment. The poor bastards don't know how to make a good show; how are you supposed to make a show that's good *and* particularly good with young people? So I would just as soon they did their best to make the most popular pro-

*This is a much greater difference than actually obtains. Becker also points out that for buying purposes the key distinction is between large and small families; but "young" and "old" are industry shorthand.

grams they're able to make and not worry their little old heads with whether it's going to be skewed a little bit younger or a little bit older. Let ABC do that. In the meantime, I'll beat them most of the time."

ABC and CBS do reason demographically when they develop shows, and in both cases the sales department, which has to sell spots for top dollar, may have its say. During the scheduling meetings, when the top programmers know they want to "pick up" a show, they often ask the sales department's advice about where on the schedule to put it. Of course, this could easily slide over into a question of whether to put it anywhere, since there are only so many slots available. In their anxiety, ABC and NBC development go farther. At times they consult with the sales department before scheduling meetings. What did sales think of the pilot? Did they laugh? Did they cry? That way, they arm themselves with marketability arguments that might prevail. Stu Sheslow, NBC's vice-president for drama, said that *Buck Rogers in the 25th Century* got onto the 1979 schedule, for example, because sales had sounded out certain advertisers, screened the pilot, and won their enthusiasm. Demographic arguments, like others, will be deployed by those who stand to benefit from them, and ignored or fudged otherwise. Since development executives move up by getting shows they've developed onto the schedule, they make all the arguments about demography, time-slots, network suitability, lead-in, competition, and advertiser zeal they can muster.

In all these calculation and ad hoc arguments, one demographic constant stands out. Since at least the early seventies, the over-sixty five audience (sometimes even over-fifty-five) has ranked least desirable. From the moment CBS shifted its programming strategy in 1969–70, as we shall see in Chapter 10, eighteen to forty-nine has been the premium group. The reason is simple: As Herman Keld puts it, "that's where your money is." Advertisers would pay less for access to older people, who had less money to dispose of. By the early eighties, however, the

population had aged significantly. In 1979–80, about one-third of the average prime-time audience was over fifty or over. Accordingly, the prime target—at least at CBS, which started with the largest share of older viewers—shifted to twenty-five to fifty-four, even twenty-five to sixty-four. As a bloc, these people now have, and spend, more money than they did ten years before. Advertisers have shifted their interests accordingly, although their computations tend to lag a few years behind reality. "For years," says one top CBS sales executive, "the beer people marketed to eighteen to thirty-four men. In recent years, those targets have changed to eighteen to forty-nine. Many food processors, like Kraft, Quaker Oats, General Mills, who used to go for eighteen to forty-nine, some years ago changed to twenty-five to fifty-four. Whatever the vicissitudes of network strategy, programmers keep at least one eye cocked in the direction of the advertisers who bankroll the whole enterprise.

Aggregate numbers, and the breakdown of those numbers, are what count, not the fate of any particular show. Moreover, the networks' grand designs shape the careers of the shows they've paid to develop in another important way. Producers produce programs, and development executives advocate them, but the top executive as a group compose schedules. Scheduling meetings dwell not only on the demographics expected but on problems of "flow": Would an eight-o'clock audience of given demographics stay tuned to show X at eight-thirty, given the competition? Many executives have also come to believe in what is called "counter-programming"—say, running a show watched disproportionately by men (*Hill Street Blues*) against a show that appeals more to women (*Fantasy Island*). Such scheduling is no longer an annual affair, but a year-long process of rearrangement, like a frantic, continuous round of interior redecoration. "I don't get gray hairs about competition from cable," says Brandon Tartikoff. "I don't own NBC. I might even be supplying some day. I get gray hairs about what movie am I going to have at eight-thirty?"

There are dissidents who think the game is not worth the candle. CBS Research's Arnold Becker, for example, makes a strong case that the preoccupation with flow is irrational from the network's point of view. He calls schedule-juggling "playing with yourself." "I have two shows," Becker argues, "A and B, and inherently they are of equal strength. I can cause A to have a good rating by putting it in a proper time period, and B a poor rating by putting it in a improper time period. If I switch those two around, B will do well and A will do poorly. The theory then follows that if I put everything in its optimum time period I would get optimum ratings. And a lot of time, energy, is spent on trying to figure out that optimum time period.…I think we have pretty well documented that there isn't an optimum schedule, that to the degree that you cause A to be high you cause B to be lower. I hate to tell you how many thousands of dollars I have paid college professors to run things through computers to try to figure out what this optimum was likely to be, or at least to give us some clues about how we should think about this. The conclusion really was, either it doesn't make any difference what you do, or we don't know how to do it."* The simplest precept of scheduling is that "lead-in," the show immediately preceding, makes a big difference to a show's ratings. But Becker makes so bold as to add, "One is hard pressed to document that lead-out [the show following], if you will, is less effective than lead-in. But everybody believes it. Even I believe it. But it's yet to be proven."

Becker is in the minority. Scheduling theories seem to impose a rational grid on decision-making. They amount to official lore; they are what network executives know. Becker and other skeptics find themselves banging their heads against a brick wall. Not only don't pro-

gramming executives believe his argument, Becker complains, "it's ridiculed as absolute nonsense. Since I've moved out to Los Angeles, I don't say this any more. I don't enjoy being hated." Programmers aren't interested in the evidence "because they can always name the one case that worked." But he thinks there are other reasons why rational argument is overlooked: "Once you have the programs, my philosophy is a very negative one, because it suggests that there is nothing you can do. There is nothing you can do but make better shows. But people like to believe that since they cannot make better shows, or they don't have better shows available to them this particular Wednesday afternoon, and they need them desperately, because they may get fired next week, that they have to do something, so they move them around and pray. It gives the feeling of doing something. It gives the feeling of movement. You don't have this feeling that you're sitting back and idly accepting your fate."

There are even a few executives and ex-executives, like Paul Klein and Deanne Barkley (formerly in charge of TV movies at both NBC and ABC) who go so far as to argue that viewers do not care much just which shows are plunked in front of them as long as they are, as Klein memorably said once, "the least objectionable programming." Klein observed that every day at the same time the number of TV sets tuned in held remarkably constant. If people simply sit in attendance, why develop so many scripts? Why make pilots and go through the rigmarole of scheduling and rescheduling? After minimal attention to demographics—you don't want to program a kids' show at 10: 00 P.M., for example—"you could choose them at random," Deanne Barkley says, "but don't you see, how does Fred Silverman justify his existence, or any of those people who are there? I maintain you could run a network with ten people. All these justify their existence by making decisions, pretending to make decisions as to what's on."

As it is, the "science" and "art" of program development and scheduling do only a few things

---

*What Becker called "the best experiment" we've done" entailed comparing the average ratings of all shows whose times were changed at midseason to the average ratings for all new shows. The conclusion was, "We weren't better off after we had made the changes than before. Some went up, some went down."

for certain. They bid up the market value of the executives themselves. They reinforce the networks' claim to be efficient servants of the popular will. Most important, they buttress network TV's position as the most efficient medium for advertisers. The numbers are both the wherewithal and the trappings of cost-effectiveness. Regardless of flaws, the presumed rationality of audience measurement and scheduling lore works just well enough to satisfy advertisers that they are getting their money's worth. That is all it really has to accomplish.

When the ratings are assembled for each week, the first-place network (usually CBS) rejoices and claims vindication for its judgments; the runner-up (usually ABC) can wax optimistic about its prospects; and the third (usually NBC) can comfort itself that it has taken some chances, or is building strength for the long run, or has stronger demographics. In any case, all three will go on competing on the common ground of ratings points. No one will pay them to do anything else.

Even by the network logic of maximum ratings, failures far outnumber successes. Of the total of sixty-two new shows introduced in the fall of 1980 and 1981, for example, only twenty did well enough to get renewed for a second year. But this bad commercial record—which television shares with the commercial theater, movies, and book publishing—is almost beside the point. In any system regulated by measures of quantity, winners require plenty of losers. As long as advertisers are content that network television gives them the most efficient access to the national market, then television's commercial failures are not too high a price for the networks to pay.

# The Triumph of the Synthetic: Spinoffs, Copies, Recombinant Culture

Safety first is the network rule. There seems safety in numbers: in test results for new and revamped shows, in extrapolations from previous ratings in the case of returning shows. But in the end, the numbers don't suffice to make decision. To build certainty, the "science" of numbers has to be joined to the "art" of hunches—consistently mostly of noting previous hits. The safest, easiest formula is that nothing succeeds like success. Hits are so rare that executives think a blatant imitation stands a good chance of getting bigger numbers than a show that stands on its own. Executives like to say they are constantly looking for something new, but their intuition tells them to hunt up prepackaged trends and then recognize the new as a variant of the old. This hedging of bets also supplies them with ready-made alibis in the frequent case of failure. Then, too, as long as the authentically and commercially new hasn't shown up, something has to be found to fill the airwaves; for time unfilled is time unsold. So why not exploit a currency already in circulation, one backed by the cachet of impressive numbers? Of course, at a certain point these gatekeepers will recognize that the market for a given formula has been stretched too far. It becomes oversaturated for cop shows, "jiggle," "fantasy," and the formula collapses. But that danger lies in the distant future, months, even years away. In the here and now, what rules is the severe pressure to show short-term results. The logic of maximizing the quick payoff has produced that very Hollywood hybrid, the recombinant form which assumes that selected features of recent hits can be spliced together to make a eugenic success. If *M\*A\*S\*H* and *Holiday on Ice* are both winners, why not army surgeons on skates? In this world without deep tradition, "why not?" is the recurrent question. The result is the absurd industrialization of mannerism, which is the industry's characteristic style.

## SPINOFFS

I asked Sy Amlen, vice-president of ABC Entertainment in New York, what was the central element of a series that determined whether it would get picked up as a potential success. With twenty-five years in research, Amlen is respected as an old pro, one of a handful of men who personify continuity in the business. Softly, but with absolute assurance, he said, "The most important thing in a show is character."

William S. Paley, Mr. Continuity himself, once wrote, "I believe the most important and virtually unfailing indication of a good program— over and above basic good writing, direction, casting, costumes, and sets—is likable, intriguing characters who capture the imagination, interest, or concern of the audience." Again and again, when I asked executives why a show had failed, I was told, "People didn't like the characters." Then came little theories about what exactly they didn't like. NBC's Gerald Jaffe said about the failed working-class series *Skag*, for example, "Anyone with a family all of whom are ugly people inside will do badly. Good people should be overcoming adversity."

The first thing network executives wonder about a new show is whether viewers will "invite" the characters back into their proverbial living rooms week after week. "The key to series television is longevity," said Tony Thomopoulos, president of ABC Entertainment. "When you look at a series's potential, you look at the character development and the longevity of those characters: Now you can deal with those characters week after week after week." These characters exist for the audience only as actors present them, which is a large reason why an idea pitched may sound so much better than the pilot looks. These actors-as-characters have to seem like reliable repeaters, since they are prospective members of the family.

Viewers strike up mysterious, quasi-personal relations with these flickering icons: squealing for Fonzie, swooning for Farrah Fawcett (or her bathing suits), loathing—and loving to loathe—J.R. Ewing, or for that matter trusting Dan Rather or Mike Wallace. Monday night may have "belonged" to Lou Grant the way it used to "belong" to the regular poker crowd at the next-door neighbors or the folks at the Kiwanis Club. We may even talk back to these characters, complain about their marriages, decry their lapses from their usual conduct. What they have in common is that they are regulars.

But there is no technological imperative behind long-running series. Limited runs of six or thirteen episodes are common in Europe.* Historians of popular culture might argue that ample precedent exists for American TV series in the eighteenth- and nineteenth-century novels that appeared regularly in newspaper and magazine installments. But the question then remains, why aren't regular characters the staples of popular culture everywhere and at all times? Are Americans more needy of familiar figures than the English, who have royalty as their continuing quasi-family? Theories that begin from audience demand always run afoul of the fact that popular taste is not born but made.

We are on surer ground when we inspect the supply side. All modern organizations aspire to order, regularity, routine, which make for efficiency and control. The networks have proved no different; but on top of this general tendency, television inherited its forms from radio. The first American radio programs, in the early twenties, were not narrative at al but one-of-a-kind musical performances. Then came dramatic series, weekly anthologies like *Great Moments in Drama* and *Biblical Dramas*. But a new precedent was set by the hit syndicated series *Amos 'n' Andy*, which played on NBC five days a week beginning in 1928. The show was all the rage, so talked about—all the way to Calvin Coolidge's White House—that regular series, constellations of fixed stars, became axiomatic. Like the film industry, whose star system arose only after 1914, radio took a while to discover that established stars were efficient draws in a consumer society. Once the discovery was made, though, advertisers joined the networks in solidifying it. Commercials and series had an affinity. In time, advertisers learned that regular characters meant reliable audiences; if characters were popular, sponsors could borrow some of that popularity.

Within a few years, television recapitulated the history of radio. In the so-called Golden Years of the late forties and early fifties the TV networks offered mostly variety show, anthology drama, music, and sports—all live, most of it produced in New York. But, by the late fifties, episodic series were considerably more popular than other forms. In 1958–59, nine of the ten most popular shows were episodic series featuring regular characters.*

The shift to episodes came with the shift from live performance to film and tape. *I Love Lucy* demonstrated that successful filmed episodic series were gold mines. The film studios belatedly recognized that television wasn't going to blow over, and switched to producing TV

---

*So are episodes of uneven lengths—fifty-eight or seventy-two minutes. In this regard, though, America is indeed driven toward uniformity by technical obstacles. With hundreds of far-flung affiliates, the networks would find it virtually imposible to synchronize their transmissions if they went out at irregular intervals.

*The tenth, *I've Got a Secret*, was really an episode series of its own: a mystery game show in which a regular cast encountered an adversary-of-the-week.

series. The networks now understood they could reach for greater profits (not to mention control) if they regularized production through film suppliers. The result was the shift of production to Hollywood and the decline of live drama. Live broadcasts dwindled from 80 percent of all network programs in 1953 to 33 percent in 1960, with the remainder split between film and videotape.* The industry came to believe that variety shows fail, anthology series fail, and an excess of movies is catastrophic.† In series, each episode is a billboard advertising the next.

The advertisers' interest in reliable characters was more than matched by the suppliers, who quickly realized that the real money was in syndication. Production costs began to climb exponentially, exceeding the license fees the networks paid for the right to broadcast the shows. But costs could be more that matched by the promise of syndication, potentially stretching to the end of recorded time. In a sense, every series developed was an investment in the chance of syndication, although only one in forty series on the air lasts long enough to be syndicated. If a show did well its first time around, and if it could last several seasons on the network—the magic number was considered to be four or five years, or roughly a hundred episodes—then it was worth a fortune to syndicators, who usually trimmed a few minutes from the original show so that more commercials could be inserted, and sold the package back to local station, or even the network itself, for daily broadcast in the morning, afternoon, or late at

night. Plainly, the route to syndication was in characters who became little household gods. All the more motive for suppliers to concoct characters who promised to wear well. Perhaps most of all, the networks care which actor is going to realize the character. Only as flesh and blood, as an actor, does the character exist for an audience. That is why the networks insist on playing a major part in casting. There is a perpetual tug of war between networks and producers over who gets the last word in casting. In these skirmishes, the networks always have the upper hand: The contracts may guarantee the producers "creative control," but the networks don't have to air the show, and the producers know who is putting up the money. In recent years many producers have been dismayed that the networks have not only usurped the casting of leads but have insisted that whole committees sit in on the casting of minor parts. "I think we should be involved in casting, it's our money," says NBC's genial number-two programming executive, Perry Lafferty. He adds, "The key to every television program's success—and this will get a lot of people mad, but it's true—is casting," Lafferty insists. "It's who plays the lead. I can't tell you any plots from *The Rockford Files*. I used to love it. I love James Garner. I loved Telly Savalas's Kojak. That's what the audience goes for. They go for the performer. They don't remember the plots; you can't write that good over a period of time. So it comes down to who do you put in there."

If the single most important factor in series success is the appeal of its major characters, then it is logical to launch a show with characters whose appeal is pretested. If acquaintanceship is ready-made, so much the better. When secondary characters are "spun off" from current series to stand on their own, presumably they have already accumulated their followings on the road. Indeed, because actor/character magnetism is so mysterious, success may be transferable even when the spun-off character and the tenor of the show change considerably from the original. One case in point is *Lou Grant*,

---

*As late as 1963, *Naked City*, one of the last shows to be shot in New York, made a considerable critical success and a decent enough showing in the ratings—though it never landed among a season's top twenty-five shows—with a format in which the regular cops faded into the background while the foreground belonged to each week's new character in the grip of the city. This figure-ground reversal was unusual, and in the squeeze of growing competition there have not been many attempts to repeat it.

†In 1976, Paul Klein at NBC decided that audiences were outgrowing series; he reserved two hours a night, four nights running, for miniseries and specials. Knowledgeable industry hands attribute NBC's precipitous decline to tht decision.

rendered serious when he moved from the comic *Mary Tyler Moore Show.* An even stranger case is *Trapper John, M.D.* This flatly written melodrama featuring a one-time *M\*A\*S\*H* character bore not the slightest tonal resemblance to its progenitor; yet with different producers it rated high on the CBS schedule for several season in a row.

Such spinoffs spring from the industry logic of putting capital to maximum use. The impulse might start with the network, the supplying company, the producer, or the actor (or even the actor's agent or business manager). Spinoffs were all the rage in the seventies and early eighties. *The Jeffersons, Maude*, and *Gloria* sprang from *All in the Family; Rhoda, Phyllis*, and *Lou Grant* from *Mary Tyler Moore; Laverne and Shirley* and *Joanie Loves Chachi* from *Happy Days; Sheriff Lobo* from *B.J. and the Bear; Facts of Life* from *Diff'rent Strokes; Enos* from *The Dukes of Hazard; Knots Landing* from *Dallas; Flo* from *Alice; Benson* from *Soap;* and in a brief third generation flash, *Checking In* from *The Jeffersons.*

This triumph of the synthetic grew into self-caricature under the successive reigns of Fred Silverman at all three networks. Silverman was head of programming at CBS in 1970–75, president of the ABC Entertainment division in 1975–78, and president of the entire National Broadcasting Company in 1978–81; his unparalleled reign over a decade demonstrates how the networks, in effect, fused in the heat of competition. Spinoffs not only seemed good bets for success, but they gave Silverman, the son of a TV repairman, a chance to exercise his craft: to plunge his own hands into a series, to rework the elements and deploy them to network advantage. As he spun with growing intensity, he also spun with declining finesse. At NBC, in his last season, Silverman tried out five different proposed spinoffs on series episodes. One made it to the air as series.

A number of other spinoffs failed over the years: *Phyllis, Flo, Lobo, Checking In, Enos,* to name only five. Evidently acquaintanceship with character did not transfer automatically. Com-

mercial success required the right context for the right characters.* On the other hand, *The Jeffersons* has lasted nine seasons, at this writing, finishing the top twenty-five for four of them. *Laverne and Shirley* ranked number one for two years running. *Rhoda, Knots Landing, Facts of Life, Benson*, and *Lou Grant* were at least modest enough successes to run more than one season.

This raises the question of how reliable spinoffs really are. I could not, however, find any network research executive who had bothered to calculate their success rate as against the normal run of shows. "You don't need research for that," said Gerald Jaffe, vice-president for research projects at NBC, humoring me for asking a naïve question. It seemed obvious that spinoffs do better than the average show. So runs the conventional wisdom, which is not always wrong.[†]

Spinoffs are lucrative not only to networks but to suppliers; indeed, the financial rewards are so great that they routinely overwhelm such aesthetic qualms as may exist. Whoever holds the "created by" credit for a series shares title to its characters, and therefore can collect a royalty of $25,000 or more per episode, whoever writes and produces the show. Moreover, any writer who devises a character is entitled to a minimum of $657 per half-hour episode, or $1,248 per hour, for each episode in which the character ever appears, no matter who writes it; for an hour-long show the payment would amount to over $27,000 over a short season. The "created by" credit is like the patent on an invention. That

---

*And at the right moment. NBC's *Bret Maverick* (1981–82) brought back the star of a bygone decade in his old role, but couldn't recapture the offhand, self-consciously spoofing charm of the original now that the western form being spoofed was no longer current. It was as if James Garner had come back to the screen telling Eisenhower jokes.

[†]In the seventies, Hollywood made a counterpart discovery, too: Sequels are to movies as spinoffs are to TV series. Faced with rising costs and declining movie attendance except among teenagers, the studios minimized risk by proliferating *Superman, Smokey and the Bandit, Star Trek, Star Wars, Halloween, Friday the 13th, Grease*…almost always to considerable payoff, although rarely as much as the original.

is why there are often heated battles over who holds title; adjudicating such matters is a central function of the Writers Guild of America.

Spinoffs are not altogether unprecedented in the history of drama and story-telling, yet television has stretched self-imitation far beyond the limits of previous forms. When Sophocles continued Creon from *Antigone* into *Oedipus the King*, he was not "spinning off Creon"; he was giving body to deep myth and carrying it to completion. Each tragedy was autonomous. When Shakespeare bore Falstaff from the two parts of *Henry IV* into *The Merry Wives of Windsor*, he may have been mindful of Falstaff's popularity, but *The Merry Wives* had a life of its own. When Balzac threaded Rastignac and Vautrin through many volumes of his *Comédie Humaine*, and Trollope did likewise in his *Barsetshire Chronicle*, they almost certainly had commercial motives, but they were not going through the motions of contriving a new situation to keep a character alive. They were populating an entire microcosm with characters who already could be said to exist, prolonging the lives of those already living. By contrast, most spinoffs are like wealthy heirs, living off capital accumulated by the forefathers.

# COPIES

If a spinoff exploits success by transferring a character, a copy exploits it by reproducing a formula. Copies are legion. As Brian Winston has aptly written, a goodly number of pilots "are to creativity what Xeroxing is to writing."

But what is exactly a copy? When I asked NBC's Gerald Jaffe about the success rates of imitation shows, he said matter-of-factly, "Everything's an imitation. You can't sort them out. Everything's and imitation of something else." And it is true that in television it is not easy to say what exactly qualifies as s copy, what is a distillation from common trendy materials, and what is simply a normal variation on run-of-the mill themes.

Only an innocent is shocked by the dryness of the tone in which the immensely successful producer Aaron Spelling says, "There are only seven original plots; you try to do them with style and moderation." In businesslike recognition of this perhaps sad but inevitable truth, the industry speaks with a single jaded voice. NBC's Brandon Tartikoff, for example, said cavalierly about three new CBS shows, "*Magnum* is *Rockford* with another guy in a moustache; *Ladies' Man* is *WKRP* sideways; *Midland Heights* is a ripoff of *Dallas*." He was talking about the competition, but his tone by no means signaled that these were venial sins. A year later, since *Magnum* was the only new hit of the bunch, it was *Magnum* that was getting cloned by other strapping, half-whimsical "hunks." With imitation so taken for granted, sometimes not even "ripoff" is a term of great opprobrium.

Of course, the entire history of art is rife with imitation. When art was one aspect of ritual, it even aspired to repetition, which hoped to approximate the transcendent. In medieval Europe, the church, crown, and nobility, who sheltered art and hired artists, were devoted principally to conserving traditions. Only as the Middle Ages waned did artists move beyond refinements of technique to search after personal style. Much later, with romanticism, the artist's calling shifted definitively from the refining to the smashing of idols. The desire to break molds now became a philosophical position. William Blake expressed the new attitude strikingly when he belittled the very formulas of rational cognition: "Man by his reasoning power can only compare and judge of what he has already perceived." From this it was only a step to Walt Whitman's call to the open road, Baudelaire's invitation to the voyage, and Pound's supreme modernist ultimatum, "Make it new."

Still, romanticism turned out Janus-faced. Romanticism invoked novelty, inviting artist and reader alike to press beyond the known; but at the same time it proclaimed that nothing was so important as the expression of true feeling. Straining for effect, romanticism invited the artist to repeat prefabricated conventions whose effects on the audience had already been demonstrated.* Romanticism encouraged not only avant-garde forays into the unknown, but academic art's repetition of the altogether known. From the formal rules of academic art to the formulas of popular culture is not so great a leap. Barbara Cartland romance novels, Agatha Christie detective stories, Marvel Comics, and *Dukes of Hazzard* episodes are all of a piece with genre paintings and the general run of sonatas and sonnets. On the premise that people want to repeat a pleasurable experience, to make it familiar, the present-day culture industry has erected an apparatus for the mass production of self-imitating artifacts.

On TV, this impulse to imitate also becomes quality control, precisely to check the individualistic excesses of episode writers. Writers are hired by the job, to write "a *Dukes of Hazzard*," "a *M\*A\*S\*H*." Once it was even commonplace for series to provide these journeymen with a "bible," which specified all the salient features of the format. Now, producers, story editors, and staff writers ensure the uniformity of the product. Accordingly, episode writing is entry-level work, the lowest-status and poorest-paid in television's writing hierarchy. (By the terms of the 1981 Writers Guild contract, the 1983–84 minimum payment for a thirty-minute prime-time script is $6,406; for story and script together, $8,933. The comparable figures for sixty minutes are $8,642 and $13,136. Pilots pay a minimum of 150 percent of the applicable episode figures, and in practice pay considerably more.) Episode writers are usually modest and often embarrassed about their labors. "You don't have to have a talent to write for television," says one vet-

eran comedy episode writer. "I thought it was writing, but it's not. It's a craft. It's like a tailor. You want cuffs? You've got cuffs." As a television product moves through the factories of the production company and the networks, the singular elements are trimmed back, the corners knocked off. Even "novelty" is stereotyped, because only certain forms of novelty are considered salable. Talk of "innovation" is relative in the extreme.

So one must distinguish between the normal imitativeness of art and the industrialized excess that is television's sincerest form of fawning on itself. Throughout the mass-market culture industries—books, magazines, pop music movies—imitation runs rampant, but in television the process was raised to self-parody by the economics of competition among the three networks. In the mid-seventies, ABC finally elbowed into serious competition with CBS by scoring with teenage shows and the new "jiggle" genre, or what the industry casually and cynically called "T&A," for "tits and ass." A new go-go competition was spawned by the coupling of greed and fear. After ABC's smash *Charlie's Angels*— did so well in 1976–77 that frequently more than half the total audience tuned in, imitation became feverish as other networks rushed in. Within the year, for example, the writer just quoted was hired to rewrite at least three pilots that were variations of *Charlie's Angels*—nubile, adventure-seeking women platonically working for (or symbolically, under) dapper men. At CBS, Mr. Paley was said to have asked his programmers, "Where are *our* beautiful girls?"

At the time, the networks were somewhat at a loss. They had been riding high with cop shows, but pressure groups led by the PTA had prevailed upon some advertisers to cut back their purchase of televised violence. Fleshly display seemed a plausible substitute for fleshly destruction. Brandon Tartikoff, then vice-president of NBC's West Coast programming, had a practical explanation for the new trend: "All of television boils down to excisable elements that you can put in twenty-second promos. If you can't

---

* This argument follows Hermann Broch, "Notes on the Problem of Kitsch." But one should not exaggerate the shift from art-as-self-contained-artifact to art-as-stimulus-to-audience. T.W. Adorno usefully reminds us: "It would be romanticizing to assume that formerly art was entirely pure, that the creative artist thought only in terms of the inner consistency of the artifact and not also of its effect upon the spectators. Theatrical art, in particular, cannot be separated from audience reaction."

have Starsky pull a gun and fire it fifty times a day on promos, sex becomes your next best handle." It was also the easiest element for executives to notice and copy.

What could be more surface than skin? By the spring of 1978, the networks had commissioned dozens of T&A scripts and pilots with titles, in case the point was obscure, like *The Beach Girls, California Girls, Pom Pom Girls, Roller Girls, The Cheerleaders, California Co-eds, The El Paso Pussycats,* and *Legs.* Only three got on the air: ABC's *The Feather and Father Gang,* about a gorgeous lawyer working with her ex-con father; CBS's *Flying High,* with three stewardesses; and CBS's *The American Girls,* with two TV reporters. Like Charlie's Angels, the American Girls worked for a male boss on a long leash. In the pilot, the "girls" were captured by white slavers in Phoenix. Like most pornography, the show contained only enough melodrama to show off the abundant jiggling. (As journalist Richard M. Levine wrote, their "biggest scoops are their necklines.") The producer couldn't reproduce the Angels' tone and the show got unplugged after six episodes. *Flying High,* meanwhile, was the brainchild of an executive producer who cast three voluptuous actresses from top New York modeling agencies. They had done commercials, but none had ever acted a script. Since the Angels formula was read as what one former executive called "three broads, one blonde," one of the stewardesses was obligingly dyed blonde. *Flying High* went down in flames within four months.

These transparent thefts were unavailing partly because *Charlie's Angels* had the gloss of coming first, but partly because the copies were only surface-deep. They copied the elements but not the aura. And the aura was everything. The great critic Walter Benjamin thought art was losing its aura in an age of photographic reproduction, but he did not live long enough to see that trash could acquire its own aura by virtue of finding its formula first. Overnight the Angels became "originals." The formula proved alluring enough to withstand a series of cast changes,

although no one ever duplicated Farrah Fawcet's pinup mystique.

Indeed, the *Charlie's Angels* formula was a bit more complicated than generally recognized. The copies failed to sufficiently fathom the Angels' attraction to women, who made up the majority of the Angels' audience. I have heard women say that they were attracted by the Angels' glamorous and frequently changed fashions, and by the spunk they displayed as they played at their Southern California "life-style." Men could tune in to ogle women's bodies; women could tune in to study what those men wanted. Moreover, without having set out to do so, producer Aaron Spelling appealed at once to elements of the new feminism and its conservative opposition. The Angels were skilled working women and sex objects at the same time. Barney Rosenzweig, who produced part of the first season, and whose "consciousness was being raised" by reading Molly Haskell's book on women in the movies, *From Reverence to Rape,* and by going out with a feminist writer, says he persuaded Spelling that the majority of the audience would be "young girls" who were going to take the Angels as role models. The Angels "must be terrific and bright and nonsexist," he said. He wanted to stop the blatantly sexist dialogue, as in one case where a man who had bought a hot dog from an Angel said, "This dog's cold," and she replied, "You should taste the buns," "You should see my buns," or words to that effect, Rosenzweig recalls. Later, after he left the show, the sexist cracks came back.

Throughout the run, The Angels got in and out of jeopardy while relying on Charlie, their unseen detective boss, to bail them out. It was probably no small part of the show's appeal to men that Charlie was heard but never seen. Male authority was invisible, and the "girls" kept free of romance. Charlie's ambassador on the scene was the sexless Bosley, eunuch to Charlie's harem. In the male viewer's fantasy, he could *be* Charlie, ever supervising, ever needed, ever returned-to monopolist of Angels. Spelling had kept Charlie off-screen as a gimmick, but it proved to be a charmed gimmick with psychological point.* The imitation Angels reported to their male bosses on-screen, and lacked the Angels' delicate balance of spunk and subservience.

The commercial problem with copies is that the numbers garnered by an "original" rarely certify an entire trend. Whatever consolation precedents provide anxious executives, the crude elements of formula are more easily observed and recycled than the singular. The truth is that when it comes to imitations, the networks lack an internal thermostat. Typically, the T&A craze ran out of control until the oversaturated audience finally tuned its channel selectors elsewhere. Then, as the trend was waning, the fundamentalist right administered the *coup de grace* with its protest against "skin," "implied sexual intercourse," and "sexual innuendo."

By 1982, necklines were up and no new jiggle was being bought. But such boom-and-bust cycles can take years to run their course, while vast sums of money and vast energies go into the copying process along the way. As long as the boom mood prevails, shows that don't fit the mold are starting with higher than normal odds against them. But complaints about executive tastelessness are somewhat beside the point. As long as commercial success is the transcendent goal in the TV market structure, competitors are always likely to copy each other's successes, reasoning that successful Product A is a litmus test that has succeeded in registering a popular desire. Moreover, imitators are always easier to find and hire than are innovators. The same logic leads to TV versions of successful movies, whether serious adaptation (*M\*A\*S\*H*), domestications (*Alice* as a comic version of Martin Scorsese's *Alice Doesn't Live Here Any More*),

or capitalizations on a hot genre (*Tales of the Gold Monkey* as a derivative of *Raiders of the Lost Ark*). Executives do not seem to know what to do instead, and don't want to be left out of a good bet. Sooner or later, the mass audience, having gone along with the fad, grows weary, bored, resentful—in its odd way, discriminating. It takes its revenge.

The cultural marketer's problem is how to know which were the magical elements in the original success. What, precisely, is to be extrapolated? The quest for borrowed glory promises security, but it is easy to guess wrong by guessing simple. In 1981, for example, Fred Silverman was by no means the only industry theorist to behold the vast ratings success of CBS's *The Dukes of Hazzard*, which regularly pulled down a 40 share, and conclude that what made it popular was the spectacle of cars crashing, cars sailing through the air, especially the successful chase that at the end of each episode proved the prowess of the show's good ole boys in time for them to gloat over the ineptitude of the hapless sheriff. But despite the show's hayseed reputation—Hollywood writers considered it synonymous with "shit-kicker," the lowest of low-life products—the show was more complex than the chase. An odd family of good-ole-boy brothers, their buxom Daisy Mae cousin (actually named Daisy, to make her archetypal origin clear), and their wise uncle, each week rose up against the wicked, white-suited Boss Hogg, a mean-spirited penny pincher who owned the bank as well as the restaurant where Daisy worked, and seemed to have the sheriff in his back pocket. Each week the town was invaded by bad-guy outsiders, the sheriff proved incompetent, and the good ole boys saved the day after a chase in their custom car, the "General Lee," with its car horn that tooted "Dixie."

The producers thought that the car and the chase were what many men tuned in for—and the show did draw an unusually high proportion of male viewers, though still, like most of television, a female majority. The writer Gy Waldron "always said that General Lee is the most critical

*After the fact, one top network executive acknowledged the show's social function when he said in all seriousness, "A series like *Charlie's Angels* performs a very important and valuable public service. Not only does it show women how to look beautiful and lead very exciting lives, but they still take their orders from a man." Rarely do executives theorize about social reasons for a smash hit; there is a virtual taboo against analyzing a golden goose to death. This makes the occasional exception all the more interesting.

character in the show," says Phil Mandelker, *Dukes's* first producer. "He was right, and so we gave it a personality." But it is a reasonable starting premise that no show draws its viewers all for the same reason. The producers and the network responsible for the original always attribute success to the magic, the "chemistry," of concept, casting, and "execution," and they may be right. But plausibly, too, an element in *Dukes's* success was its ideology: its fusion of populism, good-ole-boy fraternity, and adolescent high-jinks in behalf of law and order. Phil Mandelker thought as much. "On one level, I saw *Smokey and the Bandit* [a hit movie starring Burt Reynolds] and related very strongly to it, and felt that, wait a minute, there's something really terrific going on here. I felt [*Dukes*] was Robin Hood and Little John in Sherwood Forest. I felt that all of us have a sense that we're in Sherwood Forest today, in which the law no longer seems to work. I took that to its most extreme position, to find the comedy of it, a core of very honest people trying to do good in the middle of Sherwood Forest."*

But when NBC set out to parse the success of *The Dukes of Hazzard*, they came out with buddies and technology. And so, owing a series commitment to Johnny Carson's company, the network ordered from Carson a pilot called *The Stockers*, starring Pittsburgh Steeler quarterback Terry Bradshaw as one of a pair of southern stock-car racers. The show rated badly, and sank quickly. More clones end up in speedy demise than network executives like to think. Television audiences spot a copy when it is hurled right between their eyes. Clones beg for comparison and usually suffer by it. But they are easy to conceive, they do not stretch the imagination, and they keep the assembly line moving.

## RECOMBINANTS

If clones are the lowest forms of imitation, recombinants of elements from proven successes are the most interesting. Much of what passes for creativity in Hollywood is additive. In 1981, Fred Silverman's NBC made the movie *The Harlem Globetrotters on Gilligan's Island* and the series *The Brady Brides*, based on an earlier hit, *The Brady Bunch*. Once again, Silverman was carrying recombination to his characteristic point of self-parody. "Freddie's in some kind of time warp, and he just keeps groping into the hat for shows that were hits," as the *Hill Street Blues* writer/producer Michael Kozoll put it. But Silverman's vulgarity lay only in excess: He spliced a bit too frantically, imitated one or two decades back too far.

For in normal network doings, not only are many of the products deliberately recombinant, so is industry jargon. Grant Tinker, who had earned his reputation as a high-taste TV proprietor, still told me about a project in the works at MTM that, "just to be quick about it"—and quick is the way projects are bought and sold—he called *Hill Street in the Hospital*. (In 1982, NBC bought it under the title *St. Elsewhere*.) An ad agency referred to CBS's series *Falcon Crest* as "a taste of *The Good Earth* and a dash of *Dallas* in the middle of a California vineyard." Producer Garry Marshall told writer Sally Bedell that he conceived of *Happy Days* as "a look back, a humorous *Waltons*. In my head I was doing Norman Rockwell and *Huckleberry Finn* and *Tom Sawyer*." "I have never been in a TV development meeting," says Michael Kozoll, "where someone does not use that language and ask, 'What's it like?'"

What is good enough shorthand for shows also applies to characters. One old writing hand, Richard Powell (no relation to the actor), was writing a pilot for NBC about a man in his late

---

*Mandelker's version of Robin Hood wasn't robbing the rich to help the poor, though. His was the middle-class lament that things don't work: "Part of the trees in the forest that are surrounding us is that we assume a system of justice works, and it doesn't seem to work. We assume that if you pay a man to do a job for you, the job will be done and he will stand by it. And that doesn't work, because the man doesn't need our work. If you call the plumber he doesn't really need your work," except during economic depression.

sixties who had suffered a stroke and maintained "an acerbic relationship" with a black woman therapist. "We constantly fight," Powell said, "because they will say things to you like, 'Well, we want the man to be more like Archie Bunker, and we want the woman to be more like Maude,' and they want a kid in there who'll be like the kid in *Diff'rent Strokes.*"

This was Silverman product, too. As it happens, Silverman's network reigns were the periods of maximum competition for booming advertiser dollars, and therefore the times most given to cannibalizing programs. How easy for the press to pin the responsibility and the blame on a single powerhouse, overlooking the corporate heads and boards that promoted him to successively more powerful positions until his bubble burst. The era of recombinatory excess took off in the Silverman seventies, and many industry old hands look back nostalgically to the presumably Golden Years, when patterns of imitation had not become so automatic. Grant Tinker harks back, for instance to his earlier tenure at NBC, 1961–66, when "television was surely more varied, and because it was, I think people were hitting bull's-eyes a little more often. They weren't just clonishly following each other in a sort of futile game of program leapfrog, as we all seem to be doing now." But the trend preceded Silverman and outlasted him. Cultural recombination is not simply a convenient if self-defeating way of concocting shows to exploit established tastes. It is part of the ground rhythm of modern culture.

Of course, networks and suppliers think they are being eminently practical when they order up recombinants and imitations. After all, they are bureaucracies trying to capitalize on and mobilize demonstrable tastes. If the success rates of recombinants are not very good, what routine procedure stands a better chance of fabricating hits with minimum risk of embarrassing flops? Recombination and imitation seem like low-risk ways of getting by. Executives in any enterprise, as the organization theorist Herbert Simon argues, aim to get by—he calls it "satisficing"—

rather than seek breakthroughs on the odd chance of maximizing profits.

Recombinant talk is splendidly practical, too, providing signposts for rapid recognition, speeding up meetings, streamlining discussion about cultural goods that might otherwise seem elusive, unwieldy, hard to peg. Meetings have to be brisk, for the mass-cultural assembly line has to keep moving. Bertolt Brecht observed it in what he called the "mindless chatter" of an MGM executive in the forties: "the ongoing incest of what has been liked and bought with something else that has been liked and bought (simply rearranged)." Recombinant talk fairly begs to be parodied, but simply to parody would be shortsighted. TV executives are trying to gauge a show's appeal to consumers who, in turn, are going to make a snap judgment about whether to watch it partly, assumedly, on the grounds of whether it reminds them of pleasure and promises to repeat or extend it. But imitation too crude risks calling attention to imitativeness itself rather than the product being imitated. That is why crude imitations usually do less well than the originals. And thus the special appeal of recombination, which is imitation to the next highest power.

Beyond the immediate logic of marketability, recombinant thinking is rooted deeply throughout all modern culture and thought. Capitalism as a culture has always insisted on the new, the fashionable, the novel. Indeed, its first literary creation was precisely the novel; its second was the newspaper, with its artless juxtapositions. The genius of consumer society is its ability to convert the desire for change into a desire for novel goods. Circulation and employment depend on it. Popular culture above all is transitory; this guarantees not only turnover for the cultural marketers but currency for the customers. But curiously, the inseparable economic and cultural pressures for novelty must coexist with a pressure toward constancy. Nostalgia for "classics"—old movies, "oldie" song, antiques— is consumer society's tribute to our hunger for a stable world. Consumers want novelty but take only so many chances; manufacturers, especially oligopolists, want to deploy their repertory of the tried-and-true in such a way as to generate novelty without risk. The fusion of these pressures is what produces the recombinant style, which collects the old in new packages and hope for a magical synthesis.

As Susan Sontag points out, imitation and recombination make up a cultural set that pervades Western life in the late decades of the twentieth century. Constantly we liken experience to other experience. We attempt to assemble scraps of memory and lore, cataloguing one phenomenon as a variant of others already in repertory. Comparison saturates not only public speech but private thought. The reader thinks that Ross Macdonald writes like Raymond Chandler. The tourist thinks that this landscape has the palms of Southern California and the broad beaches of the Atlantic coast. The doctor thinks that this case resembles that one, with a twist of the other. This style of thought limits risk and gain at the same time. It is the creativity of least resistance, a managerial way to navigate the flux of incessant stimulus. Recombination conserves the mind's powers under the unrelenting pressure of the new that modernity has opened up. Classification is the essence of modern science and everyday experience alike, and recombination runs rampant through the contemporary imagination.

The recombinant style is, of course, not new in the twentieth century. Arthur Koestler even argued that recombinant thinking, the ability to apply one intellectual framework in a different context, is always the essence of creative thinking in the arts and sciences. "The creative act," he wrote, "is not an act of creation in the sense of the Old Testament. It does not create something out of nothing; it uncovers, selects, reshuffles, combines, synthesizes already existing facts, ideas, faculties, skills. The more familiar the parts, the more striking the new whole. Man's knowledge of the changes of the tides and the phases of the moon is as old as his observation that apples fall to earth in the ripeness of time. Yet the combination of these and other equally familiar data in Newton's theory  of gravity changed mankind's outlook on the world..." But Koestler missed the fact that recombination as such brings forth a hundred or a thousand banalities for each striking new synthesis, and in the process degenerates into mechanical juxtaposition to suit the rhythm of consumption and fashion in consumer society. The executive raves "unique" or "special" many time a day; the producer says he is looking for "something new" and is jolted into his new idea by seeing *Smokey and the Bandit*. And when standardization threatens the integrity of new work by collapsing it into variations on the old, it stands to reason that connoisseurship requires and commands a proliferation of varieties: twenty different varieties of ice cream, French mustard, Cabernet Sauvignon. Discriminating taste counterbalances the imitative impulse. Connoisseurs adore nuance, yet often even nuance is expressed as recombination: this with a touch of that, a hint of the other.

The recombinant style now shapes not only the marketing of new toothpastes but the marketing of high as well as popular culture. Proust was not seen as "the new Balzac," but in 1984 a publisher will no doubt promote a serious novel as "the new *White Hotel*." Willie Mays wasn't "the new Joe DiMaggio," but sports announcers now speak of basketball players who have "the speed of Dr. J. with the muscle of Willis Reed." Team owners would breed Mendelian hybrids if they could. The culture industry's sales effort, sharing in this fever, helps impose on us all a new language of shorthand. Shorthand is the semantic accompaniment of imitation and recombination. What they share is the tendency to reduce information to bits for rapid processing. Shorthand suits the computer age and the age of television, in which information comes in quick bursts, instant "hits," rapid cuts, what TV news people call "bites." If anything is communicated at all, it should be communicated quickly. By the same token, if it cannot be communicated quickly, it must not have been worth saying at all. In selling, moreover, shorthand is practical. A publisher's salesperson has thirty seconds to convince a bookseller to carry book X. Naturally, the blurb will have to tell the tale, and the sales force will prefer books whose "story line" can most easily be reduced to a thirty-second blurb, especially if the author's name is not an instant sell.

Even for the artist, in a world stripped of transcendent unities, the strategy of collage, of juxtaposition, makes the best of a bad situation. It is both recognition of, and romantic protest against, the idea that the world is finished, worn out. The best art coaxes a distinct unity out of juxtaposition; bad art deposits scrap upon scrap, endlessly reshuffling the cultural givens into pastiche, as in *Star Wars* and *Raiders of the Lost Ark*. Whether in *fin-de-siècle* assemblage or surrealist juxtaposition, in Rauschenberg or Larry Rivers, the style of conjunction is central to modern art. In poetry we see it in the fragments of Eliot's "The Waste Land" and Pound's *Cantos*, in John Ashbery's breathless swoops from image to image. The nervous editing style of most contemporary film has shaped every other art form. In the novel, we have the pop-cultural dumping ground of Joyce, the luminous lists of Jorge Luis Borges: in architecture, the postmodernism of Michael Graves and Philip Johnson among others. In a single building, postmodernism shamelessly combines the classical (columns and pediments), the decorative (ornament and trim), and the Bauhaus (simplicity and angularity). In museums, as Susan Sontag points out, the Paris Beaubourg is built with movable partitions, so that the relations between distinct exhibits can be redefined at the curator's will. The high forms of popular music are unified recombinant albums—The Beatles' *Sgt. Pepper's Lonely Hearts Club Band*, The Who's *Tommy*—and more recently, Blondie's 1980 album *Autoamerican*, which contains songs in big band, reggae, rap, religious-portentous, and rhythm-and-blues styles. Such albums with their peculiar unity assert that order can be assembled only from the juxtaposition of shards. They echo Eliot's line,

"These fragments I have shored against my ruins." In fashion, the New Wave extends the conventional assertion that all styles are born equal and juxtaposition amounts to wit. Anything goes with anything else—tuxedo jackets with candy wrappers, leg warmers with sandals—mocking and extending the recombinatory mode at the same time.

In the background stands the ultimate recombinatory form: television, the medium that perpetually levels, juxtaposing *Holocaust* to a soap commercial, news of cluster bombs in Lebanon to an appeal for hemorrhoid medicine, converting each bit into a sequel to the last and a prologue to the next, composing unintended and hitherto unimagined wholes out of parts and proposing that all images are related to all others. Scarcely a punk rock or New Wave album is complete without a song decrying television, satirizing the singer's dependency on it, skating along the slippery edge where irony and subjugation melt together. The fascination TV works on its most furious bewailers is the fascination of meaninglessness raised to a universal principle.*

Yet the mind-sets of network gatekeepers and New Wave songwriters may not be so different at least in one respect. They are both haunted by the half-felt premise that nothing is new under the sun. This is not, of course, the first cultural moment to suffer from, or revel in, a sense of exhaustion. At the turn of the century, the West did not know whether it was speeding toward universal utopia or running out of meaningful inventory. In his singular way, Nietzsche proposed both at once. At the same time, socialists and inventors and Cubists insisted there were great things to be done, a universal mankind was in the making, although Marx and the Wright Brothers disagreed over whether the

---

*Consider "T.V.O.D." by the British group, The Normal:

> T.V.O.D....
> I don't need a TV screen.
> I just stick the aerial into my skin.
> Let the signal run through my veins.

instrument of universal oneness would be the class struggle or the flying machine. Both the political and aesthetic hopes of the Second International period were crushed by the First World War; for doubters and onetime believers alike, the old sense of closure was now reconfirmed a hundred times over in the trenches of Passchendaele and Verdun.

This sense of cultural exhaustion has, if anything, swelled in the course of the century. Not unvaryingly or irreversibly: Artists are perennially animated by the hope for a breakthrough, or the allegation that they have already attained one. There have been moments of renaissance: Weimar Germany, Paris in the thirties, New York in the forties, and many places in the sixties. But without question the seventies represent the culmination of artistic weariness in more fields than television. Consider what Kennedy Fraser wrote about clothing in 1980:

> Fashion appears to have reached an impasse…has been atrophying for a decade or more. It may now simply have achieved the end toward which it has been tending: to short-circuit or completely foil spontaneity in its creators and its followers. The snag is that spontaneity is the whole point of fashion…[M]ost collections both here and in Europe continue to be absolutely saturated with more or less direct borrowings from the twenties, the thirties, the forties, the fifties—and now the sixties as well.… Now that fashion has started reviving the nineteen-sixties, it seems clear that we've reached the end of some sort of line.… There won't be anything of the seventies to revive.

Substitute "pop music" or "painting" or "theater" or "movies" or "the novel" or "television" and those lines still ring true.

So Fred Silverman was not alone when he permuted the television programs of his early years. Recombination was and remains the fashionable mode. And Aaron Spelling was speaking for the *Zeitgeist* when he said, "There are only seven original plots." Many industry hands echo Spelling, with variations: There are eight basic sitcoms, seven basic mysteries, or, even more grandly, nine or twelve or fifteen basic dramatic structures in history, period. Didn't Goethe, after all, say there were thirty-six basic plots? Gatekeepers say they are gamely looking for something new, but secretly they doubt it exists. There is barely an idea that hasn't been tried, they say, barely a plot device that hasn't been done again and again. Even gimmicks have precedents: A show featuring a monkey is patterned after a show featuring a dog; *The Six Million Dollar Man* spins off *The Bionic Woman*; and they "work," don't they?

When network executives admit something is wrong with television, they invoke shortages. Novelty and quality are scarce, they say, because in the end talent is scarce. Call this jadedness or realism, it is strikingly the same claim made by publishers of books and magazines, by producers of Broadway plays, even by many critics: There is simply not enough talent to go around. Canny studio buyers and advertising men and worn-down series producers say the same thing. "We eat our children," says Brandon Tartikoff. "It's very tough to deal with the enormous appetite of television," according to Richard H. Low, executive vice-president in charge of Broadcasting Programming and Purchasing for Young and Rubicam. "You're not going to increase the water supply by adding more spigots. We're all for more diversity and more quality, the three networks are dying for more quality—granted, quality with the requirement of large audience. The search for new writing talent that can fit that special need is continuous and enormous. Another way to look at it is to ask how many plays of quality make it to Broadway, and how many of those would appeal to 20 million people or more."

Even writers agree: "It's not a mark against the creative community,: says Larry Gelbart. "I just don't think ever in the world there have been that many talented people, all in one place, who could supply this kind of assembly-line demand." "The appetite is so voracious," said Grant Tinker when he was still at MTM, "that we wind up just feeding shit into it and that's what comes out. Nobody's setting out to make shit, but there are just so many Jim Brookses and Allan Burnses.* Television would be wonderful if it were only on Wednesday nights."

The statistics are indeed daunting. Primetime television takes up 22 hours a week on each network, for a total of 3,432 hours a year on all three. The comedy writer Michael Elias even argues that television looks so bad because so much of it is visible. If the equivalent number of oil paintings from a certain year were hung in full view, he says, painting in general might not look so stellar. The same might be said of all the new fiction published in the course of a year.

Of course, the point is arguable, unproved, unprovable and probably exaggerated. Talent is one to those mysteries, like intelligence or beauty, which is not a static national attribute like land mass. If talent is defined relative to the untalented, the argument is even tautological: Talent is always scarce. The fact is that network television works just well enough, as moneymaking machinery, to satisfy America's pop-cultural entrepreneurs. Whatever talent does exist, or might rise to the occasion under the right circumstances, the networks have no vast incentives to encourage it—and some to cut it to size, the size of network formulas. Writers in any form tend to write what they see: If they see formula, they learn to write formula, and forget they may ever have aspired to write anything else.

The television assembly line devours talent along with incompetence, not only because it runs through programs so fast, but because the system prizes slick dialogue more than story, schematic story line more than complexity, and,

in comedy, jokes more than consistency or intensity of character or situation. (Joke-writers are hired to "punch up" flagging sitcom scripts; the norm is three gags per page, which works out to three a minute.) Rainer Werner Fassbinder, Alain Tanner, Michelangelo Antonioni, Federico Fellini have made important films for West German, Swiss, and Italian television, but in American television there is no high-cultural reservation that is institutionally insulated against the pressures of mass-market thinking. Even public television is far more interested in (and subsidized for) the acceptably quaint or "high-cultural" productions of the British than native forms.

As for the actual "creative community" of Hollywood, that quite definite collection of a few hundred producers, writers, and directors who get the lion's share of the work, most have been rewarded handsomely enough and long enough for adhering to formula that it is only painful to recall they may have hoped for more. They pride themselves on what the industry calls "craft." Younger writers who loathe the conventions will shirk the business altogether, or divide themselves, writing episodes to order to make a living, while they work on the side on more serious plays and screenplays. So the business selects its own, and there is no shortage of craftsmanlike writers looking at the screen, saying "I can do that!" and catching the next plane for Los Angeles.

In the heart of the business are a hundred or so writers whose names show us again and again in the credits, composing a recombinant mosaic all their own. Once they master the standard forms and prove themselves reliable for the subdivided tasks of television writing—for "light" or "cops" or "family"—they are in demand. Routinely the networks come to them and ask if they would be interested in doing a pilot on such-and-such a subject in such-and-such a style. They wangle a respectful hearing when they "pitch" an idea back. The networks dicker with them. They are the regulars, the ones who have succeeded in internalizing the industry's values. Once in a while they are strong enough and in-

---

*Responsible, together or separately, for *Room 222*, *The Mary Tyler Moore Show*, *Lou Grant*, and *Taxi*, among others.

ventive enough and lucid enough to break through the old norms and to keep control of a show against all the network pressures to flatten it. Usually they lack either the capacity, opportunity, or will to do more than get by.

The problem is not simply that in the heat of production the writing is done by committee. With many hands stirring the broth, the Hollywood studio system succeeded in producing not only watered-down, derivative concoctions but quite a few fine movies in rapid order. Steady production does not automatically debase art; when skilled crews are kept under contract they can only help a serious repertory company, even in television. Insiders blame the pace of series production, which is more to the point. Rarely can a series stockpile enough scripts before the show starts shooting each season. The rest are being written while other episodes are being shot, edited, troubleshot. While the clock ticks away, each of the four acts of an hour drama may be farmed out to a different writer, as on *Hill Street Blues*, leaving it up to harried producers to yoke them together at the eleventh hour. Without doubt episodic television's everlooming deadlines do damage the long-term quality of a series, but deadlines by themselves can't account for the shallowness of most pilots. Most network television is simply bad—inert, derivative, cardboard—because no one with clout cares enough to make it otherwise. It is good enough for its purposes.

Many of the most talented people in the business feel, or tell themselves, that they are serving their apprenticeship, or their time, making their money and their contacts, honing—or so they want to think—their craft, hoping to sell a movie script and move up into the big leagues of feature films to stay. But most television writers don't burn to do anything different from what they already do. They only wish they had more time to do it, with less interference. The going conventions work well enough for networks, advertisers, affiliates, producers, writers, and enough of the audience. No critical mass of writers demonstrates all at once the passion to

say something different, the craft and ingenuity to make it mass-marketable, and the clout to sell it. Audiences are disgruntled with network television, but passively, and without any clear allegiance to a substantial alternative.

And so the sense of cultural exhaustion—whose most prominent symptom is the recombinant form—is at least in part self-fulfilling. In the early eighties, the networks flounder without anything that qualifies as an exciting trend even in their own terms. Old-timers proclaim that the spark is missing from the new shows, and wonder if they're only getting old. The networks whistle in the dark against the threat of competition from the new video technologies. While the official line proclaims that the networks will do fine—because ad rates are booming and the total number of homes using television is still rising even though the networks' aggregate market share is falling—in the industry's dark night more than a few executives wonder how much longer they can stay at the vital center of popular entertainment. There is anxiety about the networks' future, and the sense of a slow fadeout. It might turn out that television is not only a cause but the flickering exemplar of our larger cultural exhaustion.

The more sophisticated the numbers the executives play with, the safer the forms they employ—whether spinoffs, clones, or recombinants—the more cynical and disheartened TV's major players become, and the more their products ring hollow. The pursuit of safety above all else makes economic sense to the networks, at least in the short run, but success anxiety reduces many a fertile idea to an inert object, which usually also turns out to be a commercial dud. For all the testing and ratings research and all the self-imitative market calculation in the world does not produce the originality or energy that makes for much commercial success, let alone truth, provocation, or beauty.

In headlong pursuit of the logic of safety, the networks ordinarily intervene at every step of the development process. It is as if there were not only too many cooks planning the broth, but the landlord kept interfering as well. This presumably rational process wreaks havoc with shows, and confounds even the network's own logic. Far from a smoothly humming assembly line, the development process is clumsy, chancy political warfare. Eventually the network sets the terms, but doesn't always get the results intended. More often than not, commerce defeats not only art but commerce itself. The complex workings of network power, and its hold over production, are best pondered concretely, consider, then, the travail of a single prime-time series.

## Questions for the Gitlin readings:

1. What does Gitlin mean by "recombinant culture?" Why is this an important aspect of television production and the selection of media content?

2. What are the major goals of scheduling in network television? Why is it so important and yet so difficult to do?

# Introduction to John Fiske's "Some Television, Some Topics, and Some Terminology"

John Fiske for many years was one of the leading lights of communications research. He was a Principal Lecturer in Communications and Cultural Studies at the Curtin University of Technology in Perth, Australia and a visiting professor in the Department of Communications Arts at the University of Wisconsin at Madison. Fiske is a modern guru of the cultural studies approach to television and treats the content of programming as a text to be read. His treatment is part Marxism and part semiotics as he tries to examine the potential meanings and ideologies behind television content. Fiske develops three levels of meaning, what he calls "the codes of television,"—reality, representation, and ideology. By examining these three levels, Fiske seeks to work backwards from text to production.

The purpose is to understand the conventions of television production, its structure and the various forms that create ideological meaning. A major part of his work is designed to help us understand how polysemy works and how it exists in a social context; i.e., why different audiences can make different meanings from a singular text. Fiske suggests that such codes and meanings are imbedded in the production values and conventions of television itself.

# Some Television, Some Topics, and Some Terminology

Any book about television culture is immediately faced with the problem of defining its object. What is television? And, equally problematically, what is culture? In this book I work with a definition of television as a bearer/provoker of meanings and pleasures, and of culture as the generation and circulation of this variety of meanings and pleasures within society. Television-as-culture is a crucial part of the social dynamics by which the social structure maintains itself in a constant process of production and reproduction: meanings, popular pleasures, and their circulation are therefore part and parcel of this social structure.

Television, its viewers, and the ways it functions in society, are so multifarious that no tightly focused theoretical perspective can provide us with adequate insight. The theoretical and methodological roots of this book lie in that loosely delineated area known as "cultural studies" which derives from particular inflections of Marxism, semiotics, post-structuralism, and ethnography. This area encompasses both textually inflected and socially inflected theories of culture, and requires theoretical, analytical, and empirical approaches to rub together in a mutually critical and productive relationship. The book will focus on the problem of how the textuality of television is made meaningful and pleasurable by its variously situated viewers, though it will also consider the relationship between this cultural dimension and television's status as a commodity in a capitalist economy.

But we start by considering television as a cultural agent, particularly as a provoker and circulator of meanings. How meanings are produced is one of the central problematics of the book, but a convenient place to start is with the simple notion that television broadcasts programs that are replete with potential meanings, and that it attempts to control and focus this meaningfulness into a more singular preferred meaning that performs the work of the dominant ideology. We shall need to interrogate this notion later, but I propose to start with a traditional semiotic account of how television makes, or attempts to make, meanings that serve the dominant interests in society, and how it circulates these meanings amongst the wide variety of social groups that constitute its audiences. I shall do this by analyzing a short segment of two scenes from a typical, prime-time, long-running series, *Hart to Hart*, in order to demonstrate some basic critical methodology and to raise some more complex theoretical questions that will be addressed later on in the book.

The Harts are a wealthy, high-living husband and wife detective team. In this particular episode they are posing as passengers on a cruise ship on which there has been a jewel robbery. In scene 1 they are getting ready for a dance during which they plan to tempt the thief to rob them, and are discussing how the robbery may have been effected. In scene 2 we meet the villain and villainess, who have already noticed Jennifer Hart's ostentatiously displayed jewels.

## Scene 1

HERO: He knew what he was doing to get into this safe.

HEROINE: Did you try the numbers that Granville gave you?

HERO: Yeh. I tried those earlier. They worked perfectly.

HEROINE: Well you said it was an inside job, maybe they had the combination all the time.

HERO: Just trying to eliminate all the possibilities. Can you check this out for me. (*He gestures to his bow tie.*)

HEROINE: Mm. Yes I can. (*He hugs her.*) Mm. Light fingers. Oh, Jonathon.

HERO: Just trying to keep my touch in shape.

HEROINE: What about the keys to the door.

HERO: Those keys can't be duplicated because of the code numbers. You have to have the right machines.

HEROINE: Well, that leaves the window.

HERO: The porthole.

HEROINE: Oh yes. The porthole. I know they are supposed to be charming, but they always remind me of a laundromat.

HERO: I took a peek out of there a while ago. It's about all you can do. It's thirty feet up to the deck even if you could make it down to the window, porthole. You'd have to be the thin man to squeeze through.

HEROINE: What do you think? (*She shows her jewelry.*) Enough honey to attract the bees?

HERO: Who knows? They may not be able to see the honey for the flowers.

HEROINE: Oh, that's the cutest thing you've ever said to me, sugar. Well, shall we? (*Gestures towards the door.*)

## Scene 2

VILLAIN: I suppose you noticed some of the icing on Chamberlain's cup cake. I didn't have my jeweler's glass, but that bracelet's got to be worth at least fifty thousand. Wholesale.

VILLAINESS: Patrick, if you're thinking what I know you're thinking, forget it. We've made our quota one hit on each ship. We said we weren't going to get greedy, remember.

VILLAIN: But darling, it's you I'm thinking of. And I don't like you taking all those chances. But if we could get enough maybe we wouldn't have to go back to the Riviera circuit for years.

VILLAINESS: That's what you said when we were there.

VILLAIN: Well maybe a few good investments and we can pitch the whole bloody business. But we are going to need a bit more for our retirement fund.

## THE CODES OF TELEVISION

Figure 1 shows the main codes that television uses and their relationship. A code is a rule-governed system of signs, whose rules and conventions are shared amongst members of a culture, and which is used to generate and circulate meanings in and for that culture. (For a fuller discussion of codes in semiotics see Fiske 1983 or O'Sullivan *et al.* 1983.) Codes are links between producers, texts, and audiences, and are the agents of intertextuality through which texts

**FIGURE 1** *The Codes of Television*

An event to be televised is already encoded
by *social codes* such as those of:

Level one:
**"Reality"**

appearance, dress, make-up, environment, behavior, speech,
gesture, expression, sound, etc.
↓

These are encoded electronically by *technical codes* such as those of:

Level two:
**Representation**

camera, lighting, editing, music, sound
↓

which transmit the *conventional representational codes,*
which shape the representations of, for example: narrative, conflict, character,
action, dialogue, setting, casting, etc.
↓

Level three:
**Ideology**

which are organized into coherence and social acceptability
by the *ideological codes,* such as those of:
individualism, patriarchy, race, class, materialism, capitalism, etc.

---

interrelate in a network of meanings that constitutes our cultural world. These codes work in a complex hierarchical structure that Figure 1 over simplifies for the sake of clarity. In particular, the categories of codes are arbitrary and slippery; as is their classification into levels in the hierarchy; for instance, I have put speech as a social code, and dialogue (i.e. scripted speech) as a technical one, but in practice the two are almost indistinguishable: social psychologists such as Berne (1964) have shown us how dialogue in "real life" is frequently scripted for us by the interactional conventions of our culture. Similarly, I have called casting a conventional representational code, and appearance a social one, but the two differ only in intentionality and explicitness. People's appearance in "real life" is already encoded: in so far as we make sense of people by their appearance we do so according to conventional codes in our culture. The casting director is merely using these codes more consciously

and more conventionally, which means more stereotypically.

The point is that "reality" is already encoded, or rather the only way we can perceive and make sense of reality is by the codes of our culture. There may be an objective, empiricist reality out there, but there is no universal, objective way of perceiving and making sense of it. What passes for reality in any culture is the product of that culture's codes, so "reality" is always already encoded, it is never "raw." If this piece of encoded reality is televised, the technical codes and representational conventions of the medium are brought to bear upon it so as to make it (a) transmittable, technologically and (b) an appropriate cultural text for its audiences.

Some of the social codes which constitute our reality are relatively precisely definable in terms of the medium through which they are expressed—skin color, dress, hair, facial expression, and so on.

Others, such as those that make up a landscape, for example, may be less easy to specify systematically, but they are still present and working hard. Different sorts of trees have different connotative meanings encoded into them, so do rocks and birds. So a tree reflected in a lake, for example, is fully encoded even before it is photographed and turned into the setting for a romantic narrative.

Similarly, the technical codes of television can be precisely identified and analyzed. The choices available to the camera person, for example, to give meaning to what is being photographed are limited and specifiable: they consist of framing, focus, distance, movement (of the camera or the lens), camera placing, or angle and lens choice. But the conventional and ideological codes and the relationship between them are much more elusive and much harder to specify, though it is the task of criticism to do just that. For instance, the conventions that govern the representation of speech as "realistic dialogue" in scene 1 (Figure 1) result in the heroine asking questions while the hero provides the answers. The representational convention by which women are shown to lack knowledge which men possess and give to them is an example of the ideological code of patriarchy. Similarly, the conventional representation of crime as theft of personal property is an encoding of the ideology of capitalism. The "naturalness" with which the two fit together in the scene is evidence of how these ideological codes work to organize the other codes into producing a congruent and coherent set of meanings that constitute the *common sense* of a society. The process of making sense involves a constant movement up and down through the levels of the diagram, for sense can only be produced when "reality," representations and ideology merge into a coherent, seemingly natural unity. Semiotic or cultural criticism deconstructs this unity and exposes its "naturalness" as a highly ideological construct.

A semiotic analysis attempts to reveal how these layers of encoded meanings are structured into television programs, even in as small a segment as the one we are working with. The small size of the segment encourages us to perform a detailed analytical reading of it, but prevents us talking about larger-scale codes, such as those of the narrative. But it does provide a good starting point for our work.

## Camera Work

The camera is used through angle and deep focus to give us a perfect view of the scene, and thus a complete understanding of it. Much of the pleasure of television realism comes from this sense of omniscience that it gives us. Camera distance is used to swing our sympathies away from the villain and villainess, and towards the hero and heroine. The normal camera distance in television is mid-shot to close-up, which brings the viewer into an intimate, comfortable relationship with the characters on the screen. But the villain and villainess are also shown in extreme close-up (ECU). Throughout this whole episode of *Hart to Hart* there are only three scenes in which ECUs are used: they are used only to represent hero/ine and villain/ess, and of the twenty-one ECUs, eighteen are of the villain/ess and only three of the hero/ine. Extreme close-ups become a codified way for representing villainy.

This encoding convention is not confined to fictional television, where we might think that its work upon the alignment of our sympathies, and thus on our moral judgment, is justified. It is also used in news and current affairs programs which present themselves as bringing reality to us "objectively." The court action resulting from General Westmoreland's libel suit against the CBS in 1985 revealed these codes more questionably at work in television reporting. Alex Jones recounts their use in his report of the trial for the *New York Times*:

> Among the more controversial techniques is placing an interviewee in partial shadow in order to lend drama

to what is being said. Also debated is the use of extreme close-ups that tend to emphasize the tension felt by a person being interviewed; viewers may associate the appearance of tension with lying or guilt.

The extreme close-up can be especially damaging when an interview is carefully scripted and a cameraman is instructed to focus tightly on the person's face at the point when the toughest question is to be asked. Some documentary makers will not use such close-ups at all in interviews because they can be so misleading.

The CBS documentary contained both a shadowed interview of a friendly witness and "tight shots" of General Westmoreland. Such techniques have been used in documentaries by other networks as well.

Even the wariest viewer is likely to find it difficult to detect some other common techniques. "I can't imagine a general viewer getting so sophisticated with techniques that they could discount them," said Reuven Frank, a former president at NBC News who has been making documentaries for about 30 years.

(*NYT*, February 17, 1985: 8E)

There are two possible sources of the conventions that govern the meanings generated by this code of camera distance. One is the social code of interpersonal distance: in western cultures the space within about 24 inches (60 cm) of us is encoded as private. Anyone entering it is being either hostile, when the entry is unwelcome, or intimate, when it is invited. ECUs replicate this, and are used for moments of televisual intimacy or hostility, and which meanings they convey depends on the other social and technical codes by which they are contextualized, and by the ideological codes brought to bear upon them. Here, they are used to convey hostility. The

other source lies in the technical codes which imply that seeing closely means seeing better—the viewer can see *into* the villain, see *through* his words, and thus gains power over him, the power and the pleasure of "dominant specularity" (see chapter 2). These technical and social codes manifest the ideological encoding of villainy.

Most of the other technical codes can be dealt with more quickly, with only brief comments.

## Lighting

The hero's cabin is lit in a soft, yellowish light, that of the villains in a harsh, whiter one. (I am reminded of Hogben's (1982) anecdote about the occasion when he was given a hostile treatment in a television interview. He did, however, manage to convince the interviewer that his point of view deserved more sympathy, whereupon the interviewer insisted they record the interview again, but this time without the greenish-white studio lighting.)

## Editing

The heroes are given more time (72 secs.) than the villains (49), and more shots (10 as against 7), though both have an average shot length of 7 seconds. It is remarkable how consistent this is across different modes of television (see Fiske 1986b): it has become a conventional rhythm of television common to news, drama, and sport.

## Music

The music linking the two scenes started in a major key, and changed to minor as the scene changed to the villains.

## Casting

This technical code requires a little more discussion. The actors and actresses who are cast to play hero/ines, villain/esses and supporting roles are real people whose appearance is already encoded by our social codes. But they are equally media people, who exist for the viewer intertextually, and whose meanings are also intertextual. They bring with them not only residues of the meanings of other roles that they have played, but also their meanings from other texts such as fan magazines, showbiz gossip columns, and television criticism. Later on in the book we will discuss intertextuality and character portrayal in greater depth: here we need to note that these dimensions of meaning are vital in the code of casting, and that they are more important in the casting of hero/ines than of villain/esses.

Characters on television are not just representations of individual people, but are encodings of ideology, "embodiments of ideological values" (Fiske 1987a). Gerbner's (1970) work showed that viewers were clear about the different characteristics of television heroes and villains on two dimensions only: heroes were more attractive and more successful than villains. Their attractiveness, or lack of it, is partly the result of the way they are encoded in the technical and social codes—camera work, lighting, setting, casting, etc., but the ideological codes are also important, for it is these that make sense out of the relationship between the technical code of casting and the social code of appearance, and that also relate their televisual use to their broader use in the culture at large. In his analysis of violence on television, Gerbner (1970) found that heroes and villains are equally likely to use violence and to initiate it, but that heroes were successful in their violence, whereas villains finally were not. Gerbner worked out a killers-to-killed ratio according to different categories of age, sex, class, and race. The killers category included heroes and villains, but the killed category included villains only. He found that a character who was white, male, middle class (or classless) and in the prime of life was very likely, if not certain, to be alive at the end of the program. Conversely characters who deviated from these norms were likely to be killed during the program in proportion to the extent of their deviance. We may use Gerbner's findings to theorize that heroes are socially central types who embody the dominant ideology, whereas villains and victims are members of deviant or subordinate subcultures who thus embody the dominant ideology less completely, and may, in the case of villains, embody ideologies that oppose it. The textual opposition between hero/ine and villain/ess, and the violence by which this opposition is commonly dramatized, become metaphors for power relationships in society and thus a material practice through which the dominant ideology works. (This theory is discussed more fully in Fiske and Hartley 1978 and in Fiske 1982.)

The villain in this segment has hints of non-Americanness; some viewers have classed his accent, manner, and speech as British, for others his appearance has seemed Hispanic. But the hero and heroine are both clearly middle-class, white Americans, at home among the WASPs (White Anglo-Saxon Protestants). The villainess is Aryan, blonde, pretty, and younger than the villain. Gerbner's work would lead us to predict that his chances of surviving the episode are slim, whereas hers are much better. The prediction is correct. She finally changes sides and helps the hero/ine, whereas he is killed; hints of this are contained in her condemnation of the villain's greed, which positions her more centrally in the ideological discourse of economics (see below).

These technical codes of television transmit, and in some cases merge, into the social codes of level 1. Let us look at how some of them are working to generate meanings and how they embody the ideological codes of level 3.

## Setting and Costume

The hero/ine's cabin is larger than that of the villain/ess: it is humanized, made more attractive by drapes and flowers, whereas the other is all sharp angles and hard lines. The villain wears a uniform that places him as a servant or employee and the villainess's dress is less tasteful, less expensive than the heroine's. These physical differences in the social codes of setting and dress are also bearers of the ideological codes of class, of heroism and villainy, of morality, and of attractiveness. These abstract ideological codes are condensed into a set of material social ones, and the materiality of the differences of the social codes is used to guarantee the truth and naturalness of the ideological. We must note, too, how some ideological codes are more explicit than others: the codes of heroism, villainy, and attractiveness are working fairly openly and acceptably. But under them the codes of class, race, and morality are working less openly and more questionably: their ideological work is to naturalize the correlation of lower-class, non-American with the less attractive, less moral, and therefore villainous. Conversely, the middle-class and the white American is correlated with the more attractive, the more moral and the heroic. This displacement of morality onto class is a common feature of our popular culture: Dorfman and Mattelart (1975) have shown how Walt Disney cartoons consistently express villainy through characteristics of working-class appearance and manner; indeed they argue that the only time the working class appear in the middle-class world of Ducksville it is as villains. Fiske (1984) has found the same textual strategy in the *Dr Who* television series.

## Make-Up

The same merging of the ideological codes of morality, attractiveness, and heroism/villainy, and their condensation into a material social code, can be seen in something as apparently insignificant as lipstick. The villainess has a number of signs that contradict her villainy (she is blonde, white American, pretty, and more moral than the villain). These predict her eventual conversion to the side of the hero and heroine, but she cannot look too like them at this early stage of the narrative, so her lips are made up to be thinner and less sexually attractive than the fuller lips of the heroine. The ideology of lipstick may seem a stretched concept, but it is in the aggregate of apparently insignificant encodings that ideology works most effectively.

## Action

There are a number of significant similarities and differences between the actions of the hero/ine and the villain/ess. In both cabins the women are prettying themselves, the men are planning. This naturalizes the man's executive role (Goffman 1979) of instigating action and the woman's role as object of the male gaze—notice the mirror in each cabin which enables her to see herself as "bearer of her own image" (Berger 1972): the fact that this is common to both hero/ine and villain/ess puts it beyond the realm of conflict in the narrative and into the realm of everyday common sense within which the narrative is enacted. The other action common to both is the getting and keeping of wealth as a motive for action, and as a motor for the narrative: this also is not part of the conflict-to-be-resolved, but part of the ideological framework through which that conflict is viewed and made sense of.

A difference between the two is that of co-operation and closeness. The hero and heroine co-operate and come physically closer together; the villain and villainess, on the other hand, disagree and pull apart physically. In a society that places a high value on a man and woman being a close couple, this is another bearer of the dominant ideology.

## Dialogue

The dialogue also is used to affect our sympathy. That of the villain and villainess is restricted to their nefarious plans and their mutual disagreement, whereas the hero and heroine are allowed a joke (window/porthole/laundromat), an extended metaphor (honey and the bees), and the narrative time to establish a warm, co-operative relationship. Both the hero/ine and villain/ess are allowed irony, the use of which will be theorized and analyzed in chapter 6.

## Ideological Codes

These codes and the televisual codes which bring them to the viewer are both deeply embedded in the ideological codes of which they are themselves the bearers. If we adopt the same ideological practice in the decoding as the encoding we are drawn into the position of a white, male, middle-class American (or westerner) of conventional morality. The reading position is the social point at which the mix of televisual, social, and ideological codes comes together to make coherent, unified sense: in making sense of the program in this way we are indulging in an ideological practice ourselves, we are maintaining and legitimating the dominant ideology, and our reward for this is the easy pleasure of the recognition of the familiar and of its adequacy. We have already become a "reading subject" constructed by the text, and, according to Althusser (1971), the construction of subjects-in-ideology is the major ideological practice in capitalist societies.

This ideological practice is working at its hardest in three narrative devices in this segment. The first is the window/porthole/laundromat joke, which, as we have seen, is used to marshal the viewer's affective sympathy on the side of the hero/ine. But it does more than that. Freud tells us that jokes are used to relieve the anxiety caused by repressed, unwelcome, or taboo meanings. This joke revolves around the "feminine" (as defined by our dominant culture) inability to understand or use technical language, and the equally "feminine" tendency to make sense of everything through a domestic discourse. "Porthole" is technical discourse— masculine: "window-laundromat" is domestic-nurturing discourse—feminine. The anxiety that the joke relives is that caused by the fact that the heroine is a detective, is involved in the catch-ing of criminals—activities that are part of the technical world of men in patriarchy. The joke is used to recuperate contradictory signs back into the dominant system, and to smooth over any contradictions that might disrupt the ideological homogeneity of the narrative. The attractiveness of the heroine must not be put at risk by allowing her challenge to patriarchy to be too stark—for attractiveness is always ideological, never merely physical or natural.

The metaphor that expresses the sexual attractiveness of women for men in terms of the attraction of honey and flowers for the bees works in a similar way. It naturalizes this attraction, masking its ideological dimension, and then extends this naturalness to its explanation of the attractiveness of other people's jewelry for lower-class non-American villains! The metaphor is working to naturalize cultural constructions of gender, class, and race.

The third device is that of jewelry itself. As we have seen, the getting and keeping of wealth is the major motor of the narrative, and jewelry is its material signifier. Three ideological codes intersect in the use of jewelry in this narrative: they are the codes of economics, gender, and class.

In the code of economics, the villain and villainess stress the jewelry's investment/exchange function: it is "worth at least fifty thousand wholesale," it forms "a retirement fund." For the hero and heroine and for the class they represent this function is left unstated: jewelry, if it is an investment, is one to hold, not cash in. It is used rather as a sign of class, of wealth, and of aesthetic taste.

The aesthetic sense, or good taste, is typically used as a bearer and naturalizer of class differences. The heroine deliberately overdoes the jewelry, making it vulgar and tasteless in order to attract the lower-class villain and villainess. They, in their turn, show their debased taste, their aesthetic insensitivity, by likening it to the icing on a cupcake. As Bourdieu (1968) has shown us, the function of aesthetics in our society is to make class-based and culture-specific differences of taste appear universal and therefore natural. The taste of the dominant classes is universalized by aesthetic theory out of its class origin: the metaphor of "taste" works in a similar way by displacing class differences onto the physical, and therefore natural, senses of the body.

The meaning of jewelry in the code of gender is clear. Jewels are the coins by which the female-as-patriarchal-commodity is bought, and wearing them is the sign both of her possession by a man, and of his economic and social status. Interestingly, in the code of gender, there is no class difference between hero/ine and villain/ess: the economics of patriarchy are the same for all classes, thus making it appear universal and natural that man provides for his woman.

This analysis has not only revealed the complexity of meanings encoded in what is frequently taken to be shallow and superficial, but it also implies that this complexity and subtlety has a powerful effect upon the audience. It implies that the wide variety of codes all cohere to present a unified set of meanings that work to maintain, legitimate, and naturalize the dominant ideology of patriarchal capitalism. Their ideological effectivity appears irresistible. The resistibility of ideology is one of the themes that runs through this book, and later on, in chapters 5 and 6, we will return to this analysis, complicate it, and contradict its main implications. For the moment, however, it serves to demonstrate that popular television is both complex and deeply infused with ideology.

## SOME TERMINOLOGY

This book is not concerned with television as an industrial practice or as a profit-making producer of commodities, though it is obviously both of these, but attempts to understand it from the perspective of its audiences. For our purposes, then, television consists of the programs that are transmitted, the meanings and pleasures that are produced from them, and, to a lesser extent, the way it is incorporated into the daily routine of its audiences. We will concentrate on "typical" television—the most popular, mainstream, internationally distributed programs, for these are the ones of greatest significance to popular culture.

To understand television in this way we need to see it and its programs as potentials of meaning rather than as commodities. A program is a clearly defined and labeled fragment of television's output. It has clear boundaries, both temporal and formal, and it relates to other programs in terms of generic similarity and, more essentially, of difference. We know that an ad is not part of a program, we know when one program finishes and another starts. Programs are stable, fixed entities, produced and sold as commodities, and organized by schedulers into distribution packages. *Dallas* is the same program whether it is broadcast in the USA, North Africa, or Australia.

A text is a different matter altogether. Programs are produced, distributed, and defined by the industry: texts are the product of their readers. So a program becomes a text at the moment of reading, that is, when its interaction with one of its many audiences activates some of the meanings/pleasures that is capable of provoking. So one program can stimulate the production of many texts according to the social conditions of its reception. *Dallas* is a different text in the USA, in North Africa, and in Australia, indeed, it is many different texts in the USA alone. Texts are the site of conflict between their forces of production and modes of reception. The analysis we have just performed shows how the dominant ideology is structured into popular texts by the discourses and conventions that inform the practices of production and that are a part of their reception. But what it has not shown is how other discourses, other conventions can be brought to bear upon it that may conflict with the dominant ones structured into it. A text is the site of struggles for meaning that reproduce the conflicts of interest between the producers and consumers of the cultural commodity. A program is produced by the industry, a text by its readers.

To understand both the production of programs and the production of meanings from them, we need to understand the workings of discourse. This is, in itself, a multidiscursive term; that is, its usage varies according to the discourse in which it is situated. At its simplest, discourse is the organization of language above the level of the sentence: it is thus an extensive use of language. By extension it can cover nonverbal languages so that one can talk of the discourse of the camera or of lighting. This formalistic use does not get us very far, for it ignores the social and ideological dimension. Discourse is a language or system of representation that has developed socially in order to make and circulate a coherent set of meanings about an important topic area. These meanings serve the interests of that section of society within which the discourse originates and which works ideologically to naturalize those meanings into common sense. "Discourses are power relations" (O'Sullivan *et al.* 1983: 74). Discourse is thus a social act which may promote or oppose the dominant ideology, and is thus often referred to as a "discursive practice." Any account of a discourse or a discursive practice must include its topic area, its social origin, and its ideological work: we should not, therefore, think about a discourse of economics, or of gender, but of a capitalist (or socialist) discourse of economics, or the patriarchal (or feminist) discourse of gender. Such discourses frequently become institutionalized, particularly by the media industries, in so far as they are structured by a socially produced set of conventions that are tacitly accepted by both industry and consumers. In this sense we can talk about the discourse of news, or of advertising: these discourses still exhibit our three defining characteristics—a topic area, a social location, and the promotion of the interests of a particular social group.

Discourses function not only in the production and reading of texts, but also in making sense of social experience. A particular discourse of gender, for example, works not only to make sense of a television program such as *Charlie's Angels*, but also to make a particular pattern of sense of gender in the family, in the workplace, in school, in social clubs—in fact, in our general social relations. Social experience is much like text: its meanings depend upon the discourses that are brought to bear upon it. Just as two differently socially situated people may make a different sense of the same text, so they may make a different sense of the same social experience.

This brings us to another characteristic of discourse: discourses are not produced by the individual speaker or author, they are socially produced; the meanings that they bear preexist their use in any one discursive practice. It is often said, somewhat enigmatically, that we do not speak our discourse but our discourse speaks us. This means that discourse not only makes sense of its topic area, it also constructs a sense, or social identity, of *us* as we speak it. We all of us have an extensive repertoire of discourses that we need in order to make sense of the variety of texts and social experiences that constitute our culture. The analysis of a program can identify the main discourses out of which it is structured, but it cannot of itself identify the discourses that the viewer will bring to bear upon it to make it into a text that bears meanings for him or her. The discourses of the program attempt to control and confine its potential meanings: the discourse of the reader may resist this control.

So texts are unstable, unconfined. The ad and the program may be part of the same text in their interaction in the production of meaning and pleasure. Meanings are not confined by producers' boundaries between programs, but are part of the "flow" of television as experienced by its audiences. Neither is the television text confined by the boundaries of its medium: reading and talking about television are part of the process of making a text out of it and are determinants of what text is actually made. So, too, is our experience of other cultural media—books, films, newspapers, songs, and so on. The textuality of television is essentially intertextual.

An essential characteristic of television is its polysemy, or multiplicity of meanings. A program provides a potential of meanings which may be realized, or made into actually experienced meanings, by socially situated viewers in the process of reading. This polysemic potential is neither boundless nor structureless: the text delineates the terrain within which meanings may be made and proffers some meanings more vigorously than others. The analysis of the *Hart to Hart* segment has show how the conventional use of television codes has preferred a set of meanings that, and this is typical, fit well with the values of the dominant ideology. But other meanings may be made (see chapter 6): the text's polysemy or meaning potential may be realized differently. A white woman, for example, may find the window/porthole/laundromat joke offensive, and may read the heroine's concern for her appearance as evidence of her cleverness in being able to outwit the villain and villainess. The point to make here is that the motivation to exploit the polysemy of the program is social: the polysemy of the text is necessary if it is to be popular among viewers who occupy a variety of situations within the social structure. This variety of social situations is no harmonious relationship of roughly equal groups as modeled by liberal pluralism, but must always be understood in terms of domination and subjugation. The unequal distribution of power in society is the central structuring principle in understanding the relationship of any one group to others, or to the social system as a whole. As social groups are neither autonomous nor equal, so too the meanings they produce from the text are neither self-contained nor equal. The more positive, feminine reading of the heroine's efforts to increase her attractiveness is not a self-contained, self-sufficient one: an essential part of its meaning is its relationship with, and difference from, the dominant meanings of female attractiveness in patriarchy. As the woman reader is socially positioned in a power relationship with patriarchy, so her readings of a text enter a power relationship with those preferred by the ideological structure of the codes that comprise it. Polysemy is always bounded and structured, for polysemy is the textual equivalent of social difference and diversity.

A textual study of television, then, involves three foci: the formal qualities of television programs and their flow; the intertextual relations of television within itself, with other media, and with conversation; and the study of socially situated readers and the process of reading.

The term "readers" may seem inappropriate for the watchers of television, but it is the term I use most frequently in this book. I also use the related terms of "viewers," "audiences," and "audience" to refer in different ways to the people who watch television. "Audience," in the singular, is the easiest term to understand—and dismiss. It implies that television reaches a homogeneous mass of people who are all essentially identical, who receive the same messages, meanings, and ideologies from the same programs and who are essentially passive. The inability of the term "audience" to account for social differences and consequent differences of meanings means that it ascribes great centralizing, homogenizing power to television and its producers. Consequently it sees the audience as relatively powerless and undiscriminating, at the mercy of the barons of the industry. It sees viewers, in Stuart Hall's (1982) productive phrase, as "cultural dopes" who are unable to perceive the difference between their interests and those of the producers. Such a view of the television audience is surprisingly widely held, often by people who, on other topics, are capable of thinking quite clearly.

Pluralizing the term into "audiences" at least recognizes that there are differences between the viewers of any one program that must be taken into account. It recognizes that we are not a homogeneous society, but that our social system is crisscrossed by axes of class, gender, race, age, nationality, region, politics, religion, and so on, all of which produce more or less strongly marked differences, and that these social differences relate among each other in a complexity of ways that always involves the dimension of power. Social power is unequally distributed in society, so any set of social relations necessarily involves power and resistance, domination and subordination. The term "audiences" recognizes the heterogeneity of society and allows for that heterogeneity to be understood in terms of power relations.

The terms "viewer" and "reader" are more active than either "audience" or "audiences"; I use them with a considerable overlap of meaning, and thus, at times, interchangeably. But there are differences of emphasis between them. A "viewer" is someone watching television, making meanings and pleasures from it, in a social situation. This social situation is compounded of both the social relations/experience of the viewer (class, gender, etc.) and of the material, usually domestic, situation (which is also a product of his/her social relations) within which television is watched. The television viewer experiences a far greater variety of modes of watching than does the cinema spectator. "Viewing," then, is an active process that brings to television the social relations of the viewer (his/her point of view) and the material situation; viewing television news will be quite different for the woman who is cooking the family meal than for the man slumped in an armchair in front of the set. A viewer is engaged with the screen more variously, actively, and selectively than is a spectator.

"Viewing" is specific to television, "reading" is common to all texts. So the term "reader" means "the producer of texts, the maker of meanings and pleasures." This productive ability is the result of social experience or training, whether formal or informal. It is not an innate gift, but an acquired ability. It is a social practice, is ideological, and is the means by which sociocultural experience, the text in question, and its intertextual relationships, are brought together in a productive moment of interaction. The "reader" is less concretely situated than the "viewer" and is rather the embodiment of that central cultural process—the production of meaning.

Cultural processes are often referred to metaphorically as though they were economic ones. Bourdieu's (1980) metaphor of cultural capital is typical. By this he means that a society's culture is as unequally distributed as its material wealth and that, like material wealth, it serves to identify class interests and to promote and naturalize class differences. Thus, those cultural forms which a society considers to be "high," for example, classical music, fine art, literature, or ballet, coincide with the tastes of those with social power, whereas low brow or mass cultural forms appeal to those ranked low on the social structure. The point of this is that culture and class are closely interrelated but the discourse of culture disguises its connection with class. By using words like "taste," and "discrimination," and by appealing to apparently universal values such as those of aesthetics, the discourse of culture grounds cultural differences in universal human nature or in universal value systems. It pretends that culture is equally available to all, as democratic capitalism pretends that wealth is equally available to all. The fact that few acquire either culture or wealth is explained by reference to natural differences between individuals, which are expressed as differences in their natural talents or taste; this explanation hides the role of social class. The upshot of this is that naturally "better" people (i.e. those with "better" taste) appreciate "better" art (i.e. that which is "inherently" more universal, aesthetic) and therefore the value system that validates "high" art and denigrates "low" art is based in nature, and not in the unequal distribution of power in a class-divided society. Bourdieu's account of cultural capital reveals the attempt of the dominant classes to control culture for their own interests as effectively as they control the circulation of wealth. The consistent denigration of popular culture, such as television, as bad for people individually and bad for society in general is central to the strategy.

This theory of cultural capital explains the social function of culture as the provision of a system of meanings and pleasures that underwrites the social system structured around economic, class, and other forms of social power. Cultural capital underwrites economic capital. But the metaphor of the cultural economy must not be confined to its similarities with the material economy. The circulation of meanings and pleasures in a society is not, finally, the same as the circulation of wealth. Meanings and pleasures are much harder to possess exclusively and much harder to control: power is less effectively exerted in the cultural economy than it is in the material.

We need to extend the metaphor of cultural capital to include that of a popular cultural capital that has no equivalent in the material economy. Popular cultural capital is an accumulation of meanings and pleasures that serves the interests of the subordinated and powerless, or rather the disempowered, for few social groups are utterly without power. Popular cultural capital consists of the meanings of social subordination and of the strategies (such as those of accommodation, resistance, opposition, or evasion) by which people respond to it. These meanings of subordination are not made according to the dominant value system, they are not ones that make a comfortable sense of subordination and thus work to make people content with their social situation. Rather they are meanings made by a value system that opposes or evades the dominant ideology: they are meanings that validate the social experience of the subordinate but not their subordination.

This popular cultural capital requires a set of cultural competencies to "read" it. Brunsdon (1981), for example, argues that women fans of soap opera are highly "competent" readers. Cultural competence involves a critical understanding of the text and the conventions by which it is constructed, it involves the bringing of both textual and social experience to bear upon the program at the moment of reading, and it involves a constant and subtle negotiation and renegotiation of the relationship between the textual and the social. Cultural capital and cultural competence are both central to people's ability to make socially pertinent and pleasurable meanings from the semiotic resources of the text.

Pleasure results from a particular relationship between meanings and power. Pleasure for the subordinate is produced by the assertion of one's social identity in resistance to, in independence of, or in negotiation with, the structure of domination. There is no pleasure in being a "cultural dope"; there is, however, real pleasure to be found in, for example, soap operas that assert the legitimacy of feminine meanings and identities within and against patriarchy. Pleasure results from the production of meanings of the world and of self that are felt to serve the interests of the reader rather than those of the dominant. The subordinate may be disempowered, but they are not powerless. There is a power in resisting power, there is a power in maintaining one's social identity in opposition to that proposed by the dominant ideology, there is a power in asserting one's own subcultural values against the dominant ones. There is, in short, a power in being different. These exertions of power are all available to the subordinate and as such are all potential sources of popular pleasure. Pleasure requires a sense of control over meanings and an active participation in the cultural process. One of the central arguments of this book is that television is so popular, that is, it is capable of offering such a variety of pleasures to such a heterogeneity of viewers, because the characteristics of its texts and its modes of reception enable an active participation in that sense-making process which we call "culture."

Television and its programs do not have an "effect" on people. Viewers and television interact. So in this book I shall not talk about television's "effect," though I shall refer to its "effectivity." This rather ugly form of the word makes it more diffused and generalized, less specific. In particular it takes it out of any direct relationship with a "cause." Television does not "cause" identifiable effects in individuals; it does, however, work ideologically to promote and prefer certain meanings of the world, to circulate some meaning rather than others, and to serve some social interests better than others. This ideological work may be more or less effective, according to many social factors, but it is always there, and we need to think of it in terms of its effectivity in *society at large, not of its effects* upon specific individuals or groups. "Effectivity" is a social-ideological term, "effect" an individual-behavioristic one.

And finally, in this preview of some of the terms used in this book, we come to that most important and slippery concept of all—"culture." Culture is concerned with meanings and pleasures: our culture consists of the meanings we make of our social experience and of our social relations, and therefore the sense we have of our "selves." It also situates those meanings within the social system, for a social system can only be held in place by the meanings that people make of it. Culture is deeply inscribed in the differential distribution of power within a society, for power relations can only be stabilized or destabilized by the meanings that people make of them. Culture is a struggle for meanings as society is a struggle for power.

## Questions for the Fiske reading:

1. What does Fiske mean by the word "text?" How is a television text different from a program, and why is the distinction important?

2. Contemplate for a moment a modern program and then examine it for potentially different texts. Examine how this one example can have different texts for different audiences.

# Introduction to Jeremy G. Butler's "Style and the Camera: Videography and Cinematography" and "Style and Editing"

Jeremy G. Butler is on the faculty at the University of Alabama where he teaches courses in telecommunications and film in the Department of Communications and Information Sciences. His chapter on videography is an introduction to the idea of the camera, its use and placement in terms of producing television content. It raises the concept of composition within the camera frame and suggests that nothing in television production that is casual or unreflective. Since the camera is the mediator between us and what we watch on television, Butler states that to understand the impact of television on us as viewers, we must understand the relationship between us and the camera. The chapter starts with the technical aspects of camera lens and their varying uses and problems.

The purpose of this chapter is to present us with a lexicon of camera shots that demonstrate how moving the camera drastically changes the way we perceive the contents of the shot. Butler suggests that each camera placement creates a set of variables that determine what we see and how we see it. We must always deal with the placement of the camera, what is included and excluded with the shot, is the camera moving or staying stationary and why are these choices important. While the chapter is more technical than the others in the readings, it is vital for us to get comfortable with this terminology and what it means.

# Style and the Camera: Videography and Cinematography

When we look at television, our gaze is controlled by the "look" of the camera. What the camera "saw" on the set or on location during a production, we now see on our television screens. The camera's distance from the scene and the direction in which it is pointed, among other factors, determine what we will see in a television image. In essence, our look becomes the camera's look and is confined by the frame around the image. To understand the camera's look, it becomes necessary to understand the aesthetic, economic, and technological factors that underpin the camera's perfunctory gaze.

The camera, although a mechanical reproducing device, does not neutrally reproduce images. The camera fundamentally changes the objects it reproduces: three dimensions become two; the colors of nature become the colors of videotape or film; the perimeter of the camera frame delimits the view. The reproduction process of film and video could more accurately be thought of as one of translation, where the three-dimensional historical world is translated into the two-dimensional "language" of televisual images. This camera language is a major part of the visual style of a television program. It works in conjunction with mise-en-scene and editing to create a program's overall visual design.

Almost everything we see on television began its trip to our homes by being recorded by a camera. It would be wrong, however, to assume that this camera is always a video camera. Indeed, many television images were originally created by a film camera (although nearly everything on TV these days is edited on videotape).

Soap operas, game shows, some sitcoms, musical variety programs and specials, news programs, talk shows, and most locally produced commercials are shot on videotape or broadcast live using video cameras. In contrast, prime-time dramas, some other sitcoms, made-for-television films, music videos, and large-budget, nationally broadcast commercials are all shot originally on film (Table 6.1). The distinction is not merely technological. Even though these images all come to us through the television tube, there are still discrete visual differences between material that was originally filmed and that which was videotaped. Each technology affects the visual style of television in different ways. Each might be thought of as a separate dialect within the language of televisual style.

This chapter concerns the components of film and video camera style, the elements of **cinematography** and **videography** that record an image and affect our understanding of it. In simplest terms, cinematography refers to the characteristics of the film camera, while videography designates those of the video camera. The person overseeing the film camera is the **cinematographer**; the corresponding person in charge of the video camera is the **videographer**. Typically, in contemporary production, cinematographers and videographers leave the actual handling of the camera to the **camera operator**, who is not credited as a full-fledged cinematographer/videographer. For simplicity's sake, we will here use the term "camera operator" to refer to the combined work of cinematographers, videographers, and camera

**TABLE 6.1** *Film versus Videotape*

| Filmed | Videotaped |
|---|---|
| *L.A. Law* | *60 Minutes* |
| *Murphy Brown* | *Married...with Children* |
| *Designing Women* | *The Cosby Show* |
| *Cheers* | *Home Improvement* |
| *Murder, She Wrote* | *The Price Is Right* |
| *Northern Exposure* | *Roseanne* |
| *Beverly Hills 90210* | *The Young and the Restless* |
| *Picket Fences* | Network newscasts |
| Music videos (some of them) | MTV programs |
| National commercials | Local commercials (e.g., for car dealerships) |

operators. In any event, all three operate under the guidance of the program's director. The director designs the program's overall style, with the camera operator working within the specific province of camera style.

On the most basic level, camera-style characteristics are shaped by technological considerations. For instance, one could not have produced videographic images in the 1890s, before videotape was invented. But we should be wary of overemphasizing the importance of technology to cinematography and videography. As we have seen in our discussion of mise-en-scene in the previous chapter, the ways that film and video technologies have been used are always shaped by aesthetic convention and economic determinants. The aesthetic conventions of composition in European oil painting, for example, greatly influence the composition of TV images. And economics principally determines whether a program will be shot in film or videotape—with less expensive (and less prestigious) programs being shot on videotape. Thus, technology, aesthetics, and economics merge together in determining camera style. To fully understand cinematography and videography we must remain alert to each of these three counterbalancing elements.

In many respects, film and video share basic camera principles. In U.S. television today the two formats have begun to resemble one another more and more—especially as high-definition video nears perfection (with digital image technology not far behind). It is with these shared principles that we begin our study of cinematography and videography. Even so, there do remain some important distinctions between film and video, and they will be considered toward the latter part of this chapter.

## THE FUNDAMENTALS OF CAMERA STYLE: SHARED FILM AND VIDEO CHARACTERISTICS

### The Camera Lens

The earliest "camera," the **camera obscura** of the eighteenth century, had no lens at all. It was merely a large, darkened room with a hole in one wall. Light entered through that hole and created an image of the outdoors on the wall opposite the hole. Very little could be done by way of manipulating that image. Today's camera lens, the descendent of the camera obscura's hole-in-a-wall, permits a variety of manipulations—a catalogue of optical controls that the camera operator may exercise.

Chief among these optical controls is **focal length**. One need not be a physicist to understand focal length, although sometimes it seems like it. The focal length of a lens (usually measured in millimeters) is the distance from the lens's optical center to its **focal point**, which is that spot where the light rays bent by the lens converge before expanding again and striking the film or electronic pickup at the **focal plane**. This definition, however, tells us very little about the images that result from lenses of different focal lengths. In more familiar terms, the three conventional types of focal length are:

1. Wide angle (or short)
2. "Normal" (or medium)
3. Telephoto (or long or narrow)

The reader may already know these terms, but it is important to recognize the different and sometimes subtle effects these focal lengths have on the image.

The **wide angle lens** gives the viewer a wide view of the scene, and it also heightens the **illusion of depth** in the image. All television images are two-dimensional, of course; there is no true depth to them. They have dimensions only along two axes: horizontal and vertical (left and right, up and down). Using principles of perspective developed in the Renaissance, however, the television image creates an illusion of depth (back and front). Because of this illusion, some objects seem to be in front of other objects; the space seems to recede into the image. A wide angle lens increases that illusion of depth. Objects filmed with a wide angle lens seem to be farther apart from one another than they do with normal or telephoto lenses. When shot with a wide angle lens, the distance between the front and the rear of the piano is elongated, giving the image an illusion of great depth.

The **telephoto lens** gives a narrower view of the scene than a wide angle lens, but magnifies the scene (brings it closer). Telephoto lenses are widely used in sports coverage, to get a "closer" view of the action. Just as the wide angle lens heightens the illusion of depth, the telephoto lens diminishes it. Thus, the illusion of depth appears to be compressed in telephoto shots. The longer the lens, the more compressed the depth will appear.

The so-called **normal** focal length is medium-sized in the comparison to both wide angle and telephoto. This is the lens that has come to be accepted as "natural." However, the normal focal length does not actually approximate the human eye's range of vision (it's narrower) or illusion of depth (it's shallower). Rather, it creates an image that, to the Western world, seems correct because it duplicates that style of perspective developed during the Renaissance of the 1500s. Camera lenses that create images suggesting Renaissance perspective have come to be accepted as the norm, while wide angle and telephoto lenses are defined as deviations from the norm.

Film and video cameras may be supplied with individual lenses of different focal lengths. More commonly, today's cameras come equipped with a **zoom lens**, which in optical terms is a *variable focal length* lens. With a zoom, one can shift immediately and continuously from wide angle to telephoto without switching lenses. To **zoom in** is to vary the focal length from wide angle to telephoto, getting increasingly "closer" to the object and narrowing your angle of view. To **zoom out**, in contrast, is to vary the focal length from telephoto to wide angle—thereby getting "farther" from the object as the angle of view widens. *Closer* and *farther* are misleading terms when referring to the zoom lens, however, because the camera does not get physically closer to or farther from the object it is filming or taping. Thus, to be accurate the zoom really just magnifies and de-magnifies the object.

A characteristic of the camera lens even more fundamental than focal length is its **focus**. On television, the image is nearly always in focus. Only perhaps in sports events do we see occasional out-of-focus images as the camera operator struggles to follow a fast-moving athlete. However, in most televisual images there are areas of the image that are not in focus, parts that have been left out of focus to de-emphasize them. The camera operator can selectively focus parts of the image and unfocus other parts. In other words, he or she can use focus for specific effect.

The selective use of focus is facilitated by the photographic phenomenon of **depth of field**. (Care should be taken not to confuse depth of field with the *illusion* of depth discussed above.) Depth of field is the distance in front and behind the **focus distance** that is also in focus (the focus distance being the distance from the camera to the object being focused on). If a lens is focused at 10 feet, some objects nearer to and farther from the camera will also be in focus. This range (say, 8–14 feet in this instance) is the depth of field. Typically, the range is approximately one third in front of the focus distance and two thirds behind it. The camera operator can manipulate depth of field to influence our perception on an image—decreasing the visual impact of parts of the frame by rendering them out of focus and indistinct. A small depth of field—so that just one plane (foreground, middle ground, or background) is sharply focused—is termed shallow focus. The shallow focus of the shot is further manipulated by shifting the focus from foreground to background, which is known as **racking** or **pulling focus**. Rack focus is frequently used in expensive television productions to add some visual interest to a shot without changing to a new camera position and revising the lighting setup.

Shallow focus sounds confusingly similar to **soft focus**. However, in a soft focus shot the entire image not just a single plane within it, is slightly out of focus. Soft focus is often used in conjunction with special filters and lighting—and even Vaseline on the lens—to create an image that conventionally signifies romantic attraction, vulnerability, sweetness, or youthfulness (concealing wrinkles in an actor's face) in a character. In *Moonlighting*, for example, Cybill Shepherd was frequently shot in this fashion.

Focus does not have to be shallow or soft, however. In deep focus shots, all planes of the image are in focus—as in one shot from the television documentary, *Never Too Far from Home* (1991), where characters in the background are in focus as are the flowers in the foreground. Deep focus is often used in conjunction with deep space blocking, where background and foreground interact with one another. In the *Eerie, Indiana* shot, deep focus enables the viewer to see what is happening in the shot's background.[1]

Deep focus has been heralded by film critic André Bazin as a major advance in the realism of the cinema. He argues that:

1. Deep focus is more like the human perception of reality (we mostly see the world in deep focus); and
2. Deep focus preserves the continuity of space by maintaining the visual connections between objects in their environments.

Bazinian realism could also be applied to television (although his theories have had minimal impact on television aesthetics), but with caution. The smaller size of the television screen is a major impediment to deep focus staging of action. The background actors/objects can become so small as to have negligible impact on the shot's meaning.

## Camera Framing

The **framing** of a shot, at a most rudimentary level, determines what we can and cannot see. In the early years television (the 1940s), camera operators tended to choose a distant view of the action, which showed the entire setting. This framing was based on an aesthetic assumption (inherited from the theater) that the "best seat in the house" would be in the center, about seven or eight rows back, where one could see all of the action at once. Also, early television cameras were large and cumbersome, which made it difficult to move them around a set to achieve a variety of camera positions. Soon, however, camera technology improved. Television directors discovered the impact of a variety of framing, and began incorporating the **close-up** in their television programs.

Since the "invention" of the close-up, television directors have developed conventions of framing. It is possible to chart television's conventional framing with the human body as a standard, since that is the most common object before the camera.[2] (The conventional abbreviation of each framing is included in parentheses.)

1. **Extreme long shot** (XLS). The human form is small, perhaps barely visible. The point of view is extremely distant, as in aerial shots.
2. **Long Shot** (LS). The actor's entire body is visible, as is some of the surrounding space.
3. **Medium long shot** (MLS). Most, if not all, of the actor's body is included, but less of the surrounding space is visible than in the LS.
4. **Medium shot** (MS). The actor is framed from the thigh or waist up.
5. **Medium close-up** (MCU). The lower chest of the actor is still visible.
6. **Close-up** (CU). The actor is framed from his or her chest to just above his or her head.
7. **Extreme close-up** (XCU). Any framing closer than a close-up is considered an XCU.

In actual film and video production, these terms are imprecise. There is some variation between theatrical film shooting and shooting for television, with the latter tending toward closer framing to compensate for the smaller screen. What one director considers a medium close-up, another might term a close-up. Even so, the above terminology does provide some guidelines for discussing framing.

In fiction television, the long shot is—among other things—used for positioning the character within his or her environment, and can thereby construct aspects of the character. A long shot of a woman in a newspaper office, a prison cell, or a convent could establish her as a journalist, a convict, or a nun, respectively. Environment feeds our understanding of character, and the long shot facilitates that understanding. A long shot that helps to establish character or setting is known as an **establishing shot**. It often inaugurates a scene.

The medium shot is frequently used for conversation scenes. The framing of two characters from about the knees up as they begin a dialogue is so often used that it has been designated with the term **two-shot**. (Similarly, a **three-shot** frames three characters.) The medium shot can establish relationships between characters by bringing them into fairly close proximity.

For some, the close-up provides the "window to the soul" of the actor/character, a gateway to his or her innermost emotions. Hyperbole such as this aside, the close-up functions both to emphasize details and to exclude surrounding actions, channeling viewer perception. It thus exercises the most extreme control over the viewer's gaze.[3]

The aesthetics of framing follows certain conventions of function. The close-up is the dominant framing in television programs such as the soap opera, where the emotional states signified by the actors' faces are stressed. Television soap opera's reliance upon the close-up has coincided with the evolution of its acting style, which favors the human face over larger gestures. Television sports and action genres, in contrast, place more emphasis on medium and long shots—to facilitate the movement of automobiles, planes, and human bodies through space.

## Camera Height and Angle

In most television shots the height of the camera matches that of the actors' faces. This camera height is so ingrained in our understanding of camera style that eye level has become synonymous with "normal" height. It becomes transparent to the viewer, taken for granted. Variations on this height consequently become important, apparently signifying something about the characters. The two principal variations on eye-level camera height are

1. **Low angle**—in which camera is lower than the filmed object
2. **High angle**—in which the camera is higher than the filmed object

It has become a truism in television production manuals to observe that a low angle—where we look up at an actor—makes a character appear stronger and more powerful, while a high angle—looking down on an actor—weakens the character's impact. We can see the commonsensical basis for this assumption: when looking up at an object, it tends to appear large; and when looking down at it, small. But in actual television programs this use of low and high angles is much less systematic.

Stylistic elements such as camera angle do have meaning, but those meanings are always set within the context of the program and general aesthetic practice. Consequently, it's impossible to generalize about the "vocabulary" of television technique, where technique A = meaning B. Technique A does indeed have meanings, but only when considered within the entire textual system of a program.

## Camera Movement

Film cameras had been around for twenty years or more before tripods and dollies and other mechanical devices were developed that permitted the movement of the camera. Early films initially had little or no camera movement because of this technological limitation and because the camera operator had to hand crank the cameras, thus making their turning or movement awkward. When cameras finally did begin to move, they were limited by the practical aesthetics of early directors. Little use was seen for camera movement beyond following character action and panoramic views. Film-

makers gradually expanded the use of camera movement, and by the time television arrived, film camera movement was smooth and relatively frequent. Early television cameras, because of their enormous bulk, were as stationary as the first film cameras. Also, initial studio-based television was constricted in its camera movement by lack of space. Before long, however, television developed its own uses for the moving camera.

Principal among the functions of the moving camera are

1. To establish a space, a particular area;
2. To establish a relationship between objects/actors in a certain space;
3. To follow action;
4. To emphasize/de-emphasize one portion of a space, or an object/actor within that portion.

To achieve these functions, a variety of camera movements have evolved.

1. **Panning** and **tilting**. The most rudimentary camera movement derives its name from the affection for broad, "panoramic" views in early motion pictures. The pan is when the camera twists left and right, on an imaginary axis stuck vertically through the camera. The camera support—the legs of the tripod—does not move in a pan; only the tripod head turns. Similarly, in a tilt the camera twists up and down on an axis stuck horizontally through the camera. The camera height does not change; only its angle of vision.

Several other camera movements depend upon the movement of the *entire* camera support rather than just the tripod head: dollying/tracking/trucking; craning/pedestaling; handheld; and Steadicam. Camera technology provides the names for these movements, rather than the actual direction of the movement (as in "tilting") or what is represented (as in "panning" over panoramic views). Thus, the conventionalized method for viewers to describe these movements is to refer to presumptions of the technology used to create them.

2. **Dollying**, **tracking**, and **trucking**. In film and television there are several terms used to describe the sideways and backward/forward movement of the camera. Principal among these are **dollying**, **tracking**, and **trucking**. Each of these differs from the pan in that the entire camera support moves, rather than just the tripod head. It's like the difference between twisting one's head left and right—the human equivalent of panning—and walking in one direction or the other—human dollying.

The dolly shot is named for the device that creates it, the camera dolly—a wheeled camera support that may be rolled left and right or forward and backward. Similarly, the tracking shot earns its name from small tracks that are laid over rough surfaces, along which the dolly then rolls. In practice, "tracking" is such a broadly applied term that may be used to refer to any sideways or backward/forward movement, even if actual dolly tracks are not involved. In addition, in television studio production sideways movement is sometimes called trucking or crabbing, and a semicircular sideways movement is usually called **arcing**. Many of these terms are used interchangeably. Also, dollying need not be in straight lines that are either perpendicular or parallel to the action; dolly shots may move in curves, figure eights, and any other direction a dolly may be pushed or pulled.

To most viewers, dollying in or out is indistinguishable from zooming in or out. There are, however, important visual differences between the two techniques. Even though it takes a practiced eye to recognize them, the differences may generate disparate perceptions of the objects and humans that are presented.

When the camera operator zooms in or out, he or she changes the focal length of the camera and magnifies or demagnifies the object, but the position from which the object is viewed remains the same. The point of view of the camera is thus constant. In contrast, when the camera operator dollies forward or backward, the position from which the object is viewed shifts. And because the point of view changes in the dolly shot, we see the object from a different angle. Parts of it are revealed that were previously concealed, and vice versa.

Thus, although the zoom and the dolly share the quality of enlarging or reducing an object before our eyes, they differ in how they represent point of view and the illusion of depth. Consequently, they serve different functions on television. For example, camera movement—not zooming—is conventionally used when the viewer is supposed to be seeing through the eyes of a character as he or she moves through space—say, as a killer approaches his or her prey. Zoom shots do not conventionally serve this function, because they do not mimic human movement as convincingly as dollying does. Zooming, in turn, is more common in contemporary television production as punctuation for extreme emotion. In soap operas, camera movement is fairly limited, and zooms-in function to underline character emotions. In this case economics blends with aesthetics. Zoom shots are less time-consuming to set up than dolly shots, and thus less expensive. Consequently, the modestly budgeted soap operas favor the zoom.

3. **Craning** and **pedestaling**. A camera crane or boom looks just like a crane on a construction site, except that there is a camera mounted on one end. A camera pedestal is the vertical post of the camera support. Cranes and pedestals are the technology that permits the upward/downward movement of the camera and those movements—**craning** and **pedestaling**—take their names from that technology. Thus, in a crane shot, the camera is swept upward or downward. Additionally, since the crane is mounted on wheels, like a dolly, it can also be moved in all the directions a dolly can. A pedestal shot is one in which the camera is raised or lowered. The crane or pedestal movement is different from the tilt: in a tilt, the tripod head is twisted up or down—as if the camera were nodding—while in craning and pedestaling the entire camera body is moved higher or lower.

Crane shots serve a variety of functions. Typically a crane downs may be used first to establish a location with a wide angle shot from up high, and then particularize one element of that location by craning down to it. And cranes up are often used to end sequences or programs. Craning up and back from the character at the end of a program, we are literally distanced from him or her at a point when we are about to leave the character's story.

4. **Hand-held** and **Steadicam**. A **hand-held** shot is one that was filmed just as the name implies: with the camera held in the operator's hand instead of being placed on a camera mount. As a consequence, the hand-held shot is noticeably unsteady—especially during quick movements when the camera operator is running. A large percentage of news and sports videotaping is done with hand-held camera: shots from the field of play in sport shows (e.g., courtside shots at basketball games): documentary footage of automobile crashes; murder suspects leaving a courtroom; and so on

We might think that hand-held shots would be avoided entirely in the more controlled camera style of fiction television. Even though the majority of camera movement in fictional programs are not hand-held, hand-held shots do serve several narrative functions. First, hand-held work is used to create a documentary feel, to signify "documentariness," within works of fiction. Each episode of *Hill Street Blues* begins with a briefing in the squad room that is entirely hand-held camerawork—signifying the program's "realism." Second, hand-held movement is often used when we are seeing through a character's eyes—as was mentioned above regarding dolly shots. Indeed, hand-held camera is more frequently used in this situation than dollying because hand-held is thought to more closely approximate human movement. After all, we all have legs like a camera operator, not wheels like a dolly.

The **Steadicam** is a registered trademark for a piece of technology that has come to identify a style of camera movement that closely resembles hand-held. The Steadicam is a gyroscopically balanced device that straps to the operator's body.[4] The resulting motion is as smooth as that produced with a dolly. It is conventionally used in situations where stability is desired but economic and technical practicalities dictate that dolly tracks cannot be laid.

# DISTINGUISHING FILM AND VIDEO

As we have seen, film and video utilize many similar techniques: photographic technology that originated in still photography (focal length, depth of field, etc.) and aesthetic presumptions about framing, height, and movement of the camera. Just as significant as these similarities, however, are the two media's distinguishing characteristics.

## Aspect Radio

In television, as in pre-1952 cinema, the frame is 4 units wide and 3 units high. A screen 4 feet wide would be 3 feet high; a screen 16 inches wide would be 12 inches high; a screen 40 feet wide would be 30 feet high; and so on. This **aspect ratio** is the 4:3, which may be reduced to 1.33:1 or simply 1.33. To date, 1.33 remains the standard in television (although HDTV may change this), but since the mid-1950s the cinema has found a variety of methods to increase the screen's width: Cinerama, CinemaScope, Todd-A-O, VistaVision, Panavision, and so on. Indeed, no theatrical films are currently presented in the old 1.33 ratio. As a result, when theatrical films are shown on television, the video frame cuts off portions of the cinematic image. In other words, when we watch a theatrical movie on television, we see only a part of the image that the viewer in the theater sees. Since theatrical films still form a significant portion of television programming, it is important to understand just how the video frame modifies the film frame.

The elongation of the film frame was originally realized as response to the perceived threat of television in the decade after World War II. Film producers reasoned that theatrical films must provide viewers with something they cannot get from television. How else could they lure customers away from their television set? Thus, in the 1950s film studios attempted a variety of technological lures: color, 3-D, stereo sound, and wider screens. **Widescreen**, its advocates maintained, presented the viewer with a larger and grander and more overwhelming image. (Its detractors claimed that it was only suitable for filming snakes and dachshunds.) These new, wider screens had aspect ratios of 2.35:1 and 2.55:1, almost twice as wide as the standard ratio of 1.33:1. At first widescreen was used principally for travelogues such as *This is Cinerama* (1952) and lavish productions on the order of *The Robe* (1953). But by the 1960s widescreen films had become quite commonplace.

The first commonly used widescreen process was based on an **anamorphic lens** and is best known by its trademark labels: **CinemaScope** and **Panavision**.[5] During the shooting of the film, the anamorphic process uses a special lens that squeezes the image. If we were to look at a frame of the film itself, everyone and everything would appear skinny. When this film is projected the process is reversed; it is projected through an anamorphic lens, which unsqueezes the image and presents a broad, wide view. The 'Scope frame thus achieves an expanded aspect ratio—specifically, a 2.35:1 ratio.

The second, more common, widescreen process is created through **masking** and does not involve an anamorphic lens while shooting or projecting. Masked widescreen is created during the projection of the film, not the actual filming. A regular 1.33 frame is used, but horizontal bands across the top and the bottom of the frame as "masked" (blackened). The frame within the frame is wider than the old 1.33 ratio. This widescreen frame-within-the-frame—with a ratio of 1.85:1—is enlarged to fill the screen. Thus, masked widescreen (1.85) is not as wide as

anamorphic widescreen (2.35), but it is still wider that the pre-1952 film standard (1.33); more important, it is also wider than the current television standard (1.33). Currently, masked widescreen is the predominant format for theatrical films. Approximately 90 percent of contemporary films are presented in the 1.85 aspect ratio.

Television has adopted a variety of strategies to present widescreen theatrical movies with a minimum of viewer annoyance. The greatest widescreen challenge to TV's 1.33 ratio is the anamorphic frame's 2.35 width. In other words, television has had to find a way to fit an anamorphic film's extra-wide image into the skinnier television screen. Two processes have emerged to deal with the conversion from 2.35 to 1.33:

1. **Letterbox**
2. **Pan-and scan** or **scanning**

**Letterboxing**, the less frequently applied option for converting anamorphic films to videotape, preserves most of the original image, but shrinks it. This process closely resembles widescreen masking for the theater, in that the tops and bottoms of the video frame are blackened. In letterboxing, the anamorphic film frame is reduced and fit into the frame-within-the-television-frame. A small amount of the left and right sides of the anamorphic frame is sacrificed, but it is considerably more similar to the original framing than is a pan-and-scan version.

The **pan-and-scan** process, in contrast, reduces the 2.35 anamorphic frame to television's 1.33 by selecting the most "significant" part of the frame and eliminating the rest.

In addition, pan-and-scan can affect both camera movement and editing. The pan-and-scan frame need not remain fixed on one portion of the original frame. It can slide or "scan" left or right across the original. What was achieved with a stationary camera in the original is now presented through the "movement" of scanning.

Further, in terms of editing, the pan-and-scan version can alter the rhythms of the original edit by cutting between portions of a shot—even if there had been no cutting in the film version. What was one shot in the original has now become two. Thus, the rhythm of the original version's editing is completely altered.

In broadcast television, there is an overriding compulsion to fill the image, to leave nothing blank. The visual voids at the top and bottom of letterboxed films thus do not suit the medium, where almost all anamorphic films are panned-and-scanned. In this fashion, anamorphic films are made to conform to the norms of television. Their images are processed until they fully load the TV screen, regardless of the injury done to the original images.[6]

There have been a few, rare attempts by televisual texts to reshape the frame within the standard 1.33 rectangle. In an offbeat *ym* magazine commercial, for instance, the top and bottom of the frame have been blacked out, as in a letterboxed version of a film. This effect, which can also be observed in some music videos (e.g., Hal Ketchum's *Mama Knows the Highway*, alters the image's aspect ratio without actually changing the dimensions of the picture tube. (Wider picture tubes are, however, planned for high definition television.) Commercials and music videos can also be found that blacken the sides of the image (creating a tall, narrow rectangle), or darken all but a small rectangular or circular portion of the image. Each of these manipulations of the frame leaves blank areas in the image that would not be tolerated in conventional television. The result is an image that looks oddly distinct, that distinguishes itself from "normal" television and thereby captures our attention—which is precisely the effect needed in commercials and music videos.

The differences between film and television aspect ratios are most apparent in anamorphic films, but they are also evident in the transfer of masked widescreen films to videotape. When masked widescreen films—with an aspect ratio of 1.85—make the transition to TV's aspect ratio of 1.33, they lose a little from the edges, but not

much because of the technique used to create this form of widescreen. Recall that masked widescreen films use the entire 1.33 frame when shooting, but blackens the tops and bottoms when projected in a theater. On the actual frames of film, however, the areas to be masked are still visible. When transferred to videotape, the TV frame—which is a rounded rectangle—trims all four edges of the film frame. This maintains most of the width of a masked widescreen image and, coincidentally, it also reveals portions of the film image that are masked out in the theater. Normally this has no major effect, for today's cinematographers compose their images with television in mind. Indeed, marked in their cameras' viewfinders is the area that is "safe for television." But sometimes film directors are less cautious about the use of the areas to be masked, in which things such as boom microphone, lights, and the tops of sets may be visible. In *Pee-wee's Big Adventure* (1985), a car is driving past traffic signs at night—or so it appears in the widescreen theatrical film version. In the television version, the bottoms of the traffic signs—hidden in the masking of the original—are visible, and it is revealed that they are actually on wheels. Pee-wee's car is not moving; the signs are rolling toward the camera.

As viewers, we need to be aware of film's and television's differing aspect ratios to understand anomalies such as the wheeled signposts in *Pee-wee's Big Adventure* and *He Said, She Said*'s bizarre framing. These odd occurrences are becoming less and less common, however, as the film and television industries become more and more intertwined. Many widescreen films—both anamorphic and masked—are now composed with television's aspect ratio in mind. For this reason, even widescreen films tend to position the actors in the center of the frame—for fear of losing them when the film is transferred to videotape. Thus, the technological and economic necessities of converting widescreen film images to television images generate aesthetic results in the way the image finally appears on TV.

## Image Quality: Definition

The more clearly objects in an image appear or are defined, the higher that image's **definition**. Film and video have different levels of definition. To understand the differences between the two media, we must consider some of the technological bases of both film and video.

Definition in film is primarily determined by the size of the **grain** of the **film stock**, the specific type of film. The grains are the silver halide crystals that swim around in the chemical soup, or **emulsion**, that is attached to the celluloid backing or **base**, of a piece of film. In **fine-grain** film stocks the grain is smaller, less noticeable, and the definition is higher. Just how noticeable a film stock's grain is depends principally upon two factors.

First, film stocks that are very sensitive to light and thus may be used in dark, low-light situations are grainier than those that are less sensitive to light. These kind of film stocks are often used in documentary shooting, for example, where the light level cannot always be controlled.

Second, smaller **format** film stocks are grainier than larger format stocks. (Format here refers to film width and is measured in millimeters.) Thus, of the three most common film formats—super-8, 16mm and 35mm—the largest also has the finest grain, the highest definition. We might think therefore that 35mm's high definition would mean that it is the only film stock used in production for television. This has not been the case. Both economic and aesthetic factors have created specific niches for each of the formats. Inexpensive super-8 (and its immediate predecessor, "regular" 8mm) was the size of choice for home movie makers for over three decades, until the 1980s when low-cost videotape cameras virtually destroyed the super-8 market. 16mm film is used for documentary work and low-budget films. And 35mm film dominates filming for theatrical movies, made-for-television movies, prime-time television programs, national commercials, and music videos. Super-

8 and 16mm—with their noticeably higher grain levels—are still used within 35mm programs to achieve particular effects. For example, the fuzzy, high-grain images of a 1960s family that are used in the credit sequence for *The Wonder Years* (1988–93) denote "home movies" and connote nostalgia for a bygone era. (Those scenes have been shot in super-8 or 16mm, while the rest of the program is shot in 35mm.) High grain images—particularly black and white images—are also used to connote "documentariness" in fiction programs and have appeared in many music videos and commercials.

Definition in video is not a factor of graininess, since video images are not composed of chemical crystals or grains. Moreover, although video image quality is defined somewhat by the material used to record that image—as do film stocks in the cinema—it is not exclusively so defined. This is because, unlike film, the video image can exist *without being recorded in any fashion*. Indeed, video images existed long before there was videotape to record them. Film's existence, in contrast, depends upon an elaborate mechanical-chemical process that fabricated a piece of film which runs through a projector. It cannot exist without that recording medium. In contrast, all that television needs to create an image is a camera to produce an image and a television set to receive it. An immediate image may be instantaneously generated on a video screen, even if it is never recorded on videotape. What this means in terms of understanding image quality is that we may separate the quality of the video image from the quality of the video image *as it appears on videotape*. This distinction would be impossible to make in regard to the cinema because the medium does not exist separate from its presence on a physical strip of film.

At the most basic level, the video image is made up of phosphorescent dots—**pixels** or **phosphors**—that are arranged in horizontal lines on the TV screen. An **electron gun** (three electron guns, in most color TVs) in the rear of the picture tube, or **cathode ray tube** (CRT), fires an electron beam at these pixels, scanning

line by line across the 525 lines of the TV image?[7] When struck by the beam the pixels glow and thereby create the television image. The pixels in standard U.S. broadcast television are so large that the **scan lines** are visible to the naked eye—if one should care to sit so close to the TV. Because the video pixels in these scan lines are much larger than the grain in 35mm film stock, the video image is less clear—has lower definition—than the 35mm film image (although it is roughly equivalent to the 16mm film image). And, though it may seem somewhat strange, when film images are converted to video signals they still retain a higher degree of definition than images originally shot with a video camera. Thus, filmed images on television are clearer and more sharply defined than video images. What all of this boils down to is that filmed images can hold more visual information than video images.

The superior definition of 35mm film is soon to be challenged by new developments in video. By increasing the number of scan lines in the video image and decreasing the size of the pixels, the video image may be made much clearer, more highly defined. This is the intent of so-called **high-definition television (HDTV)**, which uses more than twice as many scan lines as the North American standard does—1125 and 525, respectively. Consequently, HDTV's image definition is roughly twice that of conventional broadcast television. The technology for HDTV has existed for several years now, but implementation has been held up mostly by its incompatibility with current systems. For U.S. broadcasters to use HDTV the entire television system would have to be replaced. Nevertheless, HDTV has already found uses in commercials and, on an experimental basis, theatrical movies—areas that would normally have opted for 35mm film. It seems clear that many of the visual differences between film and video are short-lived; but still, these differences do influence the style of television as it exists today.

When the recording of video signals is factored into the image-quality equation, we may see that the different videotape formats can have a marked impact on image definition. As in film, formats in videotape are largely determined by the width of the medium: **8mm**, 1/2", 3/4", **1**", and **2**". Home videographers are most familiar with 1/2" VHS and 8mm videocassette formats. Broadcast news operations use videocassette cameras for location shooting (**electronic news gathering [ENG]**), but they have larger formats (e.g., 3/4") or different systems (e.g., Betacam) than home camcorders. Studio television programs, such as the ones listed in Table 6.1, are recorded on one- and two-inch formats, which do not use videocassettes at all. Instead, the tape is recorded on machines with reels of videotape.

There are many variables in videotape formats other than width that affects image quality. For this reason, it would be inaccurate to say that the wider the format, the better the image quality and the more expensive the video system. Still, it is obviously true that 2" videotape delivers images of much greater definition than 1/2" tape. The latter finds limited use in broadcast television. Like super-8 film, 1/2" VHS tape is sometimes used in videotaped narrative programs to denote home movie-style videotaping.[8] And, parallel to 16mm film, the video formats used in television news are sometimes used in videotaped/filmed fiction programs to signify "news style."

Home videotaping formats also make occasional appearances on television news when "amateur" videotapes of news events (tornadoes, earthquakes, police brutality) or surveillance videotapes of crimes are broadcast. The poorer resolution of these tapes—their difference from broadcast-quality tapes—becomes significant in these instances. It marks the tapes as "authentic," as unposed and spontaneous and supposedly a pure piece of the historical world. Regardless of how that footage was obtained, it appears to be part of reality because we consciously or unconsciously link it with other amateur videotapes we have seen. Thus, the technology (1/2" VHS videotape) creates a visual style (poor resolution images) that carries certain significations based on our association with other videotaped images.

## Image Quality: Color and Black and White

There are a few basic color characteristics that are described the same in both video and film: **hue**, **saturation**, and **brightness**. Hue designates a specific color from within the visible spectrum of white light: e.g., red, green, blue. The level of saturation defines a color's purity—how much or little grayness is mixed with the color. Deep, rich, vibrant colors such as those in a brand-new U.S. flag are said to be heavily saturated. They become less saturated as the weatherbeaten flag's colors fade. Saturation is also termed **chroma** or **chrominance** in video color. Brightness or **luminance** in video indicates how bright or dark a color is.

Despite these similarities, video and film take different approaches to creating color images. Video constructs color by adding them together (additive color). A single phosphor on the TV screen is colored red, green, blue. The electron gun (or guns) ignite three nearby phosphors and combine their individual colors, thus generating a broad variety of colors. Film, in contrast, is a subtractive color process. As white light from a projector lamp passes through a piece of motion picture film, yellow, magenta (reddish), and cyan (bluish) colors are filtered out of the light. The colors that are not filtered out form the many colors of the spectrum.

Thus, both video and film rely upon three-color systems to generate color images. Different video systems and film stocks **balance** these three colors in different ways. Some are more sensitive to red, others to blue; some appear more naturalistic under sunlight, others under tungsten light (as in household light bulbs). No video system or film stock captures color exactly as it exists in nature, but this is not necessarily a drawback. Rather, it presents a wide range of color options to the camera operator. Color may be manipulated through the choice of video system and film stock, as well as through lens filters and colored gels on the lights.

In the 1980s, long after television had been a strictly color medium, black-and-white video and film began to be reintroduced. Although black-and-white images are uncommon in narrative programs, they have been used to indicate dream sequences or events that occurred in the past. In these cases, black-and-white's contrast from color has been used to communicate narrative information. It becomes **diegetically** significant—significant in the world the characters inhabit. Black-and-white is also used in nonnarrative television such as commercials and music videos. In these situations the color-less images cannot always be anchored in specific meanings. Yes, there have been several commercials in which everything is black-and-white except for the product advertised (a rather obvious use of black-and-white); but there are also black-and-white music videos in which the significance of the lack of color is ephemeral or elusive. In any event, black-and-white video/film is still another option that the camera operator may use to affect the viewer.

## Special Effects

Special effects are not, strictly speaking, part of the style of the camera. Very few special effects are achieved solely by using a camera. Rather, most are accomplished by other machines transforming the video or film images created by the camera. (Also, special effects are commonly used to generate transitions between shots, as we discuss in Chapter 7). Still, a few comments on special effects seem in order at this point so that we do not innocently presume that the images we see on television could not have been somehow processed and manipulated.

Film and video take different approaches to special effects creation. For decades, television programs shot on film and movies originally shown in theaters have depended upon an optical printer to generate everything from simple fade outs to the illusion of spaceships attacking the Death Star (in the first *Star Wars* [1977]). The results are known as **optical effects**. Technicians fabricate optical effects by re-photographing pieces of film and manipulating them in a broad variety of ways, but this process is awkward and time-consuming.

Since the 1960s, however, increasingly sophisticated technology has been developed for producing special effects without an optical printer—using video technology, some of which is aided by computers. Today, even theatrical films use video to generate special effects—transferring the video image to film for the end product. Video dominates special effects in both film and television because, economically, video effects are much less expensive than optical effects; and, aesthetically, video effects appear equally plausible.

Among the first **electronic effects** to be developed for television was **keying**. In this process a portion of a video image is electronically cut out and another image is placed in that video "hole." The simplest form of keying is the insertion of letters and numbers into an image. (To achieve the same effect on film with an optical printer would take hours.)

**Chroma Key** is a special type of keying in which a particular color (blue or green, usually) is subtracted from an image and a new image is inserted in its place. Weather forecasters, for example, stand in front of a blue screen, which is transformed into map or radar images. The forecaster is in a studio gesturing toward a blue screen. The map that appears behind him has been created by a computer and inserted into the image, taking the place of the blue screen.

Keying and similar electronic effects have been surpassed, technologically, by **digital video effects** (DVE), which are generated by computers. A computer is able to translate the pixels of a video image into a series of numbers (or digits, hence *digital* video effects). Once the image has been digitized it becomes completely malleable. The image can be shrunk, stretched, duplicated, colored, twisted, rotated, and turned on it head. Bits and pieces of older images may be seamlessly patched together, as done in the Paula Abdul ad for Diet Coke. Moreover, one object or person can even be effortlessly transformed into another—as in the so-called morphing process

used in Michael Jackson's *Black or White* video, *Terminator 2: Judgment Day* (1991), a Miller beer commercial, and numerous other commercials. The options open to the DVE technician seem virtually limitless.

# SUMMARY

This chapter has been filled with more technological information—mechanical, electronic, and chemical—than the other chapters. This is because camera style is inevitably described in technological terms—words borrowing from technological roots for their meanings: *dolly shot, anamorphic framing, telephoto shot.* To discuss television style, then, it becomes necessary to understand television technology. Technology does not exist in a vacuum, however. The use of specific technological inventions—videotape, camera dollies, etc.—depends upon the TV program's budget and the aesthetic conventions of the time. Moreover, many elements of camera style are not all determined by technology. Framing and camera height decisions, for example, do not depend upon specific technological devices. Instead, they result from shifting aesthetic conventions.

Technology, economics, and aesthetic convention blend together in the videographer's, cinematographer's, and/or director's manipulation of camera style. The persons responsible for visual style choose initially between video and film, and thereby determine much about the definition and color of the final product. But—regardless of the choice of video or film—focal lengths, depths of field, framings, camera heights, and movements will be selected to maximize narrative informational or commercial effect. Each of these camera-style aspects serves many functions on television, affecting our understanding of a program. As critical viewers, we need to remain alert to the significance of camera-style techniques. We can then understand their function within television and their impact on television's construction of meaning.

# FURTHER READINGS

Video and film camera style is discussed in many of the readings suggusted at the end of Chapter 5.

Readers interested in the specifics of film camera technology should consult J. Kris Malkiewicz, *Cinematography: A Guide for Film Makers and Film Teachers*, 2nd ed. (New York: Simon & Schuster, 1989).

# NOTES

1. In the cinema, deep focus was not used much until the 1940s, when directors such as Orson Wells and cinematographers such as Gregg Toland began incorporating it. In *Citizen Kane* (1941) and *The Magnificent Ambersons* (1942), Welles uses deep focus to coordinate simultaneous action on several planes: for example, in *Citizen Kane*, while a young boy's mother and father discuss the boy's future, he (the boy) is visible through a window, playing in the snow in the far background.

2. Although some refer to framing solely in terms of camera-to-object distance, it is inaccurate to do so because framing is the result of camera-to-object distance in conjunction with focal length. Focal length determines framing as much as the distance of the camera from the object.

3. To film critic André Bazin, this aspect of the close-up made it the framing least like our perception of reality, where we can pick and choose where and at what we look.

4. It can accommodate both film and video cameras; but if film is used, the operator still views the image on a video monitor rather than looking through a viewfinder.

5. CinemaScope originated the first popular anamorphic process in the U.S., but today they have been superseded by Panavision.

6. Letterboxing is more popular in laserdisc versions of theatrical films than in their videocassette versions.

7. The number of scan lines varies in different countries which use different broadcasting systems. Two European formats, for example, use 100 (PAL) and 307 (SECAM) more scan lines than the North American standard does. The U.S. standard was set by the NTSC (National Television Standards Committee) back in 1941.

8. More typically, however, filmed programs use videotape in this fashion. The contrast between the filmed image and the videotaped image is more striking than that between 2" videotape and ½" tape.

# Style and Editing

Editing is at once the most frequently overlooked and the most powerful component of televisual style. We are seldom conscious of a program's arrangement of shots, and yet it is through editing that television producers most directly control our sense of space and time, the medium's building blocks. For many theorists of television, editing is the engine that powers the medium.

At its most basic, editing is deceptively simple. Shot 1 ends. Cut. Shot 2 begins. But in that instantaneous shot-to-shot transition, we make a rather radical shift. We go from looking at one piece of space from one point of view to another piece of space from a different perspective. Perspective and representation of space suddenly become totally malleable. Time, too, can be equally malleable. Shot 2 need not be from a time following shot 1; it could be from hours or years before. The potential for creative manipulation is obvious.

Within broadcast television, however, editing is not completely free of conventions—far from it. Most television editing is done according to the "rules" of two predominant **modes of production**: **single-camera** and **multiple-camera**. By mode of production we mean an aesthetic style of shooting that often relies upon a particular technology and is governed by certain economic systems. As we have seen before, television forever blends aesthetics, technology, and economics.

Single-camera productions are filmed with just one camera operating at a time. (As noted in Chapter 6, most single-camera work is done in film, not videotape, although the film is often transferred to tape to be edited.) The shots are not taken in the order in which they will appear in the final film, but instead are shot in the sequence that is most efficient in order to get the production done on time and under budget.

Consider, for example, a scene between two characters named Eugene and Lydia, in which shots 1, 3, 5, 7, and 9 are of Eugene and shots 2, 4, 6, 8, and 10 are of Lydia. The single-camera approach to this scene would be to set up the lighting on Eugene, get the camera positioned, and then shoot the odd-numbered shots one after another. Then Lydia's lighting would be set up and the camera would shoot all the even-numbered shots of her. Later, the shots would be edited into their proper order.

Multiple-camera productions have two or more cameras trained on the set while the scene is acted out. In our hypothetical ten-shot scene, one camera would be pointed at Eugene while the other would simultaneously be pointed at Lydia. The scene could be edited while it transpires or it could be cut later, depending on time constraints. Sequences in daily soap operas and game shows tend to be edited while they are shot, but weekly sitcoms are generally edited after shooting.

These modes of production are more than just a matter of how many cameras the cinematographer/videographer brings to the set. They define two distinct approaches, whose differences cut through

- **Pre-production**—the written planning for the shoot
- **Production**—the shoot itself
- **Post-production**—everything afterward

And yet, both modes rely upon similar principles of editing.

Historically, the single-camera mode of production came first. It developed initially in the cinema and has remained the preeminent way of making theatrical motion pictures. On television, it is the main mode used to create prime-time dramas, made-for-television movies, music videos, and nationally telecast commercials. As it is also the site for the development of most editing principles, we will begin our discussion of editing there. Subsequently we will consider the multiple-camera mode of production, which is virtually unique to television and is only rarely used in theatrical films. Sitcoms, soap operas, game shows, sports programs, and newscasts are shot using several cameras at once. Although multiple-camera shooting has developed its own conventions, its underlying premises are still rooted in certain single-camera conceptualizations of how space and time should be represented on television.

# SINGLE-CAMERA MODE OF PRODUCTION

Initially it might seem that single-camera production is a cumbersome, lengthy, and expensive way to create television images, and that television producers would shy away from it for those reasons. But television is not a machine driven solely by the profit motive. Just as we must be cautious of technological determinism (i.e., that television producers will use new technology as it becomes available), we must also be wary of slipping into an economic determinism. That is, we must avoid the mistaken belief that television producers' aesthetic decisions and technological choices will *always* be determined by economic imperatives. In a study of how and why the Hollywood film industry adopted the single-camera mode of production, David Bordwell, Janet Staiger, and Kristin Thompson contend that technological change has three basic explanations:

1. Production efficiency—does this innovation allow films to be made more quickly or more cheaply?
2. Product differentiation—does this innovation help distinguish this film from other, similar films, and thus make it more attractive to the consumer?

3. Standards of quality—does this innovation fit a conventionalized aesthetic sense of how the medium should "evolve"? Does it adhere to specific sense of "progress" or improvement?[1]

Although single-camera production is less efficient than multiple-camera, it compensates for its inefficiency by providing greater product differentiation and adhering to conventionalized aesthetic standards. Because single-camera mode offers more control over the image and the editing, it allows directors to maximize the impact of every single image. Consequently, it is the mode of choice for short televisual pieces such as commercials and music videos, which rely upon their visuals to communicate as powerfully as possible. Commercials in particular need a distinctive style to distinguish them from surrounding messages that compete for our attention.

## Stages of Production

### Pre-production

To make single-camera production economically feasible, there must be extensive pre-production planning. Chance events and improvisation are expensive distractions in a single-camera production. The planning of any production—whether a made-for-TV movie or a Pepsi commercial—begins with a script. Actually, there are several increasingly detailed stages of scripting:

- **Treatment**—a basic outline
- **Screenplay**—a scene-by-scene description of the action, including dialogue
- **Shooting script**—a *shot-by-shot* description of each scene
- **Storyboard**—small drawings of individual shots

For our purposes it is not important to go into the differences among these written planning stages, but it may be helpful to consider the storyboard, which consists of drawings of images for each shot (with more than one image for complicated shots). Storyboards indicate the precision with which some directors conceptualize their visual design ahead of time. Alfred Hitchcock, for example, was well known for devising elaborate storyboards. For him, the filmmaking process itself was simply a matter of creating those images on film. Commercials and music videos are also heavily storyboarded. Each frame is carefully plotted into a particular aesthetic, informational, or commercial system.

## Production

A single film camera is used on the set and the shots are done out of order. (Most narrative single-camera productions, as well as many music videos and most nationally broadcast commercials, are shot with *film*, not video, cameras; see Chapter 6. Actors typically rehearse their scenes in entirety, but the filming is disjointed and filled with stops and starts. Because the final product is assembled from all these fragments, a **continuity person** must keep track of all the details from one shot to the next—e.g., in which hand the actor was holding a cigarette and how far down the cigarette had burned. Nonetheless, small errors do sneak through, illustrating just how disjointed the whole process is. For instance, a frame enlargement from a *Northern Exposure* (1990—) scene that is analyzed below, a dishrag is on actor Janine Turner's shoulder. At the very beginning of the next shot, the dishrag has disappeared.

The "production" stage of making television is under the immediate control of the **director**. He or she chooses the camera positions, coaches the actors, and approves the mise-en-scene. Most television directors do not write the scripts they direct (which is done in pre-production), and most do not have control over the editing (post-production). However, the actual filming/videotaping process is their direct responsibility.

## Post-production

The task of the technicians in post-production is to form the disjointed fragments into a unified whole. (The exposed film may be cut together on film editing equipment, or, as is becoming more and more common, the film may be transferred to videotape for editing.) Ideally the parts will fit together so well that we will not even notice the seams joining them. At this point in narrative television production, the **sound editor** and **musical director** are called upon to further smooth over the cuts between shots with music, dubbed-in dialogue, and sound effects (see Chapter 8). Of course, in music videos and many commercials the music provides the piece's main unifying force and is developed well before the visuals. Indeed, the music determines the visuals, not vice versa, and becomes part of the pre-production planning.

## The Continuity Editing System

In Chapter 2 we discussed Hollywood classicism as the major narrative system in theatrical film. Accompanying this narrative structure is a particular approach to editing that has come to be known as **continuity editing**. It operates to create a continuity of space and time out of the fragments of scenes that are contained in individual shots. It is also known as invisible editing because it does not call attention to itself. Cuts are not noticeable because the shots are arranged in an order that effectively supports the progression of the story. If the editing functions correctly, we concentrate on the story and don't notice the technique that is used to construct it. Thus, the editing is done according to the logic of the narrative.

There are many ways to edit a story, but Hollywood classicism evolved a set of conventions that constitute the **continuity system**. The continuity editing system matches classicism's narrative coherence (discussed in Chapter 2) with continuities of space and time. Shots are arranged so that the spectator always has a clear sense of where the characters are and when the shot is happening—excepting narratives that begin ambiguously and clarify the "where" and "when" later (e.g., murder mysteries). This spatial and temporal coherence is particularly crucial in individual scenes of a movie.

A scene is the smallest piece of the narrative action. Usually it takes place in one location (continuous space), at one particular time (continuous time). When the location and/or time frame change, the scene is customarily over and a new one begins. To best understand the continuity system, we will examine how it constructs spatial and temporal continuity within individual scenes. How these scenes then fit together with one another in a narrative structure is discussed in Chapter 2.

## Spatial Continuity

In the classical scene the space is oriented around an **axis of action**. Let's say that the action of this scene is Brent and Lilly talking to one another in a cafeteria. The axis or line of action, then, runs through the two of them. The continuity system dictates that cameras remain on one side of that axis. The arc defines the area in which the camera may be placed. If you recall your high school geometry, you'll recognize that this arc describes 180°. Since the cameras may be positioned only within the 180° arc, this editing principle has come to be known as the *180° rule*.

The 180° rule helps preserve spatial continuity because it ensures that there will be a similar background behind the actors while cutting from one to the other. The cafeteria setting that is behind Brent and Lilly recurs from shot to shot and helps confirm our sense of the space of the room. A shot from the other side of the axis (position X) would reveal a portion of the cafeteria that had not been seen before, and thus might contain spatial surprises or cause disorientation.

More important than similar backgrounds, however, is the way in which the 180° rule maintains **screen direction**. In the classical system, the conventional wisdom is that if a character is looking or moving to the right of the screen in shot 1, then he or she should be looking or moving in the same direction in shot 2. To cut from

camera A to camera X would break the 180° rule and violate screen direction. In a shot from camera A, Lilly is looking screen left. If the director had cut to a shot of her from position X, Lilly would suddenly be looking screen right. Even though the actor herself had not changed position, the change in camera angle would make her *seem* to have changed direction. This is further illustrated by camera position B. A cut from Brent (camera B) to Lilly from the hypothetical X position would make it appear as if they were both looking to the right, instead of toward one another. Breaking the 180° rule would confuse the spatial relationship between these two characters.

Maintaining screen direction is also important to action scenes filmed outdoors. If the director is not careful about screen direction, he or she will wind up with car chases where the vehicles appear to be moving *toward* each other rather than following. And antagonists in confrontational scenes might appear to be running in the same direction rather than challenging one another.

There are, of course, ways of bending or getting around the 180° rule, but the basic principle of preserving screen direction remains fundamental to the classical construction of space. For this reason, the continuity system is also known as the *180° system*.

Built upon the 180° rule are a set of conventions governing the editing of a scene. Although these conventions were more strictly adhered to in theatrical film during the 1930s and 1940s than they are on television today, there are several that still persist. Some of the most prevalent include:

- The establishing shot
- The shot-counter shot editing pattern
- The re-establishing shot
- The match cut—including the match-on-action and the eyeline match
- The prohibition against the **jump cut**

This may best be illustrated by breaking down a simple scene into individual shots.

The first shot of a classical scene is typically a long shot that shows the entire area and the characters in it. This **establishing shot** introduces the space and the narrative components of the scene: Maggie, Joel, her cabin, a dinner cooked by her. In a sense, the establishing shot repeats the exposition of the narrative, presenting specific characters to us once again. If the establishing shot is from a very great distance, it may be followed by another establishing shot that shows the characters clearly in a medium shot or medium long shot.

From there the scene typically develops some sort of alternating pattern, especially if it is a conversation scene between two persons. Thus, shots of Maggie are alternated with shots of Joel, depending on who is speaking or what their narrative importance is at a particular point (camera positions B and C. Note that once again the 180° rule is adhered to, as the cameras remain on one side of the axis of action. Note also that the angles of positions B and C crisscross each other, rather than being aimed at Joel and Maggie from positions D or E. These latter two positions do not violate the 180° rule, but positions B and C are preferred in the continuity system for two reasons. First, these angles show more of the characters' faces, giving us a three-quarter view rather than a profile. We look into their faces without looking directly into their eyes and breaking the taboo against actors looking into the camera lens and at the viewer. Second, since we see Joel's shoulder in Maggie's shot and vice versa, the space that the two share is reconfirmed. We know where Maggie is in relationship to Joel and where he is in relationship to her.

Shots which are said to be the counter or reverse angle of shots such as B, go by the name **shot-counter shot** or **shot-reverse shot**.

Once shot-counter shot has been used to detail the action of a scene, there is often a cut back to a longer view of the space. This **re-establishing shot** shows us once again which characters are involved and where they are located. It may also be used as a transitional device, showing us a broader area so that the characters may move into it or another character may join them. Often it is immediately followed by another series of shots-reverse shots.

The *Northern Exposure* scene does not contain this type of re-establishing shot, but provides a variation of it. After a series of fifteen shots in fairly tight close-up, the camera cuts back to a *medium* close-up as the tone of Joel and Maggie's conversation shifts. The scene is then played at medium close-up for seven shots, as Joel and Maggie drift apart emotionally. Just when Maggie is most disenchanted with Joel, he compliments her and their intimacy is regained. This is marked in the framing with a tighter shot of Joel, as he raises his glass to toast her. She reciprocates his intimacy and is also framed tighter. After one more close-up of Joel, the camera cuts to the original medium shot of the two of them, which tracks back and out the window. Thus the framing has gone from medium shot to medium close-up to close-up, coming closer to the characters as the scene intensifies. But it does not remain at close-up. The camera cuts back to medium close-up and then returns to close-up before ending the scene with a track backward from a medium shot. The key to any classically edited scene is variation, closer and farther as the narrative logic dictates.

Two other editing devices are among those used to maintain space in the continuity system: the **match cut** and the **point-of-view** or **subjective shot**.

In a match cut, the space and time of one shot fits that of the preceding shot. One shot "matches" the next and thereby makes the editing less noticeable. A **jump cut**, in contrast, results in a disruptive gap in space and or time, so that something seems to be missing. Jump cuts were regarded as mistakes in classical editing, but they were made fashionable in the 1960s films of Jean-Luc Godard and other European directors. Today, jump cuts similar to this are quite common in music videos and commercials, and even find their way into more mainstream narrative productions. *Homicide: Life on the Street*

(1993—) is peppered with them. But then, *Homicide* is not a conventionally edited show. In most narrative television programs, match cuts remain the norm and jump cuts are generally prohibited.

Matching may be achieved in several ways. Two of the most common are the **match on action** and the **eyeline match**.

In a match-on-action cut, an activity is continued from one shot to the next. In the *Northern Exposure* scene, Maggie begins to sit down; at the start of the next shot she continues that movement. The editor matches the action from one shot to the next, placing the cut in the midst of it. This, in effect, conceals the cut because we are drawn from one shot to the next by the action. We concentrate on Maggie's movement, and the cut becomes "invisible."

An eyeline match begins with a character looking in a direction that is motivated by the narrative. For instance, in *L.A. Law* the boardroom scenes are edited based on the looks of the characters. Jonathan looks in a specific direction and the editor uses that look as a signal to cut to Leland, toward whom Jonathan had glanced. Jonathan's *eyeline* provides the motivation for the cut and impels the viewer toward the new space. In an eyeline match such as this, the second shot is *not* from the perspective of the person who is looking, but rather merely shows the area of the room in the eyeline's general direction. The shot of Leland is from a camera position in the middle of the table, not from the chair where Jonathan was sitting, even though his glance cued the shot of Leland.

A shot made when the camera "looks" from a character's perspective is known as a **point-of-view** shot. A point-of-view shot is a type of framing in which the camera is positioned physically close to a character's perspective. The shots of Joel and Maggie, for example, are all point-of-view shots. In each, we see from Joel's or Maggie's point of view. If the camera is positioned as if it were inside the character's head, looking out his or her eyes, then it is known as a subjective shot. Frequently, point-of-view and subjective shots are incorporated in a simple editing pattern: in shot 1 someone looks and in shot 2 we see what he or she is looking at from his or her perspective. In another *Northern Exposure* scene, Maggie draws Joel's attention to his brother, Jules. Joel turns and looks in the first shot. The camera cuts to a close-up of the brother that is taken from Joel's perspective. Subjective shots such as this are very similar to eyeline matches, but the eyeline cut does not go to a shot that is the character's perspective.

## Sample Decoupage

The best way to understand editing is to take a scene and work backward toward the shooting script, thereby deconstructing the scene. The process of breaking down a scene into its constituent parts is known as decoupage, the French word for cutting things apart.

In our discussion of *Northern Exposure* we have created a sample decoupage. You may want to perform a similar exercise with a videotape of a short scene of your own choosing. Watch the tape several times with the sound turned off. Try to diagram the set and each of the camera positions from a bird's-eye view. Draw a shot-by-shot storyboard of the scene. Ask yourself these questions:

1.  How is the scene's space, the area in which the action takes place, introduced to the viewer? Does an establishing shot occur at the start of the scene (or later in it)?
2.  What is the narrative purpose or function of each shot? What does each shot communicate to the viewer? Does an establishing shot occur at the start of the scene (or later in it)?
3.  Why was each shot taken from the camera position that it was? Do these angles adhere to the 180° rule? Is screen direction maintained? If not, why is the viewer not disoriented? Or if the space is ambiguous, what narrative purpose does that serve?

4. If the characters move around, how does the editing (or camera movement) create transitions for one area to another?

5. Is an alternating editing pattern used? Is shot-counter shot used?

6. How does the camera relate to the character's perspective? Are there point-of-view or subjective shots? If so, how are those shots cued or marked? That is, what tells us that they are subjective or point-of-view shots?

7. Is match-on-action used? Are there jump cuts?

8. How does the last shot of the scene bring it to a conclusion?

9. In sum, how does the organization of space by editing support the narrative?

## Temporal Continuity

Within individual scenes, story time and screen time are often the same. Five minutes of story usually takes five minutes on screen. Time is continuous. Shot 2 is presumed to instantaneously follow shot 1. Transitions from one scene to the next, however, need not be continuous. If the story time of one scene always immediately followed that of another's, then screen time would always be exactly the same as story time. A story that lasted two days would take two days to watch on the screen. Obviously, story time and screen time are seldom equivalent on television. The latter is most commonly much shorter than the former. There are many gaps, or ellipses, in screen time. In addition, screen time may not be in the same chronological order as story time. Through flashback, for example, and action from the story past is presented in the screen present. So, both time's *duration* and its *order* may be manipulated in the transition from one scene to the next.

To shorten story time or change its order without confusing the viewer, classical editing has developed a collection of scene-to-scene transitions that break the continuity of time in conventionalized ways, thus avoiding viewer disorientation. These transitions are marked by simple effects that are used instead of a regular cut.

1. The **fade**. A **fade-out** gradually darkens the image until the screen is black; a **fade-in** starts in black and gradually illuminates the image. The fade-out on one scene and fade-in to the next is often used to mark a substantial change in time.

2. The **dissolve**. When one shot **dissolves** into the next, it means that one shot fades out at the same time the next shot fades in, so that the two images overlap one another briefly. The final shot from the *Northern Exposure* scene above illustrates this. The final shot is a long shot of Joel and Maggie, as seen through the window of her cabin. From there it dissolves to a close-up of Joel's face in his own bed. The two shots both appear on screen for a short period of time, overlapping one another. Here the dissolve serves to mark the transition from Joel's dream state to "reality." Dissolves are more conventionally used to signal a passage in time; and the slower the dissolve, the more time has passed.

3. The **wipe**. Imagine a windshield wiper moving across the frame. As it moves it wipes on one image off the screen and another on to take its place. This is the simplest form of a wipe, but wipes can be done in a huge variety of patterns. Wipes may indicate a change in time, but they are also used for an instantaneous change in space.

In addition to these transitional devices, classical editors also use special effects to indicate flashbacks. In films of the 1930s and 1940s, the image may become blurry or wavy as the story slips into the past (or in a dream). The special effect signals to the viewer, "We're moving into the past now. During the prime of the classical era, changes in time were inevitably clearly marked, and these techniques continue to be used (as is suggested by the dissolve in *Northern Exposure*).

Fades, dissolves, and wipes were part of the stock-in-trade of the film editor during the cinema's classical era, and they are still evident in today's singe-camera productions. Historically, however, narrative filmmakers have used these devices less and less. Initially, this was due in large part to the influence of 1960s European filmmakers, who accelerated the pace of their films through jump cuts and ambiguous straight cuts (no special effects) when shifting into the past or into dream states. The jump cuts in Jean-Luc Godard's *Breathless* (1960) revolutionized classical editing, breaking many of its most fundamental "rules." And Luis Bunuel's films enter and exit dream states and flashbacks without signaling them to the viewer in any way, creating a bizarre, unstable world.

Classical editing is not a static phenomenon. It changes according to technological developments, aesthetic fashions, and economic imperatives. Current fashion favors straight cuts in narrative, single-camera productions, but fades, dissolves, and wipes are still in evidence. Indeed, the fade-out and fade-in are television's favorite transition from narrative segment to commercial break and back. In this case, the fade-out and fade-in signal the transition from one type of television material (fiction) to another (commercial).

## Nonnarrative Editing

Not all television material that is shot with one camera tells a story. There are single-camera commercials, music videos, and news segments that do not present a narrative in the conventional sense of the term. They have developed different editing systems for their particular functions. Some bear the legacy of continuity editing, while others depart from it.

### Commercials and Music Video Editing[3]

First, note that many commercials and music videos actually involve narrative. Many do tell stories—very brief, highly condensed stories.

Advertisements for McDonald's often show characters involved in some sort of rising action that leads to a climactic encounter with a Big Mac. The video for Bruce Springsteen's "I'm On Fire" casts him as a mechanic repairing a car for a wealthy woman and confronting his desire for her. The editing for these short narratives is appropriately compressed, with some classical components left out. But the principles of continuity persist. The editing still establishes characters in a specific space and guides us through that space through the (somewhat abbreviated) conventions of continuity editing.

But what of the commercials and music videos that do not tell stories? What editing systems(s) do they use?

As we discussed in Chapter 4, the principal strategy behind commercials is an expository one. Commercials need to convince us of the importance of a product—or at least the difference between it and other similar products. To achieve product differentiation, the commercial-makers must quickly present the dissimilarities between this product and all the others. This may result in shots that contrast the advertised product with others. Or it may result in a listing of the advertised product's advantages. Or, finally, the product may be associated with other desirable objects or person—as when a beer commercial presents images of slender men and women in brief swimwear (none of whom are actually drinking beer because television regulations prohibit it). Thus, the shots in a nonnarrative commercial tend to be organized according to:

- Product contrast
- A categorization of the product's virtues, and/or
- The association of the product with other objects/humans/values

Music videos, in their own way, are also selling "product" differentiation, for bands need to differentiate themselves from other groups to sell their music. But music video also represses its function as musical advertising, creating the illusion of aesthetic expression for its own sake.

This has led to the occasional music video in which the editing is rather abstract. A variety of techniques are used to hold the editing together, to make disparate shots cohere. The main tools that impart coherence to a music video are the musical recording that the video illustrates and the image of the performers themselves. For example, in *Red, Hot, and Blue* (a collection of Cole Porter songs), David Byrne's video links close-ups of a number of people mouthing the same song lyric. Byrne is among them, but the consistency lies in the images of one face after another—it doesn't matter whose—singing, "Don't Fence Me In." In this video, consistency arises from another, more abstract, property: unlike most television, it was produced in black and white. Another video from the same collection offers a more vivid example: *I've Got You Under My Skin* connects images of performer Neneh Cherry (a dancer in a skintight, leathery body stocking) and a head-on view of a loudspeaker—all in a glistening, high-contrast monochrome, tinted a deep blue. By far, however, the property that lends music videos their visual coherence is movement itself. Many videos exemplify a form of match-on-action, with more accent on the action than on the match. Whether a body, an object, or the camera itself, generally something is moving. In a drama or sitcom, the possible spatial disruption caused by a cut may be smoothed by connecting shots depicting similar movement by the same character. In a video, spatial unity may be less important than temporal continuity. One shot may be entirely different from the next—even if they both depict the same person, the performer may be wearing a costume in one shot and dressed differently in the next—but movement, supported by the continuity of the music, helps bridge the transition.

**News Editing**

Although the in-studio portion of the nightly newscast is shot using multiple cameras, most **ENG (Electronic News Gathering)** work is done with a single camera. That is, the stories filed by individual reporters are shot in the field with a single video camera. The editing of these stories, or **packages** (ranging in length from 80 to 105 seconds), follows conventions particular to the way that the news translates events of historical reality into television material (see Chapter 4). The conventional news story contains:

- The reporter's opening **lead**
- A first **sound bite**, consisting of a short piece of audio, usually synched to image, that was recorded on the scene: e.g., the mayor's comment on a new zoning regulation, or a bereaved father's sobbing
- The reporter's transition
- The reporter's concluding **stand-up**, where he or she stands before a site significant to the story and summarizes it

This editing scheme was inherited, with variations, from print journalism and a specific concept of how information from historical reality should be organized.

The reporter typically begins by piquing our interest, implicitly posing questions about a topic or event. The sound bites provide answers and fill in information. And, to comply with conventional structures of journalistic "balance" (inscribed in official codes of ethics), two sound bites are usually provided. One argues pro the other con, especially on controversial issues. The news often structures information in this binary fashion: pro/con, yes/no, left/right, on/off. The reporter then comes to represent the middle ground, with his or her concluding stand-up serving to synthesize the opposing perspectives. Thus, the editing pattern reflects the ideological structure of news reporting (as discussed in Chapter 4).

# MULTIPLE-CAMERA MODE OF PRODUCTION

Although a good deal of what we see on television has been produced using single-camera production, it would be wrong to assume that this mode dominates TV in the same way that it dom-

**TABLE 7.1**  *Top Ten Prime-Time Shows: 1992–93*

All of the following are multiple-camera productions except for *Murder, She Wrote* and *Northern Exposure*, which use single-camera production.

1. 60 Minutes
2. Roseanne
3. Home Improvement
4. Murphy Brown
5. Murder, She Wrote
6. Coach
7. NFL Monday Night Football
8. Cheers
9. Full House
10. Northern Exposure

**TABLE 7.2**  *Top Ten Prime-Time Shows: 1950–51*

Of the following, all but the Westerns (*The Lone Ranger* and *Hopalong Cassidy*) and *Fireside Theatre* were telecast live using multiple camera technology. (1950–51 was the first season during which the A.C. Nielsen Company rated programs.)

1. Texaco Star Theater
2. Fireside Theatre
3. Philco TV Playhouse
4. Your Show of Shows
5. The Colgate Comedy Hour
6. Gillette Cavalcade of Sports
7. The Lone Ranger
8. Arthur Godfrey's Talent Scouts
9. Hopalong Cassidy
10. Mama

inates theatrical film. The opposite is true. It would be impossible to calculate exactly, but roughly three-quarters of today's television shows are produced using the multiple-camera mode. Of the top ten most popular prime-time shows in the 1992–93 season, only two were shot in single-camera mode (Table 7.1). This is misleading in that the current popularity of sitcoms, most of which are shot in multiple camera, skews the sample. But still, it indictes just how ubiquitous multiple-camera production is. Furthermore, this doesn't even take into consideration non-prime-time programs such as daytime soap operas and late-night talk shows, all of which are also done in multiple-camera. Obviously, multiple-camera production is the norm on broadcast television, as it has been since the days of television's live broadcasts—virtually all of which were also multiple-camera productions (Table 7.2).

It is tempting to assume that since multiple-camera shooting affords the director less control over the image and is less expensive and faster

to produce than single-camera, it is therefore a cheap, slipshod imitation of single-camera. This is the hierarchy of style that television producers, critics, and even some viewers themselves presume. In this view, multiple-camera is an inferior, though necessary, mode. However, ranking one mode of production over another is a futile exercise. It is more important to discuss the differences between the two and understand how those differences may affect television's production of meaning. In short, how do the different modes of production influence the meanings that TV conveys to the viewer? And what principles of space and time construction do they share?

## Stages of Production

### Pre-production

Narrative programs such as soap operas and sitcoms, that utilize multiple-camera production start from scripts much as single-camera productions do, but these scripts are less image-oriented and initially indicate no camera directions at all. Sitcom and soap opera scripts consist almost entirely of dialogue, with wide margins so that the director may write in camera directions. Storyboards are seldom, if ever, created for these programs. This type of scripting is emblematic of the emphasis on dialogue in multiple-camera programs. The words come first; the images are tailored to fit them.

Nonnarrative programs (game shows, talk shows, etc.) have even less written preparation. Instead, they rely upon specific structure and a formalized opening and closing. Although the host may have a list of questions or other prepared material, he or she and the participants are presumed to be speaking in their own voices, rather than the voice of a scriptwriter. This adds to the program's impression of improvisation.

## Production

A multiple-camera production may be filed or videotaped or even broadcast live. *Murphy Brown* is filmed; *Roseanne* is videotaped. Some local news programs and *Saturday Night Live* are telecast live. If a program is filmed, the editing and the addition of music and sound effects must necessarily come later, after the film stock has been processed. If a program is videotaped, there are the options of editing later or while it is being recorded **live-on-tape**. (Obviously, a live program must be edited while it is telecast.) Time constraints play a factor here. Programs that are broadcast daily, such as soap operas and game shows, seldom have the time for extensive editing in post-production. Weekly programs, however, may have that luxury.

The choice of film or videotape is, once again, dependent in part of technology, economics, and aesthetics. Since the technology of videotape was not made available until 1956, there were originally only two choices for a multiple-camera program: either broadcast live and record the broadcast on kinescope or shoot in film.[4] *I Love Lucy*, among the first multiple-camera *filmed* programs, made the technological choice to use film because of the economic imperative of making it easier and cheaper to syndicate the program after its first run. After the introduction of videotape, this economic incentive no longer held true. Today, producers who shoot film in a multiple-camera setup do so primarily for an aesthetic reason. They use the higher resolution of the film image to distinguish their programs from videotaped ones (see Chapter 6 on film-video visual differences).

Narrative programs that are filmed and those videotaped narrative programs that are edited in post-production follow a similar production procedure. The actors rehearse individual scenes off the set, then continue rehearsing on the set, with the cameras. The director maps out the positions for the actors and the two to four cameras that will record a scene. The camera operators are often given lists of their positions relative to the scene's dialogue. Finally, an audience (if any) is brought into the studio.

The episode is performed one scene at a time, with 15- to 20- minute breaks between the scenes—during which, at sitcom filmings/tapings, a comedian keeps the audience amused. One major difference between single-camera and multiple-camera shooting is that, in multiple-camera, the actors always perform the scenes straight through, without interruption, unless a mistake is made. Their performance is not fragmented, as it is in single-camera production. Each scene is filmed or videotaped at least twice and, if a single line or camera position is missed, they may shoot that individual shot in isolation afterwards.

Further, in multiple-camera sitcoms, the scenes are normally filmed or taped in the order in which they will appear in the finished program—in contrast, once again, to single-camera production. This is done largely to help the studio audience follow the story and respond to it appropriately. The audience's laughter and applause is recorded by placing microphones above them. Their applause is manipulated through flashing "applause" signs that channel their response. (This response is augmented in post-production with recorded laughter and applause. The resulting **laugh track** is made through a process known popularly as **canned laughter**, and called **sweetening** in the industry.)

The entire process of filming or videotaping one episode of a half-hour sitcom takes about three to four hours—if all goes as planned.

Live-on-tape productions, such as soap operas, are similar in their preparation to those edited in post-production, but the recording process differs in a few ways. Once the videotape starts rolling on a live-on-tape production, it seldom stops. Directors use a **switcher** to change between cameras as the scene is performed. The shots are all planned in advance, but the practice of switching shots is a bit loose. The cuts don't always occur at the conventionally appropriate moment. In addition to the switching/cutting executed concurrently with the actor's performance, the scene's music and sound effects are often laid on at the same time, though they may be fine-tuned later. Sound technicians prepare the appropriate door bells and phone rings and thunderclaps on audiotape and then insert them when called for by the director. All of this heightens the impression that the scene presented is occurring "live" before the cameras, that the cameras just happened to be there to capture this event—hence the term live-on-tape. The resulting performance is quite similar to that in live theater.

In soap operas, individual scenes are not shot like sitcoms, in the order of appearance in the final program. Since soap operas have no studio audience to consider, their scenes are shot in the fashion most efficient for the production. Normally this means that the order is determined by which sets are being used on a particular day. First, all the scenes that appear on one set will be shot—regardless of where they appear in the final program. Next, all the scenes on another set will be done, and so on. This allows the technicians to light and prepare one set at a time, which is faster and cheaper than going back and forth between sets.

As we have seen, narrative programs made with multiple cameras may be either filmed or videotaped and, if taped, may either be switched during the production or edited afterward, in post-production. Nonnarrative programs, however, have fewer production options. Studio news programs, game shows, and talk shows are always broadcast live or shot live-on-tape, and never shot on film. This is because of their need for immediacy (in the news) and/or economic efficiency (in game and talk shows). Participants in the latter do not speak from scripts, they extemporize. And, since these "actors" in non-narrative programs are improvising, the director must also improvise, editing on the fly. This further heightens the illusion of being broadcast live, even though most, if not all such programs, are on videotape.

## Post-production

In multiple-camera programs, this varies from the minimal touch-ups to full-scale assembly. Live-on-tape productions are virtually completed before they get to the post-production stage. But programs that have been filmed or videotaped and not switched at the time of taping must be compiled shot by shot. The editor of these programs, like the editor of single-camera productions, must create a continuity out of various discontinuous fragments.

It might appear that sitcoms and the like would have a ready-made continuity, since the scenes are performed without interruption (except to correct mistakes) and the cameras roll throughout. What we must recall, however, is that there are always several takes of each scene. The editor must choose the best version of each individual shot when assembling the final episode. Thus, shot 1 might be from the first take and shot 2 from the second or third. The dialogue is usually the same from one take to the next, but actors' positions and expressions are not. Inevitably, this results in small discontinuities. In one *Murphy Brown* scene, for instance, TV producer Miles argues with his girlfriend Audrey and her former boyfriend, Colin. In one shot, Colin, on the far left of the frame, is holding a sandwich in his right hand. The camera cuts to a reverse angle and instantaneously the sandwich has moved to his left hand. Evidently, the editor selected these two shots from alternative takes of the same scene.

To hide continuity errors from the viewer, the editor of a multiple-camera production relies on editing principles derived from the single-camera 180° editing system (e.g., match cuts, eyeline matches, etc.). Also, the soundtrack that is created in post-production incorporates music, dubbed-in dialogue, sound effects, and laugh tracks (in sitcoms) to further smooth over discontinuities and channel our attention.

## Narrative Editing: The Legacy of the Continuity System

It is striking how much multiple-camera editing of narrative scenes resembles that of single-camera editing. In particular, the 180° principle has always dominated the multiple-camera editing of fiction television. This is true for the simple, technology based reason that, to break the 180° rule and place the camera on the "wrong" side of the axis of action would reveal the other cameras, the technicians, and the bare studio walls. Obviously, violating the aspect of the 180° system is not even an option in television studio production.

However, acceptance of the continuity editing system in multiple-camera production goes beyond marinating screen direction due to an ad hoc adherence to the 180° rue. It extends to the single-camera mode's organization of screen space. As you read through the following description of typical scene development you might refer back to the description of single-camera space above. Note also that the following applies to all narrative programs shot in multiple-camera, whether they are filmed or videotaped (or recorded live-on-tape).

A scene commonly begins by introducing the space and the characters through an establishing shot that is either a long shot of the entire set and actors, or a camera movement that reveals them. On weekly or daily programs, however, establishing shots may be minimized or even eliminated because of the repetitive use of sets and our established familiarity with them. In any event, from there a conventionalized alternating pattern begins—back and forth between two characters. In conversation scenes—the foundation of narrative television—directors rely upon close-ups in shot counter shot to develop the main narrative action of a scene. After a shot-counter shot series, the scene often cuts to a slightly longer view as a transition to another space or to allow for the entrance of another character. Standard, single-camera devices for motivating space (match on action, eyeline matches, point-of-view shots, etc.) are included in the multiple-camera spatial orientation.

The differences between multiple-camera programs and single-camera ones may not be noticeable to us. But they do occur, and they do inform our experience of television. The main difference between the two modes is how action, especially the physical movement of the actors, is represented. Although multiple-camera shooting arranges space similarly to the space of single-camera productions, the action within that space is represented somewhat differently. In multiple-camera shooting, some action may be missed by the camera and wind up occurring out of sight, off-frame, because the camera cannot control the action to the degree that it does in single-camera shooting. For example, in one scene from *All My Children* that was shot in multiple-camera, the following two shots occur:

1. Medium close-up Erica, over Adam's shoulder. She pushes him down and is left standing alone in the frame at the end of the shot.
2. Medium close-up Adam, seated, stationary at the very beginning of the shot.

Here, we do not see Adam fall, as we would if this scene had been shot in single-camera. Multiple camera editing leaves out "significant" action that single-camera editing would include.

Single-camera continuity editing would probably have matched these shots by cutting in the middle of Adam's fall, showing his action fully, and establishing his new position in the chair.

Small visual gaps such as this and other departures from the continuity editing system occur frequently in multiple-camera editing. What significance do they have? They contribute to the programs' illusion of "liveness." They make it seem as if the actors were making it up as they went along and the camera operators were struggling to keep up with their movements, as if the camera operators didn't know where the actors were going to go next. Of course, they do know the actors' approximate positions, but not their exact ones. In single-camera shooting the action is controlled precisely by the camera, bound by the limits of the frame. In multiple-camera shooting that control is subtly undermined. As a result, in their editing, multiple-camera narrative programs (soap operas and sitcoms, principally) come to resemble talk shows and game shows. The visual "looseness" of multiple-camera editing comes to signify "liveness" when compared to the controlled imagery of single-camera productions. The spatial orientation of the two modes is quite similar, but the movement of actors through that space is presented a bit differently.

## Nonnarrative Editing: Functional Principles

The nonnarrative programs that are shot with several cameras in a television studio include, principally, game shows, talk shows, and the portions of news programs shot in the studio. (Sports programs and other outdoor events such as parades also use several cameras at once, but that is a specialized use of multiple-camera production.) These programs do not share the need of narrative programs to tell a story, but their approach to space is remarkably similar to that of narrative programs. Typically, their sets are introduced with establishing long shots, which are followed by closer framings and inevitably (in conversation-oriented genres such as talk shows) wind up in shot-counter shot patterns. Game shows also follow this pattern of alternation, crosscutting between the space of the contestants and that of the host. The mise-en-scene of nonnarrative programs (discussed in Chapter 5) is quite distinct from narrative settings, but the shot-to-shot organization of that mise-en-scene follows principles grounded in the continuity editing system.

## SUMMARY

In our consideration of editing on television, we have witnessed the pervasiveness of the continuity system. Although originally a method for editing theatrical films, its principles also underpin both of the major modes of production for television: single-camera and multiple-camera.

The continuity system functions, in a sense, to deceive us—to make us believe that the images passing before us comprise one continuous flow, when actually they consist of many disruptions. Or, in other terms, the continuity system constructs a continuity of space and time. Many techniques are used to construct this continuity. The 180° rule maintains our sense of space and screen direction by keeping cameras on one side of an axis of action. Shot-counter shot conventionally develops the action of a scene in alternating close-ups. Match cuts (especially matches-on-action and eyeline matches) and the basic point-of-view editing pattern motivate cuts and help prevent viewer disorientation.

Time on television is not always continuous. Indeed, gaps and ellipses are essential to narrative television if stories that take place over days or months are to be presented in half-hour, hour, or two-hour time slots. Through editing, the duration and order of time may be manipulated. Within the continuity system, however, our understanding of time must always be consistent. We must be guided through an alteration of chronological order. Fades, for instance, are used to signal the passage of time from one scene to the next.

These principles and techniques of the continuity system are created in both single-camera and multiple-camera modes of production. An understanding of the stages of production—pre-production, production, and post-production—helps us see their subtle differences. The key distinction is that single-camera shoots the scene in discontinuous chunks, while multiple-camera (especially live-on-tape productions) allows the scene to be planted out in entirety while the cameras "capture" it. Even so, both modes of production must find ways to cope with discontinuity and disruption, and it is here that the continuity system's principles come into play, regardless of the actual production method used to create the images.

Nonnarrative television is not as closely tied to the continuity system as narrative programs are, yet it does bear the legacy of continuity-style editing. Establishing shots, shot-counter shot editing patterns, and the like are as evident on talk shows and game shows as they are on narrative programs.

The power of editing, the ability to alter and rearrange space and time, is a component of television that is taken for granted. Its "invisibility" should not blind us, however, to its potency.

## FURTHER READINGS

Editing style and mode of production are discussed in many of the readings suggested at the end of Chapter 5.

The evolution of single-camera production is comprehensively described in David Bordwell, Janet Staiger, and Kristin Thompson, *The Classical Hollywood Cinema: Film Style and Mode of Production to 1960* (New York: Columbia University Press, 1985). John Ellis, *Visible Fictions: Cinema: Television: Video* (Boston: Routledge & Kegan Paul, 1982) is not as exhaustive, but it does begin the work of analyzing the multiple-camera mode of production. Few other sources make such an attempt.

In the cinema, the principles of editing have long been argued. This stems from the desire to define film in terms of editing, which was at the heart of the very first theories of the cinema. These initial forays into film theory were carried out in the 1920s by filmmakers Eisenstein, Kuleshov, and Pudovkin. See, for example, Sergei Eisenstein, *Film Form: Essays in Film Theory*, edited and translated by Jay Leyda (New York: Harcourt, Brace & World, 1949); Lev Kuleshov, *Kuleshov on Film*, edited and translated by Ronald Levaco (Berkeley: University of California Press, 1974); and V.I. Pudovkin, *Film Technique and Film Acting*, translated by Ivor Montagu (New York: Bonanza, 1949).

Editing has also been a central component of recent debates within film studies over the position of the spectator, as can be seen in Jean-Louis Baudry, "Ideological Effects of the Basic Cinematographic Apparatus," in *Narrative, Apparatus, Ideology*, edited by Philip Rosen (New York: Columbia University Press, 1986), 286–98; Nick Browne, "The Spectator-in-the-Text: The Rhetoric of *Stagecoach*," in Rosen, 102–19; and Daniel Dayan, "The Tutor-Code of Classical Cinema," in *Movies and Methods*, edited by Bill Nichols (Berkeley: University of California Press, 1976). Kaja Silverman, *The Subject of Semiotics* (New York: Oxford University Press, 1983) reviews this debate.

Ken Dancyger, *The Technique of Film and Video Editing* (Boston: Focal Press, 1993) offers a broad historical and critical overview of film editing that includes a limited section on editing for television.

Despite the obvious impact of editing on television style, television criticism has been slow to articulate its significance. However, this work has been begun in Jeremy G. Butler, "Notes on the Soap Opera Apparatus: Televisual Style and *As the World Turns*," *Cinema Journal* 25, no. 3 (Spring 1986):53–70; and the previously cited Herbert Zettl, *Sight Sound Motion*.

Further, Steven E. Browne, *Videotape Editing: A Postproduction Primer*, 2nd ed. (Boston: Focal Press, 1993) approaches television editing from a hands-on perspective—explaining editing principles and the operation of videotape editing machines.

# NOTES

1. David Bordwell, Janet Staiger, and Kristin Thompson, *The Classical Hollywood Cinema: Film Style and Mode of Production to 1960* (New York: Columbia University Press, 1985), 243–44.

2. Many people use *point-of-view* and *subjective* interchangeably. Here, however, we will distinguish between subjective shots from within the head of the character and point-of-view shots that are nearby, but not through the character's eyes.

3. We group music videos together with commercials because (1) mustic videos are, in esssence, commercials for compact discs (Cds) and cassettes, and (2) music videos and commercials have come to resemble one another more and more, especially in their editing.

4. Ampex Corporation marketed its Quadruplex ("Quad") videotape system to the broadcast industry in 1956. Programs that were broadcast live before then did have the option of being recorded on motion picture film while they were telecast. In these kinescopes, as they were called, a movie camera filmed directly from a television screen. The result is rather primitive, but this is how live programs such as *The Honeymooners* were made available for syndication.

# Introduction to Horace Newcomb's "Situation and Domestic Comedies: Problems, Families, and Fathers"

Horace Newcomb is another of the founding fathers of television criticism. He started in the 1960's as a television critic for the *Baltimore Sun* and produced dozens of influential pieces on television genres and media production. He moved on to the University of Maryland where he became a lecturer in American Studies and author of several major texts on media studies.

*TV: The Most Popular Art* is a genre studies work in which Newcomb dissects all the major genres produced in the first twenty-five years of television. The chapter we are focusing on is his defining work on the situation comedy and all the possible variations that particular formula genre might have to viewers. Newcomb's strength is his ability to examine the formulaic parts of any genre and discuss how they relate to meaning for the television audience. He is particularly adept at suggesting what the formula elements mean in terms of audience values. In this way, he is reflecting the semiotic work of Seiter and Fiske (see elsewhere), but his work claims that meaning is buried in the structural aspects of television content, not simply its images.

# Situation and Domestic Comedies: Problems, Families, and Fathers

Lucy's daughter, Kim, arrives home to find her mother preparing for a date. She is thrilled that her mother is going out, and her pleasure is heightened by her mother's enthusiasm. Lucy has met a suave, handsome, polite man—everything a middle-aged television widow could wish for. In the next scene Kim meets the date at the door. Played by Robert Cummings, he is indeed everything her mother has indicated. The two of them make polite conversation until Lucy comes downstairs, reversing the classic pattern of parent waiting for daughter's dramatic appearance. Lucy is glowing in a new dress, her hair strikingly down. As the couple leaves, the daughter calls them back and explains to Bob that her mother is to be dealt with carefully and returned home at a reasonable hour, furthering the reversal of roles. Big laugh on the sound track. Kim waits up for her mother, who promises to tell all in the morning.

The following morning—scene shifted to the kitchen—Kim is having breakfast alone before Lucy's entrance. The milkman, a neighborhood gossip, arrives with the daily delivery. The daughter asks if he delivers Bob's milk. Of course, replies the milkman, and he begins to supply frightening details concerning the young women who are in and out of the apartment at all hours. Kim is increasingly alarmed; the milkman is increasingly comic. He envies the bachelor's freedom, his lack of responsibility, and his consequent harem. With each detail he sighs with desire as Kim cringes in fright. As Lucy comes in for breakfast, Kim hurries out of the house. She rushes to her mother's office and

there solicits the aid of Uncle Harry in a plot to protect her mother from the menacing Bob. They plan a dinner party that will demonstrate Lucy's "true" nature and consequently frighten away the deceiving bachelor.

The wolf is met at the door by Uncle Harry, who casually reveals Lucy's wedding gown, hung prominently in the coat closet. It is kept there, he explains, in perpetual readiness. While Lucy is out of the room, Bob is told that she is actually older than he had been led to believe and is quite hard of hearing. He will have to speak loudly to her. Kim, meanwhile, has prepared a plate of special canapés for Bob, spiked with great quantities of hot sauce and pepper.

The following scene is the classic: yelling, mugging, strangling, confusion, and the gulping of huge glasses of water, all to the accompaniment of riotous laughter supplied by the sound track. Following a commercial break, we return to the scene. There, in summary form, we learn that the problem has been remedied. All characters are present and apologetic, for Lucy has explained that Bob is an agent for a modeling firm and does indeed use his apartment for interviews. She had known this all along. Kim and Uncle Harry are somewhat chagrined, but all in all it was a funny show and no one was ever really worried. The fade-out comes to a cast enjoying one another's company and laughing at its own misunderstandings, laughing at itself.

This is television's own form of comedy. Its roots go deep, of course, to farce, slapstick, to the confused comedies of the eighteenth-century stage, to the raucous silent films, even to Punch and Judy. But it is a standard format for television. No season is without a supply of new versions, but no season removes all of its old faithful, star-supported series, either. So stable—and so staple—is situation comedy that it has given rise to the parallel form, the domestic comedy. The only other comic forms on television are the monologue, a form not essentially visual, and the skit, usually a parody in situation comedy form.

The fact that Lucille Ball has starred in some type of situation comedy for over twenty years, however, does not mean simply that the form is a profitable time filler. More than any other television personality, she has found herself in situations like that described above. How many times has the audience watched in delight as she leaves the boss's theater tickets in a suit destined for the cleaners, calls the police to search for the kidnapped chimpanzee which turns up asleep in the neighbor's house? How many times have we marveled at the responses, the wide-eyed mugging, the bawling tears, the gleam of conspiracy? And there is something here that goes deeper than a superficial level of appeal.

This form allows Lucy to excel and in it we find many of the elements essential to any understanding of television as popular art. It is a paradigm for what occurs in more complex program types, and its perennial popularity is probably due to the relatively simple outline it follows. There is something here that allows us to do more than enjoy and laugh. Something makes us "love" Lucy.

In the delineation of the elements of the formula present here we can discern a meaning that goes beyond the element of "story." As we have seen in Chapter 1, the formula becomes the particular way of ordering and defining the world. Much of that ordering in situation comedy and in other television forms will have a strong sense of the "unreal." I suggest, however, that in situation comedy and in all of television there is the creation of a "special" sense of reality. The total effect of specific formulas is this reality. Each has its own meaning, its own structure, its own system of values. Indeed, as we

will see later, to break with this reality is to create a new formula, and in some cases a new form of television art. We begin with situation comedy precisely because its rigid structure is so apparent and because we find elements there that will carry through to other television formulas. A shift in emphasis, of focus, a different tone, a different sort of content, and we may find many of these same elements in mysteries, Westerns, doctor and lawyer shows, and many others.

Like all television forms, situation comedy creates its own special physical world. In part the worlds are defined by what is economical and what is feasible depending on varying advertisers and budgets. The southern California locale, for instance, predominates because that is the home of the film industry. But because content must be molded to this world, the physical circumstances take on a primary importance in defining the special nature of the formulas. As we will see, any change in setting—a movement, a change in decor, in design—reflects a change in attitude and in the meaning of the formula. These physical limitations, though they appear to limit the possibilities, delineate a great deal of the formulaic meaning that we are searching for.

The situation comedy depends on the one-room set. In the Lucy show recounted above, there are three of these sets: the living room, the kitchen, and the office in which Lucy and Uncle Harry work. For the eye of the viewer there is nothing of substance "between" these sets—that is, there is no concrete, physical world of things. Movement is always accomplished by means of a fade-out–fade-in sequence, and to move from house to office the viewer is never allowed to see the street, to "enter" a car or a subway. We see no houses, no yards, no trees. The formula is, in this sense, internal. We become accustomed to the shift in scenes that occurs during the commercial break.

Stylistically, the rooms that we see in situation comedy are stale with repetition. Always middle to upper-middle class in tone, they are carefully crowded with stuffed couches and comfortable chairs, coffee tables on which there are small "objects," and walls on which hang conventional paintings. Somewhere in the room is a passageway to another part of the house, a stairway or a door to bedroom or kitchen. Because the most important rooms are the living rooms and the kitchens, the sets frequently depend on the "modern" suburban arrangement of these rooms, and our eye is allowed to flow through a dining "area" connecting the two important rooms in one space. Bedrooms and baths are hidden in the recesses, though in the more "sophisticated" series such as the Dick Van Dyke show, we may be admitted to them. In "The New Dick Van Dyke Show" we may even see the star and his wife occupying a double bed, in contrast to the "old" show in which the couple discreetly slept in twins.

Such homes reflect prosperity but not elegance. The standard of living is based on comfort; the rule of existence is neatness. During the meal scenes there is always plenty to eat, and a teen-ager frequently opens a refrigerator to pour another glass of milk. There is shabbiness or disarray only when called for by the script, and in such circumstances care is taken to indicate that it is an arranged form of clutter; the audience is immediately cued by the laugh track and the opening shots that this episode depends on a rearranged set of physical expectations.

The severity of this middle-class rule is indicated for us by the upturned world of "The Beverly Hillbillies." There in the midst of the millionaire's luxury they reflect the values of rural America—or perhaps it is more accurate to say that they reflect the values of rural America as conceived by middle-class Americans. At any rate, the mixture is decidedly more middle class as they insist on wearing their own, but very neat and clean, overalls. Their food is exotic, true, but the recipes are from the mountains and stewed possum is the staple dish. Much of the show's success depends on the continuing

praise of middle-class virtues and the rejection of luxury as a way of life.

When one thinks of the living rooms in which the shows were viewed, a mighty contrast comes to mind. Where, on the television programs, are the scattered magazines and newspapers; where are the stacks of toys left by rumbling children? Does anyone ever run out of milk? Such scenes and events do not appear for good reason. We are not concerned with characters and their homes as representatives of what "we" are like, of what our homes are like. We are concerned with what happens to a set of characters, and only incidentally will that character's physical surroundings and his attitudes toward them reflect our own. Indeed, the television version of the American living-dining-kitchen complex reflects a sort of idealized version which many of the viewers would choose over their own if given the opportunity, a factor that takes on greater importance as we now discover what it is that happens in these rooms.

What, in "real" life, is a situation? More aptly, what in "real" life is not? It is a strange word with which to define a formula, to define a type of comedy. Clearly, it is not meant to be universally applicable or we could find ourselves with situation tragedies or situation mysteries. In situation comedy the situation is simply the broad outline of events, the special funny "thing" that is happening this week to a special set of characters. The characters will appear at the same time the following week in another funny situation which will be entirely nondependent on what happens tonight. In the Lucy show episode the situation might be stated as follows: a reversal of the parent (mother) protects child (daughter) situation. In such terms this is a totally undeveloped situation, but clearly it has humorous possibilities.

In one sense the elaborate development of situation as it occurs in the Lucy show is rather roundabout; some minutes and three scenes are required to establish the situation fully. These scenes are required to define this episode's comic difficulty. In another manner, however, producers take a more direct route with the "built-in" situation. What happens when a man discovers that his beautiful young wife is a witch with incredible supernatural powers? Anything happens, and with great regularity. As the idea begins to wear a bit thin, there is always the possibility of introducing the mother-in-law, delightfully increasing the humor of the "my mother-in-law is a witch" idea. Similarly, it is possible for the young couple to have a child who is also a witch and who uses her "powers" in a typically childish fashion. If such a situation seems too extreme, one can always populate Beverly Hills with a family of mountain folk or marry a liberated Jew to a liberated Irish Catholic. Shipwreck a couple of millionaires, an actress, a professor, and a young girl with their pleasure boat crew, an inane captain and his zany crewman, and leave them on an island for a few years.

In such form, however, these descriptions are only bald outlines. In order for the situation to develop into something resembling a story, two other elements common to the formula must be added: complication and confusion. The complicating element in the Lucy episode is Kim's discovery of the suitor's "true" nature. The show cannot remain the same from this point on. Given the situation, the daughter must take it on herself to protect her mother, and to do this she must enlist the aid of the uncle. His concern, adult wisdom, maleness, and age are crucial. Basically, the complication of any situation is any element that begins the events of the particular show. It comes early, as soon as possible after the situation has been established. In an episode of "Bewitched," for example, where the situation is built in, Samantha and her daughter, Tabitha, shop for a doll. When the mother goes to pay for the item, the salesman chats with the small witch, remarking that he would like to be a child

again. The laugh track begins to chuckle in anticipation and is rewarded when the little girl wiggles her nose manually and the salesman gapes at himself in the body of a nine-year-old-boy. In the action that follows we are taken through all the contortions of convincing Tabitha that the man really wishes to be a grown-up again so that she can remove the spell.

Complications in situation comedies may take many forms, but most generally they are involved with some sort of human error or mistake. The source of the complication on the Lucy show has to do with the daughter's well-intended attempts at protection, but it rises basically out of the misinformation of the milkman. He is the low-comedy character, sighing and dreaming of a fuller life as he offers detail after detail which seem to indict Lucy's date. With each tidbit the daughter gasps and the milkman leers. It is an eloquent scene and the audience can thoroughly enjoy both performances, for the audience knows that this scene is the one that will precipitate the action that follows. Similarly, we may be treated to errors of a more physical nature. When Lucy leaves a winning lottery ticket in her boss's trousers, it is to the great delight of the audience that she must follow them through the entire cleaning process, emerging at last stiffened with starch.

It is such action that I refer to as confusion, the heart of what is comic about situation comedy. Situation comedy, like most television formulas, does not conform to the artistic standards of "high" art in the development of action, character, event, and conclusion. Events, the things that "happen" in sitcom, are composed solely of confusion, and the more thorough the confusion, the more the audience is let in on a joke that will backfire on the characters, the more comic the episode. Individual shows are frequently structured on various layers of confusion that can be generated out of a single complication. Like parentheses within parentheses, the characters slip into deeper and deeper confusion. Expression and reaction follow complication, gesture follows reaction, slapstick follows gesture. The broader the element, the louder the laughter.

After Bob has gulped several glasses of water in his attempt to drench the fiery canapés, he runs for the door and escapes. Lucy, who still does not understand what has been created by her guardians, eats one of the spiked appetizers. Before her daughter and Uncle Harry can stop her—their attempts are elaborately comic gestures—she swallows it whole and begins to steam, reaches for a pitcher of water and drinks it down as the fade-out begins. This is what we have waited to see, this moment of ultimate confusion in which the star proves her ability to out-mug the other members of her family. There is no development, the "plot" is not getting anywhere. There are simply characters involved with one another in confusing sequences. The only movement is toward the alleviation of the complication and the reduction of confusion.

At the center of the situation, complication, and confusion stand the characters of the situation comedy. They are cause and effect, creator and butt of joke, the audience's key to what the formula means. As we have seen, that formula allows for little real development, no exploration of idea or of conflict; the stars merely do what they have always done and will continue to do so well. The characteristics of these favorites, the things that identify them, cut across program types and create not individual actors, but situation comedy stars, a television unit. We expect these characters to behave in certain ways, and if we have our favorites—Lucy, Gilligan, Granny—they will more than likely do the same things, react in the same ways, within their stylistically individual manners.

Physically the stars are easy to identify. With the rural exceptions they are young American suburbanites. Lucy's TV age is around forty or forty-five. In her earlier shows she could not have been cast as over thirty. Only the older Clampetts, of "The Beverly Hillbillies," exceed this top limit, and their actions belie their age as the "eternally youthful" Granny outdoes her grand-children in physical prowess and mental exasperation. As becomes such youth, the characters are beautiful and healthy. They match the neatness of their living rooms, and if the opening shots of a show depict a character as ill or frazzled, we know that it is called for in the script, that the situation depends on it.

All the characters are prosperous enough to afford their suburban "ranch-style" homes. The husbands are employed as advertising account executives, young lawyers, or doctors. Dick Van Dyke in his earlier show portrayed a comedy writer for a television variety show, and Jeannie's husband is a career officer in the Air Force. As with sickness, extreme fatigue is almost always a function of the script. These people simply do not work themselves out of the sitcom "look."

Emotionally, the characters correspond to this same standard. They are never troubled in profound ways. Sorrow cannot touch their lives. Stress, as the result of confusion, is always funny.

Surrounding these central characters are two sets of supporting characters. They offer a more natural spread of types. In some cases they are older or younger than the central characters—Uncle Harry and Kim in "The Lucy Show," for example. In other cases they are not as carefully "beautiful": Miss Jane, the secretary, in "The Beverly Hillbillies" is typical of this class. Children of various ages, occasional cousins, aunts, and uncles appear as needed.

One group of supporting characters is almost incidental. These people most nearly represent the audience. They appear in shops, banks, or offices. They are run over by fleeing characters, amazed and bewildered by unnatural events and unusual circumstances. Though they "populate" the comedy world, they almost never realize what the "situation" is, and they are often victims of the central characters' foibles.

More important is the set of regular characters who serve as foils for the antics of the stars. Ricky Ricardo and Fred and Ethel Mertz, of the "I Love Lucy" series, fall into this category. So do Ann Marie's father and her boyfriend Don in "That Girl." Banker Drysdale and Miss Jane, of

"The Beverly Hillbillies," are classic patterns for the type.

Given such solid established worlds, it would seem strange that the characters should find themselves in difficulty. But difficulty is a mild word for the confusion that reigns in this formula. Again and again we run into horrible complications, plots involving policemen and postmen, mistaken identities and misplaced objects. Our middle-class characters come into possession of clues threatening gangsters, or formulas for secret weapons. Though the gangsters turn out to be funnier than guys and dolls and secret weapons fizzle in actual tests, it seems for the moment that we are beset on all sides by maddening complexities and problems. Ultimately, this is because of the most prominent aspect of the central character's makeup, a lack of any sense of probability. They are, in some way, out of touch with our day-to-day sense of how things happen, with the set of laws that allows us to predict the outcome of our actions. Again, Lucy is the prime example. She has no such sense of probability—not because she is stupid, for her schemes demonstrate exactly the opposite, but because she is innocent. Gilligan and Ann Marie are similar examples. They are without malice, and if their actions precipitate a chain of events that weighs heavily on other characters, it is not because they are cruel, for just as often they suffer the consequences themselves. Indeed, as often as not they do not "do" anything, but act "naturally" and are consequently done to. What they lack, or what they refuse to recognize, is a knowledge of the order of the world. If one did not suspect that the word had been invented precisely for the advertising of a new situation comedy, they would have to be called "wacky."

The supporting characters live somewhere between the improbable world of the central characters and the world as most of the audience experiences it. Uncle Harry knows that his suit is very wet after Lucy tips the water cooler over him, but it is unlikely that he will break her jaw in response. It is probable that the humor of the formula would be apparent simply in the audience's comparison of the events of the show with the events of its own world. There is no doubt, however, that the placement of a set of characters in the show, who will react similarly to the audience, is an advantage.

Such characters are all the more important in the show that depends on the built-in situation. If the fractured sense of probability is a workable component, if the audience accepts a Lucy innocent of the consequences of her own actions, then there is no need for central characters to conform to the laws of probability and reality in any way. It is only a short step, then, to a world in which the suburbs are inhabited by witches and genies, and a shorter step still to rich hillbillies in a Beverly Hills mansion, complete with mountain folk values and barnyard menagerie. An uncharted island in the South Pacific, a small rural community complete with pet pigs within commuting distance of New York? No problem at all. In fact, the problems are eased, the plot is simplified. All that is necessary now is a misdirected nose wiggle and the boss is turned into a monkey.

The supporting character is caught directly in the middle. Darren knows that his wife, his daughter, and his mother-in-law are witches. He is surrounded by "situation." There is no way for him to avoid involvement and the continued jarring of his sense of the real. Finally, even he accepts the new order of reality as we see him pleading that Samantha not give up her powers in order to preserve their marriage. He married her for what she is, he says, and that means witchness along with everything else.

These supporting characters serve a crucial function in that they stand, dramatically, closer to the value structure of the audience than to that of the central characters. Uncle Harry is a tightwad. He will not give Lucy a raise, though he should know by now that every refusal to do so will result in a scheme on her part and that he will most likely suffer in the outcome. His straightforward attitude precipitates an often incoherent sequence of events. Similarly, Banker

Drysdale of "The Beverly Hillbillies" stands in awe of both the Clampetts' money and their value structure. Because he does not share their simplistic view of the world, however, he cannot share their wealth, despite his attempts to do so. But, then, very few people in the audience are hillbillies, much less millionaires, and cannot see the relationship between their world and the "situation" that entertains them.

For the supporting characters and for the audience to whom they directly relate, the world of such situations is an amusing and frustrating one. It is an embarrassing sort of frustration because the audience always knows more than the characters involved and watches time after time as an innocent or not-so-innocent character walks into the trap of his or her own actions. If the situation comedy consisted solely of the antics of the characters, if we were repeatedly forced to involve ourselves merely in laughing at the pie-in-the-face aspects of the formula, it would remain at the level of embarrassment. But there is a recurring structure that outlines every episode of situation comedy, and that outline is ultimately the defining factor of the formula.

Lucy takes a fall and lodges her hand in a coffeepot just prior to serving at an exclusive social function. Gilligan swallows a radio that suddenly receives signals from a spacecraft. Jeannie, the genie, sends her husband to the base without his pants. How should a character behave under such circumstances? In many cases the stars of situation comedy avoid the most natural conclusion to such a sequence of events. Lucy, for example, never tells her hostess that a coffeepot is stuck on her wrist; Jeannie's husband never admits to having married a genie. For if natural solutions were sought, the stories could never exist. Finding contorted paths out of such inane thickets is precisely the business of situation comedy.

The action involved will fall into four basic parts: the establishment of the "situation," the complication, the confusion that ensues, and the alleviation of the complication. The essential factor is the remedying of the confusion. It is rather like a mathematical process, the removing of parentheses within parentheses. In some cases it is accomplished merely by the explanation scene. In the Lucy episode that has served as our primary example, the entire show was given over to the creation of confusion in a single central scene which gave full play to the talents of the central characters. The clarification of that confusion was accomplished in a simple verbal explanation following the final commercial. In the episode of "Bewitched," however, in which the salesman was changed into a small boy, there was much more to do. In the attempt to clarify the physical elements of the confusion, more confusion followed. The removal of the spell was not an easy task, and time was spent demonstrating that the man's life would be seriously impaired by his nine-year-old body. In addition, the man learned the foolishness of wishing for a world of eternal childhood. But in both cases, the structure finally brings us full circle to a state of "normalcy."

Such "normalcy" is obviously "unreal." What does it mean to return to the normal state in which the witches are behaving like the good humans who surround them? Each of these shows is built on a complication that could never arise in "real" life. What, then, accounts for the success of such a formula? Why does it sell so well? What sense of need does this pattern tap so that it draws audience after audience, year after year? Clearly, though there is a sense of entertainment in the fantastic nature of some of the situations, and in the antics of the comic stars whom we enjoy watching, there is more than that, too. I would suggest that the more fundamental appeal of the situation comedy is found precisely in the fact that everything always "comes out all right."

What we see in the situation comedy is the establishment of a problem and an absolutely thorough solution to that problem. As suggested earlier, the audience always knows that the solution will be found. It is impossible that Lucy will be hurt by a scheming Bob, out to take advantage of her middle-aged dreams. It is impossible that the toy salesman will remain forever bewitched, an adult trapped unwillingly in a young boy's body. Rather, we know that all the parties involved will not only solve their problems but laugh at them, and laugh together, at each other. There is a warmth that emerges from the corrected mistakes, a sort of ultimate human companionship.

Such a feeling arises from the basic formula of human failure and human response. No one intends to cause pain in the shows, no one intends evil. The problems exist solely at the level of misunderstanding. Drysdale may desire the Clampetts' money, but he is not willing to steal and kill for it. Uncle Harry may not be free with salary raises, but he is quick to defend Lucy from emotional harm. So what if it is a one-sided world populated by characters totally innocent of our reality, or even if the characters are not of our order of reality at all? The possibility of the fantastic solution, of the magical paths out of our troubles, is a recurring human dream. And it is, as we observed in Chapter 1, one of the basic characteristics of popular art. The audience is reassured in its beliefs; it is not challenged by choice, by ambiguity, or by speculation about what might happen under other "realistic" circumstances. The character is not forced to examine his or her values, nor is the audience. In the situation comedy, there is no particular set of beliefs to be dealt with. There is only the barest, most basic outline, the paradigm. Human beings create problems for themselves; human beings resolve those problems, even in nonhuman situations. It is the upturned line of comedy in its barest form, and the result is a sigh of relief along with the laughter.

One need only recall the closing scenes of the old "Perry Mason" series to see that this outline is involved in a direct relationship with the rest of television. There, following the tortuous solutions to murders, kidnappings, extortions, and intimidations, following the disintegration of criminals on the witness stand, we could always find Perry and Paul and Della and their clients, smiling over cigarettes and coffee, laugh-ing at another case solved. In formulas other than situation comedy, however, the problems that our television stars must solve become more brutal. They also become more social and political in nature. Consequently, the values that are embodied in these formulas take on the same sort of specified, identifiable nature.

The closest step, however, is the most gentle. We move down the suburban streets and enter other homes where the humor is not quite so riotous and where the problems are a bit closer to those that most of us know. Those problems occur in the formula for domestic comedy.

The ritualistic, paradigmatic world of situation comedy is clearly antecedent to that of domestic comedy. Its dependence on people, on some sort of family setting, and on human error as the basis of plot structure offer many elements to its more "homey" counterpart. These similarities, however, rarely extend beyond the structural level, and there is a great difference in the mass of detail that defines the two forms. In a sense, the world of the situation comedy is much more tightly controlled than that of the domestic comedy because the insistence on the problem-solution outline forces each episode into a lockstep of regularity. Similarly, with character and event determined by formula, interaction among characters is minimized, and the result is a world that will not allow for changes or for development. There is simply no room for growth.

The domestic comedy, though restricted in other ways, is more expansive. There is less slapstick; less hysterical laughter. There is more warmth and a deeper sense of humanity. The cast built on the family as group is capable of reducing dependence on a single star, a single style. A richer variety of event, a consequent deepening of character, and a sense of seriousness enable the formula to build on the previous comic outline in significant ways.

The establishing shots in the various series introduces us immediately to the more physical aspects of these differences. In "The Lucy Show" and in "Bewitched" cast names and credits are run while cartoonized versions of the central characters mimic their human counterparts. The fantastic world of the situation comedy is defined by the fact that these characters are structurally "unreal," just as the cartoons are unreal. In "The Beverly Hillbillies" and "Gilligan's Island" opening songs recount in narrative form the events that lead up to the built-in situation on which each show is based.

The domestic comedy offers, by contrast, not an introduction to situation, but an introduction to setting. The camera follows Jim Anderson's car down a quiet street where houses are surrounded by large trees and picket fences. We turn with him into a driveway, and as he steps out of the car, we are introduced to the world of "Father Knows Best." A photograph of a large frame house fades into reality, and we are welcomed to the world of "My Three Sons." The camera picks up a cowboy hat rising over a hill in yet another tree-lined street, and we watch as Jimmy Stewart emerges, riding a bicycle into the front yard of a large old Victorian house, typical for the role of college professor he plays. We are "at home" in "The Jimmy Stewart Show."

What the producers have taken pains to establish is a strong sense of "place." The houses we see are residential rather than suburban, found in small towns or older, more established portions of cities. Here the streets wind naturally, the sidewalks are neatly trimmed. Even the variations bear out the pattern. The family of "Family Affair" lives in a modern apartment building in New York. Care is taken, however, in the opening shots to show us the outside of the building and to locate it specifically adjacent to a lovely city park. In "The Mary Tyler Moore Show" we are treated to shots of an interstate highway, of downtown Minneapolis' familiar landmarks, and of a Victorian mansion remodeled to house several apartments.

Such settings, of course, are archetypically American. The use of older houses in small town settings is a conscious attempt to build on a set of responses to that pattern. The city park as surrogate lawn recalls an older time when parks were considered the play yards of the municipal family, visited as safely as one would visit a neighbor's garden. Even for those of us who do not experience such scenes daily they are a part of our consciousness. They inform us of older meanings, link us with a more familiar reality than that provided by the situation comedy. The reality, it turns out, may not be the one in which we live, but it is one that defines much of what we do.

Internally, the houses continue to reflect the rooted sense of reality begun outdoors. The sitcom interior was space that existed primarily for the purpose of the formula: it offered a setting in which things could happen. Such space needs no actual definition and could be a stage setting as well as the setting for a television program. The interior sets of the domestic comedy, however, are defined by the uses of the typical American family. Rooms are defined by function and by personality, used for certain purposes, commanded by certain individuals.

The kitchen, for example, is a special place. It is the domain of the mother, whose sex role is more stereotyped than that of the lead comedienne of the situation comedy. Whenever personal problems are taken to the kitchen, they are soon to be defined or solved in the softer, more "feminine" manner. Here, Mother counsels the children and nurses minor wounds. And when Father cannot sleep, we find him in the kitchen pouring a glass of milk. Mother will soon appear to prepare a midnight snack or to warm the milk.

The living room is most appropriately the room of the father, though in some cases there is also a den or an office that serves him. In the living room other members of the family are welcome, but Father relaxes here. The furnishings are more worn than those of the sitcom living room. Father can sit here in a favorite chair, waiting until an appropriate hour for a daughter to return from her date. Past that hour he must go to the kitchen to worry.

Bedrooms are highly personal in nature and are defined by the individuals who occupy them. They are decorated in keeping with children's ages and occupations. The bedroom of the parents is more private, the area of important discussion. But privacy is a function of all bedrooms, and brothers and sisters do not violate the space of their siblings. Any number of plots may be generated from the theme of violated space, and ultimately any room in the house can be explored and exploited for its possibilities in creating plot.

Such possibilities are realized because the houses and rooms of domestic comedy, by contrast with those of situation comedy, are used. There is a sense of movement and activity there because by definition domestic comedy is dependent on people. Movement can begin as children rumble down the stairs for breakfast or as the father hurries out the door, late for work. It can begin as he enters the kitchen in the afternoon or as the children return from school. As a consequence of such movement, there is always a feeling of use about these sets, a sense of clutter that makes us aware of the ways they are lived in.

The movement enhances our sense of life most strongly by indicating the existence of a world outside the house. It is a world of offices for fathers, schools for children, and shops and clubs for Mother—the perfectly stereotyped pattern. In the situation comedy all such external factors would have to be connected in some way to the current situation or complication. There is no sense of going to work other than for purposes of finding out what will happen to the character. There is no way for the central character in a sitcom to enter a grocery store without precipitating some sort of comic action. The world of the domestic comedy is a world that creates, by contrast, the illusion of being lived in rather than acted in, and consequently

there is a sense of involvement. To some degree it is this involvement that creates a seriousness even in the midst of exceptionally funny events.

These differences in setting, in the more physical aspects of the two formulas, are not meant to suggest that there are no direct relationships among them. Indeed, when we begin to translate out some of the significances of the setting, we see immediately that the two forms are directly related. Once again we find ourselves rooted firmly in the upper-middle class. With no outrageous variations designed to facilitate situations the sense of the average is, if anything, more pronounced. Again the homes are exceptionally comfortable. This is true in the emotional as well as in the physical sense, for there is always the feeling that the homes are long since paid for. There is no sense of brief tenure, of the transient family. The children are well-dressed and well-fed. If they do ask for something that the father cannot "afford," they are taught to work for it in the best middle-class manner.

The shift in meaning comes when we realize the importance of the greater emphasis on persons than on situations. We simply see more people. We see more of their homes and we see their toys, clothes, food, and other evidences of life. It is a matter of degree, of tone. The concern exhibited for Lucy by Kim and Uncle Harry is basically a family concern. Such concern could easily be the focus of a domestic comedy episode, though there is less likelihood of the extreme measures taken by Lucy's protectors. The prosperity and the personal emphasis indicate that this world is one of great stability. Such stability is grounded in part in possession and ownership.

In a much more important sense, however, the stability grows out of the family unit itself. Here are people who support each other, who share each other's problems and joys. The real basis for domestic comedy is a sense of deep personal love among the members of the family. Essential to such families is a sense of groupness, of interdependence. The interdependence is impossible without a strong sense of role definition. Members of families in domestic comedies know who they are. When there does occur some doubt, when a son challenges his father's wisdom or a daughter is unsure of her responses to a young man, we have the components for a plot conflict. The resolutions to such conflicts leave us with a stronger sense of the family as a unit in which the roles are redefined and re-established.

The father stands at the center of the family. In the most traditional sense he provides leadership and wisdom, and it is not so important that Father knows *best* as it is that Father *knows*. Much of his wisdom and authority rise from the fact that he has a much stronger definition of his function outside the home. In specific episodes the action centers on the role he plays in the home, but we are not allowed to forget that he is the provider and that he faces situations that require serious judgment throughout the day. Jim Anderson is, significantly, an insurance salesman. Other fathers may be engineers or government consultants. They must care for families other than their own, and in their professional capacity their ability to care and to decide is continually defined and tested.

Such men become centers of authority in their families because they are practiced in decision-making, in exercising their "power." Within the family, however, we consider them doubly wise because they never allow such authority to exceed the bounds of wisdom. They are rarely harsh in their judgments. They present familial justice tempered with much mercy. Essentially their role is that of advisor, and if it is at all possible, they much prefer allowing a member of the family to become aware of his or her own errors without resorting to explicit measures.

The role of the mother is in keeping with the cultural stereotype. She reassures us by acting as the provider of physical comforts within the home. Though she is not the primary judge of actions within the family, she is often the source of behind-the-scenes wisdom. She is the one who can point out to Father the folly of his initial decision. Her wisdom is increased by her choice to allow the father the appearance of superiority in his role, even though she has directed the decision.

The roles of children are equally well defined and depend heavily on standard, popular stereotypes for their content. Often they appear to have arrived fully defined from movies of the forties or fifties, even when they are updated in terms of dress or actions. Physically they must be in the process of "growing up." This is especially true for boys, though both sexes go through the pangs of sexual initiation and encounter, within the discreet bounds of what is permissible on TV, of course. The problems they face in all areas must eventually be turned over to the parents, who, in their wisdom, will solve them in the most gentle manner.

Small children occupy special places in these homes. They appear as dolls or toys, and they are always handled with care. Because they see the world from a different perspective, they often add to the action that takes place. Their view of the adolescent and adult worlds frequently reminds adolescents and adults of their shortcomings, and "out of the mouths of babes" is a frequent plot device. Ultimately their presence is almost always a tempering agent, and it is not uncommon for an episode to end with the delightful and perceptive remarks of a seven-year-old.

As in the situation comedy there are a variety of characters who play only incidental roles. One group of supporting characters, however, is much more important in domestic comedy than in situation comedy. These characters are not actual members of the family, but in many cases, especially when the family is not biologically complete, they fulfill surrogate family roles. Early domestic comedy offered its audiences exceptionally simple family groups. "The Life of Riley," "Ozzie and Harriet," and "Leave It to Beaver" bring us varying arrangements of siblings. Then followed a series of shows in which families seem to have suffered repeated patterns of loss. One of the parents was missing. In some later cases, these partial families find other partial families, and the result is a huge, multiple group such as "The Brady Bunch."

In the intervening period, however, it was necessary to replace the missing parent with some sort of substitute. In "Family Affair," Mr. French, the butler-maid-chef-jack-of-all-trades, fills the role of mother, offering a gentler, more indirect sort of influence than that offered by Uncle Bill, the authority figure for the show. The same role is filled by Mrs. Livingstone in "The Courtship of Eddie's Father," and here care is taken that she is both older and Oriental in order to preclude sexual interest on the part of the father. In a somewhat different vein, in "The Ghost and Mrs. Muir," the ghost of a long-dead sea captain acts as the authority figure for a fatherless family.

Such factors lead us to define the television "family" in rather nontraditional terms. Any group that is united by ties of love, of warmth, and of mutual concern can be termed a family. In almost every case the two major roles of the authoritative father and the counseling mother must be filled in some way. The essential factor is a set of shared values which define the "groupness" of the family. The growth of these ideas is crucial in developing a sense of probability for the show.

These extensions of the typical family make it possible for the concept of family to be developed even in units or groups in which there are no blood ties. One speaks, for example, of the "family" of "The Mary Tyler Moore Show." Mary, the star of the show, is clearly the central character. She portrays a single girl pursuing a career as a television associate producer. The supporting cast, however, rather than comprising a group of foils who serve only to highlight Mary's talents, performs familial functions. Rhoda, another single-working girl, lives in the same group of apartments in the remodeled house. She is much like a sister and is often found in Mary's apartment. She is also a parody of the Jewish mother, remembering her own mother's advice and making fun of it. Mary's boss, Lou Grant, is

also a parody, of the authoritarian father. His rantings get him into more trouble than the conventional father, but he knows, finally, what he is talking about. Murray, Mary's colleague in the newsroom, is even-tempered and "realistic" in the manner of many television mothers. Ted Baxter, self-centered and comical anchor man for the evening news, suffers exactly the same conflicts and problems of an adolescent son. Much of what Mary does on the show resembles the sort of advisory problem-solving performed by fathers and mothers on the other shows. The group is tightly knit and the comic hostility that the members exhibit toward each other is based on an intergroup affection much like that of a traditional family. A number of episodes have explicitly explored these relationships, and a favorite theme deals with the fact that the most "disliked" member of the family, Ted, is really the most vulnerable and most in need of group protection. Clearly, the concept of family can extend to other members of the household who are not blood relations, to co-workers, or even to whole towns in which the cast is closely united by deep personal concern.

The complex family structures of domestic comedy generate innumerable problems on which to contrive plots. The problems build on the human failure syndrome we noted in the situation comedy, and the problem-solving paradigm carries directly into the other formulas. In the earlier form, however, the failures were centered in physical problems: mistaken identities, misplaced objects, physical mishaps, and so on. Though such problems also arise in domestic comedy, they establish far fewer of the plot structures than in sitcom. Here the problems are more likely to be mental and emotional. Failure takes place in the area of complex human interaction, though the plots themselves could seldom be called complex. Because each member of the family plays a well-defined, highly stereotyped role, it is possible for any member of the family to become the center of an individual episode. The extended family thus serves the function of allowing action and emphasis to be spread among larger numbers of individuals. This, too, contrasts with situation comedy in which our attention is continually drawn back to the star.

Paralleling this change in the nature of the problems is a change in the manner of resolving problems. While it is true that the outcome is never in doubt, that the problem will be resolved in a manner that will release the built-up tension, it is also true that there is more room for ambiguity and complexity, admittedly of a minimal sort. Characters do seem to change because of what happens to them in the problem-solving process. Usually they "learn" something about human nature.

This learning process is directed toward three major groups. If the problem has something to do with the terrors and trials of "growing up," it is likely that the lesson will be directed toward one of the children. If the problem is directed toward a broader concept and the lesson has to do with human nature in general, the learner will probably be an adult. Frequently, the adult, in the course of guiding the child through a problem, will learn a general truth and both functions will be served in the same involvement. More importantly, however, is the way in which the audience learns. This learning process is enhanced by many of the physical details we have noted. It is largely for this reason that we have been treated to outside views of houses and to living rooms that are cluttered instead of the sterile interiors of sitcom. If the wife of the family burns the dinner or the child seems brokenhearted over the loss of a toy, the world seems somehow closer to our own, and with the lessened distinction between the two worlds the morals of domestic comedy become direct statements to the audience.

One of Mary Tyler Moore's neighbors desperately asks that Mary inform her ten-year-old daughter of the facts of life. When all the contortions are completed, when Mary sits down with the child and begins her speech, the child informs her that she knows all about *that* from biology class. What she really needs to know

about is "love." Mary has learned how to deal with the child, and her advice directs the girl toward her own self-discovery of love. The audience has been reassured that there is still a distinction between sex and love, that old notions still prevail.

In a similar episode of "The Jimmy Stewart Show" we are confronted with the apparently simple problem that Father needs a new briefcase. Everyone in the family decides, without group consultation, to buy one for his birthday. His wife goes to the local luggage shop and selects a sealskin case which, unfortunately, costs over a hundred dollars. She settles for a more utilitarian model. The older son, after much thought and discussion with his wife, buys the expensive model. The close friend of the family buys a handsome attaché case. All of the gifts are presented at the same time and with various expressions of great love and respect. The older son points out that his expense has been small return for what he has received from his father. The friend fumbles for words of affection. The wife acknowledges her continuing love. Finally, though, all of the cases are stored away. The favored gift comes from the very young son who has sewed a book bag from cloth given to him by his mother. Because of the deeply personal concern, his own handicraft, the father chooses to honor this gift, and he explains this to the family.

He also explains it to the audience. His actions and statements to his family during the events of the episode make clear to the audience the values of love and support that we discussed earlier. But "The Jimmy Stewart Show" does not let the comment rest with such indirect presentation. Making explicit what is implied in all the domestic comedies, Stewart addresses the audience directly at the end of each show. It is difficult to tell whether or not he speaks as his character or as Jimmy Stewart. Indeed, the two "people" are woven tightly together. In either case, he speaks to "us," without the fictional frame of the show. Each week he comments on the outcome of the episode and then concludes by telling us that he and his family wish each of us and our family "peace, love, and laughter."

These concepts—peace, love, and laughter—are the central virtues of the world of the domestic comedy. In the situation comedy there is much laughter, there is a form of love, and there is very little peace of the sort indicated here. The domestic comedy is filled with such peace. It grows out of the love, and in the context of these two we discover a gentler form of laughter.

These values are grounded in the belief in the family as a supportive group. Within the family strength abides. The strength grows out of the mutual support that each of the family members is willing to offer and for which he or she receives like support in return. Many episodes are built on the minor ways in which family members hurt one another, sometimes consciously, sometimes not. With each resolution of such a problem, however, the family unit is strengthened. The group is the sheltering unit, particularly when we are made aware of the difficulties of the world surrounding the family.

Such support is grounded on the mutual respect of individuals. Any episode may be built on problems of privacy rights in the home, on problems with bullies and exploiters at school, and on all the problems rising from sibling rivalry, reinforcing the idea that the individual is the unit on which families are built.

The first to recognize these factors and the most able at articulating solutions to most of them is the father, or the authority center of the group. The wisdom of the father, with assists from the mother, is the prime value asserted by the structures of domestic comedy. This is not to suggest a value placed on domination or authoritarianism. Quite the contrary, such wisdom is strongest as an expression of that sense of group warmth and support. The father speaks from age and experience; his concern is to guide his children through problems so that they will learn from their errors but not be destroyed by them. In most cases it is the father who, by his actions or by his direct explanation of what has

happened, points the moral that we take from domestic comedy.

Once again we must remember that such morals and the values they reflect are the morals and values of an older time. The white frame houses with picket fences, the spreading, sheltering trees, and the flower gardens mirror a time when families did not move about the country several times during their lives. They remind us of times when uncles and grandparents lived with their children and grandchildren. They recall the possibility of young men entering their fathers' businesses. In a sense the structures of domestic comedy form a world more like that of the nineteenth or early twentieth centuries than that of present-day America.

What is important here is that we know that the nineteenth or early twentieth centuries were not so thoroughly warm and tender. But those years are far enough removed from our present experience to be cloaked in an ideal obscurity. This television version of the past, when things were simpler and when order was more prevalent than chaos, becomes more and more crucial as we examine other forms of television drama. The use of history to express another set of values becomes a major device in the creation of various forms.

This is not to say that these values—peace, love, and laughter—are outdated, or that they are no longer present in America. On the contrary, they are among the old verities. The problem arises when we compare their expression in the domestic world of television's happy homes with their expression in our own world. Domestic comedy may not be untrue, but it is unfinished. No matter how serious the problem, no matter how critical the conflict faced by the child, the problem will emerge as solved. This factor remains constant from situation to domestic comedy. There remains the magic of the wise father, the counseling mother, the obedient child. The sense of completeness, of the happy ending, is the popularity factor. Yet one is left with the image of fathers and mothers delighting in the antics of "My Three Sons" while they are slightly unsure of the whereabouts of their own children.

The deep cultural appeal of this form is made clear when we realize that the most significant innovations in television rise from it. When the problems encountered by the families become socially or politically significant, this form can be expanded. The frame of the ordered world is shattered. Families find themselves living in the world of the present without magical solutions and, to some extent, without the aid of peaceful and laughing love. Comedy, in the form of "All in the Family" or "Maude" or "M*A*S*H" is changed into the perfect vehicle for biting social commentary. Clearly this has long been the case with traditional comic forms: from Aeschylus to Chaplin artists have recognized this power. For television, however, the sense of satire and commentary was long in coming. When it did begin to present answers that were not totally acceptable at the mass cultural level, a new stage had been reached. In the meantime, other forms and formulas applied the same sort of acceptable answers to larger and more crucial social problems which became, without question, the content of the more action-oriented series.

# Introduction to Bonnie J. Dow's "Hegemony, Feminist Criticism and *The Mary Tyler Moore Show*"

Bonnie Dow brings a different perspective—a feminist viewpoint—to the idea of mass communications studies. Feminist theory, while always a part of critical studies, has only really begun to develop a convincing body of research since the 1970's. Practitioners such as Dow examine questions of gender and how it relates to the distribution of power in mass media. To place her work in a social context, *The Mary Tyler Moore Show* was hailed as ground-breaking television because it depicted a single woman supposedly more interested in a career than a husband and family. But as Dow points out, with ideological messages, what we see is often not exactly what we get.

The concept of Hegemony Theory is an often difficult idea to grasp. This theory, created by Antonio Gramsci in his seminal 1971 work, *Selection From the Prison Notebooks* (lest you think ideas not important, he was in prison for publishing Marxist propaganda during the 1960's) deals less with economics as a determinant for class based structure and more on ideology itself. Hegemonic theory believes that the reproduction of oppressive ideology survives and flourishes with the compliance of its victims. Such ideology shapes the consciousness of those peoples most oppressed. Ideology then becomes a form of distortion in perceived reality so that, as Dow points out, what we consume in terms of media messages reaffirms basic dominant values. For feminists and hegemonic theorists, this dominance must work at a subconscious as well as conscious level. The purpose is to maintain the *status quo*. What Dow suggests is that even in a program as highly liberalized and regarded as this one, hegemonic principles are at work.

# Hegemony, Feminist Criticism and
# *The Mary Tyler Moore Show*

This essay claims that the feminist premise of *The Mary Tyler Moore Show* is contradicted by the patriarchal relationships and role definitions developed within its narrative, hegemonic devices that are bolstered by the conventions of the situation comedy genre. The conclusion explores the ideological tension produced by the show's narrative that allows for differing evaluations of the program's message, and discusses the implications for feminist criticism of television's hegemonic patterns.

Recent scholarly essays call for greater attention to feminist issues in media studies (Dervin, 1987; Treichler & Wartella, 1986). The feminist agenda in communication is a broad one, encompassing a myriad of issues, contexts, methodological approaches, and goals. This situation reflects the fact that feminist analysis of communication is a dynamic and growing concern. This essay contributes to this dialogue through a critical study of *The Mary Tyler Moore Show*, illustrating the hegemonic processes at work in television discourse about women.

Initially, this essay offers a brief review of feminist perspectives on popular culture and discusses the place of this analysis within a feminist critique of television. Moreover, the essay details the basis for a critical approach to television that focuses on its hegemonic effects, particularly in the negotiation of oppositional ideology. The usefulness of these concepts will be illustrated through an analysis of *The Mary Tyler Moore*

*Show* (TMTMS) as an example of television programming that was, in many ways, an early response to social changes brought about by the feminist movement of the late 1960's. *TMTMS* will be used to illustrate conclusions about the working of hegemonic devices that contradict feminist ideology on television. Finally, this analysis will be used as the basis for discussing the further implications of an awareness of hegemony for a feminist critique of television.

## FEMINIST PERSPECTIVES ON POPULAR CULTURE

"Feminist perspective" may be an ambiguous phrase to some. The recent interest in popular culture criticism with a feminist focus has produced a variety of works from differing perspectives. Some critics appear to view popular culture as a sphere that is largely opposed to valorization of the female in any form; much feminist psychoanalytic work on film contains this discouraging message (De Lauretis, 1984; Kuhn, 1982; Mulvey, 1989). Other perspectives argue for a resistant reading through which discourse of the seemingly dominant ideology can be interpreted as empowering for women (Byars, 1987) or through which we can begin to discover a "feminine aesthetics" (Modleski, 1982, p. 105). In addition, Radway (1984) has highlighted the usefulness of reader-response methods in understanding how women read romance novels and through her critique of the politics of

From *Critical Studies in Mass Communication*, 7 (1990), 261–274. Used by permission of the National Communication Association.

mass culture analysis (1986). More recently, a collection of essays edited by Baehr and Dyer (1987) has extended the feminist critique of television to examine women's situations as writers, actors, producers, and audience.

All of these perspectives contribute to the ongoing dialectic about the role of women within popular culture, as producers, products, and spectators. The present analysis is intended to add to the body of work on feminism and popular culture by illustrating the possibilities for contradiction of feminist premises through hegemonic processes. One of the projects of an ongoing feminist critique (Press, 1989) must be to examine how women are devalued in the process of cultural reproduction. The critical perspective chosen here explores the subtle manifestations of hegemony in television by focusing on narrative structure and character interaction.

While literary study is the birthplace of feminist criticism, television and literature cannot be easily transposed. For example, while feminist critics of literature can focus on literature produced by women as a way to explore a feminine poetics or to ameliorate the historical white male bias of literary studies and the literary canon, feminist critics of television always deal with the discourse of the dominant ideology. Despite recent labor gains by women, it is no stretch to acknowledge that the institutions that sponsor and produce popular television are largely controlled by men and are permeated with patriarchal ideology that is revealed in television programming. However, in the years since the resurgence of the feminist movement, the television industry has attempted to respond to the changing social climate. Thus, we now have more women in television production, as well as increased numbers of women in more powerful roles on the screen, in both news and entertainment programming (Baehr & Dyer, 1987). Despite these numerical increases, however, the hegemonic process limits possibilities for substantive change: the effects of that process are the focus of this analysis.

# HEGEMONIC PROCESSES IN TELEVISION

Gitlin's (1982) work on television on hegemony provides a compelling and persuasive account of television's incorporation of social change and oppositional ideology. Drawing on Gramsci, Gitlin (p. 429) offers what he calls "a lexicon for discussing the forms of hegemony in the concrete." Generally, hegemony or hegemonic processes refer to the various means through which those who support the dominant ideology in a culture are able continually to reproduce that ideology in cultural institutions and products while gaining the tacit approval of those whom the ideology oppresses. In Gitlin's view, television furthers hegemony through incorporation of radical ideology, or what Barthes (1973, p. 150) has called "inoculation." In this process, one protects the dominant ideology from radical change by incorporating small amounts of oppositional ideology.

Thus, television adjusts to social change by "absorbing it into forms compatible with the core ideological structure" (Gitlin, 1982, p. 450). So, for instance, the demands made for increased minority and female representation result in higher visibility for these groups on television, although the situations and characters through which they are depicted may implicitly work to "contain" the more radical aspects of the changes such representation implies. Some limited changes in content result, but the general hegemonic values remain intact (Gitlin, 1982). Thus, those who champion the oppositional ideology may be satisfied that their demands are having an impact on television, while those who create the programming actually have made only cosmetic changes in representation of the disputed group.

However, the hegemonic system is not a perfect monolith; it does not produce inescapable ideology. When subversive ideology is incorporated, some of it sticks, albeit in a less stringent form. To retain its dominance, the hegemonic system must change, and these changes produce "leaks" or contradictions (Gitlin, 1982, p. 449). The point of a hegemonic perspective is not that television never changes—it clearly does—but that it is less progressive than we think. The medium adjusts to social change in a manner that simultaneously contradicts or undercuts a progressive premise.

## TMTMS, FEMINISM AND HEGEMONY

The enormous popularity of *TMTMS* in its first run (1971-77) makes the program a particularly appropriate subject for an analysis of how television responds to social change. After a slow start, the show was consistently in the top twenty rated programs for six of the seven years it was broadcast (Brooks & Marsh, 1985). *TMTMS* was popular with critics as well as viewers. Hough (1981, p. 221) described it as "one of the most believable, lucid, and lovable portrayals of the single woman in American society of the seventies" and noted that, "while there are a thousand sitcoms in television history, 'The Mary Tyler Moore Show' will probably still be among the top ten in terms of historical and social significance."

Moreover, the point in social and television history at which the show appeared makes it noteworthy as a feminist text. Arriving as it did on the crest of the developing women's liberation movement, *TMTMS* was informed by and commented on the changing role of women in American society. One of the show's creators, James Brooks, observed that although the show did not explicitly address the issues of the women's movement, "we sought to show someone from Mary Richards' background being in a world where women's rights were being talked about and it was having an impact" (quoted in Bathrick, 1984, pp. 103-104).

Indeed the character of Mary Richards as in independent career woman on *TMTMS* challenged a television tradition that had stereotyped women as "goodwives," "bitches," "victims," and "courtesans" (Meehan, 1983). Although the "single woman" premise had been successful in *That Girl* (1966-1971), its Ann Marie character had been watched over and protected by her father and her fiancé. Her adventures in the big city seemed like little more than a premarital fling, and by the end of the series she was headed for domestic bliss. In contrast, Mary Richards was in her thirties, mature, and ambitious. When the show ended, she was thirty-seven and remained romantically unattached.

*TMTMS* was undoubtedly influenced by the developing women's liberation movement. If the show had appeared even five years earlier, its chances for success would have been lessened (Gitlin, 1983). Both James Brooks's comment and the premise of the show itself demonstrated that *TMTMS* was intended to be a departure from the tradition of sexist portrayals of women on television. Consequently, the show's popularity is surprising, both because of the audience's exposure to decades of traditional depictions of women on television and because of general resistance to many aspects of the feminist movement. Thus, analysis of *TMTMS* reveals ways in which television adapts to social resistance as well as social change.

A number of hegemonic devices work to contradict the progressive feminist premise of *TMTMS*. This section concentrates on three: family roles, intra-gender relationships, and the generic constraints of situation comedy. In the following sections I argue that, despite its workplace setting, *TMTMS* offers a traditional picture of the female within the family through Mary Richards's implicit roles as wife, mother, and daughter. The relationship of Mary Richards to the larger female community reinforces the public/private dichotomy that devalues women's relationships as well as positioning Mary as an idealized token version of the successful, single woman. The conventions of the situation comedy as a genre constrained the development of positive and progressive female characterizations on *TMTMS*. Arguments are supported by examples of specific episodes that exemplify dramatic patterns in the program's history.

# THE *TMTMS* "FAMILY"

The presentation of a family structure is common to many of the most successful comedies in television history, from *I Love Lucy* to *All in the Family* to *The Cosby Show*. Because a sitcom is short in length and typically limited in setting, the situation and the characters tend to change little from episode to episode. Consequently, the characters have strong connections to each other and to the situation.

The "domestic" situation comedy inherently limits role possibilities for women. In the sitcoms preceding *TMTMS*, leading female characters were primarily wives and/or mothers who had no identity beyond the home and little real power within it, at least in comparison to the husbands/fathers. Programs such as *Father Knows Best, The Donna Reed show, The Dick Van Dyke Show,* and *The Brady Bunch* are examples. The patriarchal structure of the traditional, white, middle-class family was reinforced in years of sitcom programming in the 1950's and 1960's.

Although *TMTMS* was not the first comedy to feature a woman in the workplace, the program is often noted as the precursor of a number of successful comedies in the 1970's that used a workplace setting. The regular cast of the show, which was set in a Minneapolis television newsroom (WJM-TV), included Lou Grant, producer of the news; Mary Richards, associate producer and later, producer; Murray Slaughter, news writer; and Ted Baxter, anchor. For the first four years of the show, Mary Richards's neighbor and best friend, Rhoda Morgenstern, and their landlady, Phyllis Lindstrom, were also regulars. Although scenes were occasionally set in Mary's home, the majority of the action took place in the newsroom, the focus of the show. In the last four years of the show, the character of Sue Ann

Nivens, the hostess of the *Happy Homemaker* show at WJM, was added, and the role of Georgette Franklin Baxter, Ted Baxter's girlfriend and later his wife, was expanded.

It can be argued that these characters behaved in many ways as an extended family. Although "all sitcom is 'domestic' or family-oriented if we expand the definition to non-blood-related groups that function as families" (Mintz, 1985, p. 116), programs differ in the extent to which the groups they feature function as *traditional* families. Indeed, it could further be argued that, while programming had previously concentrated on blood or legal relations, *TMTMS* ushered in an era of nontraditionally structured television families that included such programs as *Laverne and Shirley, Kate & Allie,* and *Who's the Boss*. All cases involve a group of people who care about each other, are committed to their relationships, and form bonds because they live and/or work together. Allowing this broader "family" circumscription, then, the concept of "patriarchy" may refer to "any kind of group organization in which males hold dominant power and determine what part females shall and shall not play, and in which capabilities assigned to women are relegated generally to the mystical and aesthetic and excluded from the practical and political realms" (Rich, 1979, p. 78).

In considering *TMTMS* as representing nontraditional family relations, we can analyze Mary Richards in terms of her three major roles: daughter, wife, and mother. While these roles are not always kept distinct, each plays out repeatedly.

## Mary as Daughter

*TMTMS* may be characterized in terms of Lou Grant's paternalism toward Mary Richards and, in turn, her submission to his professional and personal authority. Mary consistently seeks Lou's approval and advice; he guides and protects her. For example, in one episode, Sue Ann Niven's boyfriend makes a pass at Mary. Mary becomes upset and takes her problem to Lou, who with fatherly indignation, offers to "kill him" and then, more seriously, advises Mary to tell Sue Ann. Ultimately, Mary listens to Lou and comforts Sue Ann, and the situation is happily resolved. This illustration echoes the pattern of the classic father-and-child problem-solving plot familiar from *Father Knows Best* or *Leave It to Beaver*: The child has a problem and goes to the father, who tells the child to do "the right thing," which the child intuitively knows she should do anyway. With the advice and pressure of the parent, the child overcomes her reluctance and does what is required; the situation is happily resolved, demonstrating the father's wisdom.

An episode in which Mary asks for a raise also demonstrates the parent/child nature of Mary and Lou's relationship. Lou tells her that they must confront the station manager together, arguing that the station could afford to lose one of them but not both. When they are refused and threaten to quit, the station manager does not object. Mary is thoroughly demoralized by unemployment, but Lou is confident that the station manager will eventually give in. At the end of the episode, she and Lou go back to see the station manager, who offers them a $5000 raise for them to split—double what Mary had expected. Once again, despite Mary's reluctance, Lou's recommendation proves successful.

Lou's patriarchal superiority is underscored by the negative consequences that result when Mary refuses his advice. After being promoted to producer, Mary meets a female swimmer and is convinced she would make a good sportscaster for WJM. Lou ridicules the idea, and Mary accuses him of sexism. However, Lou grants Mary the ultimate authority as producer and Mary hires the woman. In her first broadcast, the new sportscaster reports nothing but swimming news because, we find out, she does not believe in contact sports. Mary is forced to fire her. At the conclusion, Mary tells Lou that she was wrong about the sportscaster and bemoans her failure to strike a blow for women. Lou assures her that she has indeed proven something: "that

a woman has the chance to be just as lousy in a job as a man." Like a good parent, Lou allows Mary to make and learn from her own mistakes, (and it is doubly interesting that this object-lesson involves female "incompetence").

*TMTMS* was replete with similar episodes in which Mary, the daughter figure solicits advice from the older and wiser Lou, the father figure.[1] Under Lou's tutelage, Mary copes with her problems. The daughter role can be viewed as a hegemonic device that works to contain Mary's independence. *TMTMS* tells us that Mary cannot really "make it on her own" either personally or professionally without fatherly guidance. In this fashion, Mary's independence is domesticated.

## Mary as Wife and Mother

At the same time that Mary is Lou's dutiful daughter, she also acts as a nurturing wife/mother to Lou and other characters. It is her general responsibility to maintain interpersonal relations, and she does this through personal advice, support, and mediation of conflict.

Mary is constantly accessible; her friends, who drop by at any time, are received warmly. When Ted Baxter cannot have a child, he comes to Mary, who reconciles him to the idea of adoption. When Ted has sexual problems, his wife Georgette comes to Mary for advice. When Sue Ann feels threatened by her sister, she seeks comfort from Mary. Later in this same episode, Sue Ann becomes so demoralized that she takes to her bed, convinced that she is no longer wanted or needed. Although Sue Ann has consistently treated Mary unkindly, Mary assumes nurturing responsibility.

Mary's role as nurturer is established in the series' first episode, when Lou shows up drunk at Mary's apartment the night after he hires her. His wife is out of town and he decides to write her a letter on Mary's typewriter. Despite the fact that he interrupts a visit from Mary's former boyfriend, she accommodates him, viewing his behavior as "kind of sweet" rather than intrusive.

Later in the series, Lou decides to redecorate the living room as a surprise for his wife. He seeks Mary's advice, and she enlists Rhoda, her neighbor, for the job. Following Lou's divorce, he consistently turns up at Mary's apartment for dinner, seeking the wifely/motherly functions that he misses. Whenever a "woman's touch" is needed, Mary is there.

Mary is the ideal mother-surrogate in these situations. Like other typical sitcom mothers such as Harriet Nelson or June Cleaver, she is other-centered, sublimating her own feelings or needs to those of her "family." The idea that only Mary can adequately fulfill these "womanly" functions is reinforced in the rare instances in which she flatly refuses to perform. Even when she attempts to assert herself, she returns to her accommodating patterns by the end of the episode. For example, when a former WJM staff member returns for a visit, Lou decides that a party at Mary's home would be appropriate (most social interaction outside the office takes place in Mary's apartment). Mary refuses this imposition, suggesting Lou's house for the party. On the given night, she arrives early at Lou's to assist with preparations, only to find Lou in a state of total and carefree unreadiness. It is clear that Lou has counted on Mary's last-minute assistance, and when, recognizing the manipulation, she refuses to comply, Lou redirects his manipulation. The guests, he claims, knowing Mary, will *assume* that she helped him, and so she will be blamed for the mess. Mary frantically begins to clean.

Two aspects of this situation are significant. First, Mary is obviously concerned about how others assess her traditional "womanly" qualities and would not want to be viewed as an inadequate homemaker or hostess. Second, this example emphasizes Mary's role as social facilitator for the group. Lou's confidence that Mary will take over the preparations demonstrates his (and the guests') realization of her role, and Mary's acceptance of it is clear when she in fact gives in. The nurturing aspect of Mary's character is not just an extension of the fact that she is a "nice" person. Her friend and colleague Murray Slaughter is a nice person too, but he does not perform the nurturing and interpersonal facilitation that Mary does.

Mary's sensitivity, relationship skills, and willingness to spend her time and energy on the problems of others are symptomatic of her status as mother to the group. Like the traditional mothers of domestic sitcoms, she derives her value as a person from what she can do for others. Interestingly enough, the lyrics of the theme song from *TMTMS* echo this assumption: "Who can turn the world on with her smile? / Who can take a nothing day and suddenly make it all seem worthwhile?" In *TMTMS* Mary is a woman in a man's world, and her primary function is to enhance the lives of others in ways men supposedly cannot: "The patriarchy looks to women to embody and impersonate the qualities lacking in its institutions…such qualities as intuition, sympathy, and access to feeling" (Rich, 1979, p. 80).

This analysis illustrates the contradictions that exist within *TMTMS*. Although it took the sitcom from the home to the workplace, it did not significantly alter the traditional male/female roles of the genre. Superficially *TMTMS* seems progressive, but the interaction of its characters demonstrates the hegemonic patterns that undercut Mary's status as a liberated woman.

## THE FEMALE COMMUNITY ON *TMTMS*

The above section demonstrates how Mary Richards' situation as a familial adjunct to other characters can be seen as a hegemonic device defusing the threatening aspects of the "independent" woman. In their traditional forms, as they are used on *TMTMS*, the daughter/wife/ mother personae are demeaning to women, suggesting that their judgments and concerns are less important than those of others, particularly males.

This section examines Mary's relationships with other women. Assessing the portrayal of female relationships on television can provide insight into the nature of women's valuation as a group. Two major issues arise from the portrayal of interaction within the female community on *TMTMS*: the division between Mary's public and private lives, and the extent to which Mary is depicted as a token successful female.

It can be argued that television, by focusing on women's relationships with men and thereby assuming their ultimate importance in women's lives, undermines the importance of female community (see Tuchman, 1978). *TMTMS* conforms to this pattern. Mary's relationships with women are consistently depicted as secondary to her relationships with men. In the primary dramatic arena, the newsroom, Mary is the only woman. While this may suggest that Mary is a woman who can make it in a man's world, it also suggests that women's public success depends on them cooperating with male-defined structures of power. Sue Ann Nivens enters the show not as a "newsman" but as the host of the *Happy Homemaker* show; her character is sketched so as to prevent female bonding. Sue Ann's job and her interests fall in traditionally female areas. She is man-hungry and constantly in pursuit of Lou, which makes her relationship with Mary competitive rather than cooperative.

In the first four seasons of the show, Mary has close relationships with Rhoda Morgenstern, her neighbor, and Phyllis Lindstrom, her married landlady. Because Rhoda and Mary are closer in age and both single, their bond is closer. In many ways, the relationship between the two women is positive; they are supportive, caring, and cooperative with each other, and neither views their relationship as a substitute for satisfying relationships with men (see Bathrick, 1984). However, Mary's successful interpersonal relationships with Rhoda and Phyllis at home further extend the division between the public and the private in *TMTMS*.

## Public and Private Realms

Traditional thought prescribes that women are suited for the private, personal realm, and men for the public professional one. The stereotypical characteristics assigned to men and women reflect this division; men are aggressive, competitive breadwinners, and women are passive, nurturing homebodies (see Welter, 1966). *TMTMS* does not deny this perspective. Mary's interaction with close female friends is home-centered and largely involves personal rather than professional issues. At work, Mary is surrounded by men, and her one female relationship (with Sue Ann Nivens) is neither close nor supportive.

Another aspect of the private/public division is that its boundaries are more fluid for men than for women. Men are able to work and compete successfully in the public sphere and still return home to fulfill private roles as husbands and fathers. This is evident in *TMTMS* as well. While Rhoda and Phyllis rarely appear in work contexts, Mary's male colleagues are frequently seen outside of the newsroom.

## Female Tokenism

On the surface at least, Mary is a positive character. She is bright, attractive, well liked, has a good job that she performs well, and is generally happy. The other female characters on *TMTMS* do not fare as well. Sue Ann is constantly seeking fulfillment through men; Georgette is an addle-brained blonde who is devoted to the egocentric and insensitive Ted; Rhoda has a less than satisfying job, is overweight, and is unsuccessful in romantic relationships; and Phyllis is an eccentric, narcissistic wife and mother who often is frustrated by her circumscribed role. Moreover, Rhoda and Phyllis cannot get along with each other despite their common friendship with Mary, again reinforcing the idea that only

Mary can be successful in all contexts, and perhaps, that non-extraordinary women cannot get along with each other.

Mary's isolation as the sole woman in the newsroom and her portrayal as the only reasonably successful and fulfilled woman in *TMTMS* demonstrate her tokenism. Mary succeeds in the public realm only by succumbing to male expectations that she fulfill traditional female roles. She is successful, likable, and admirable in the eyes of the other women and men on *TMTMS* *because* she is submissive and unassertively nurturing and, thus, has successfully adapted herself to the male culture. Moreover, Mary's isolation as the only thoroughly positive female character in the private realm promotes perception of her as an ideal woman who is different from most. The token woman is "separate[d]...from the wider female condition; and she is perceived by 'ordinary' women as separate also, perhaps even stronger than themselves" (Rich, 1986, p.6). As the sole well-adjusted female character, Mary is figuratively isolated from and literally outnumbered by the unfulfilled female characters of Rhoda, Phyllis, and Sue Ann.

In the end, Mary is no one's equal. She is inferior to other, specifically male, characters in the public realm, where her success depends more on interpersonal than professional skill, and she is superior to other female characters in the private realm. This imbalance posits Mary Richards as a token stab at a positive portrayal of female independence. In contrast to Mary, *TMTMS* tells us, most women, like Rhoda, Sue Ann, Georgette, and even Phyllis (who constantly looks for ways to improve her marriage), are dissatisfied and continue to seek fulfillment through men. Mary's superiority comes from a particular kind of power that she has gained through compliance with male expectations. She has learned to adapt better than other female characters. In their own ways, Rhoda, Phyllis, and Sue Ann still resist or simply cannot meet the demands of patriarchy, while Mary has met those demands and is rewarded for her efforts. The hegemonic message derived from a comparison of Mary with other female characters is that compliance produces more happiness than resistance.

# GENRE CONSIDERATIONS

The hegemonic devices at work in *TMTMS* cannot be separated from generic considerations. The familial roles within which Mary Richards operates are a product of the conservatism of situation comedy as a genre and the replicative nature of television. In his discussion of the medium's "recombinant" nature, Gitlin (1983, p. 63) notes that "executives like to say they are constantly looking for something new, but their intuition tells them to hunt up prepackaged trends and then recognize the new as a variant of the old." *TMTMS* presents us with a "new" premise and old characters. A sitcom about a single, ambitious woman is daring until you surround her with a recognizable husband/father figure and a group of children to nurture. At that point, she becomes Donna Reed repackaged as a working woman.

The tendency of television programming to rehash traditional themes and roles is intensified by the conservatism of the sitcom, which is "committed to the prevention of change and the protection of the present" (Grote, 1983, p. 72). At the end of the episode, no radical change has occurred, and "everything goes back as it was at the beginning of the episode" (Grote, 1983, p. 68). Once the character's personalities, relationships, and interaction patterns have been established, program makers are unlikely to change them without risking damage to the success of the show.[2] Although one or all of these factors are challenged in some way within each episode, the problem ultimately is resolved in a fashion that requires no fundamental adjustment of the situation (Grote, 1983).

The first few episodes of a sitcom are designed to establish the situation firmly. The elements that make *TMTMS* problematic from a feminist perspective can be seen in the first episode of the series, in which Mary arrives in Minneapolis and gets her job at WJM. In the first scene we see an argument between Phyllis and Rhoda over Mary's apartment. Instantly, Mary is the mediator, trying to satisfy both women. Rhoda, who has been outside washing the windows, is swathed in bulky clothes and looks particularly unattractive next to the perky, pretty Mary. Phyllis reveals to Rhoda Mary's reason for moving to Minneapolis: the man she had dated for two years was unwilling to marry her. Thus, it is established that Mary did not come to the city seeking her independence for its own sake, but as a reaction to being refused the traditional role she desired.[3]

The next scene shows Lou Grant interviewing Mary for a job at WJM. Mary clearly has no qualifications for the job, yet Lou comments on her "spunk" and decides to give her a chance. Thus, we have the first example of Lou's paternalism toward Mary. Lou tells her, "If I don't like you, I'll fire you. If you don't like me, I'll fire you." It is interesting that Lou's standards for Mary are based on personal factors rather than professional ones, indicating that Mary's success in the newsroom will depend on her likability rather than her professional merit. At this point, we have already seen several indicators of patterns that will recur in the series: Mary's superiority to Rhoda, Lou's paternalism, and the importance of Mary's interpersonal qualities.

Indeed, the first episode displays most of Mary's eventual roles; by the end of it, she is nurturing a drunken Lou in her apartment. In this scene, Mary is saying a final good-bye to her boyfriend, who has followed her to Minneapolis. On the surface, Mary's refusal to continue a relationship with him seems to testify to her conviction to be independent. However, the fact that Lou is there as well suggests an opposite conclusion: that Mary is able to reject her possibilities for traditional bliss with the boyfriend because she has found new possibilities in her developing daughter/mother relationship with Lou.

Having established its basic premises in the first episode, in typical sitcom fashion *TMTMS* does not tamper with them. Mary grows older and more mature, but her patterns do not change significantly. Many episodes center on threats to these patterns, as Mary variously tries to reject Lou's authority, assert herself, and reject the nurturing role. However, the show always travels its circular path and returns Mary to docility by the conclusion. Indeed, in the last episode, the patriarchal patterns remain. As the WJM "family" prepares to split up after the station has been sold, Lou, in his paternal role, arranges to bring Rhoda and Phyllis, who have left Minneapolis, back to console Mary. Even on this occasion, Phyllis and Rhoda bicker over Mary's attention, reinforcing Mary's superiority and bringing her mediating skills to the fore. Significantly, Mary acknowledges the relationships she has formed, saying, "Thank you for being my family."

The problems of *TMTMS* and its portrayal of women are neither minor nor obvious. To depict Mary as a truly self-sufficient and self-determined woman would have required a complete reworking of the very basics of the series' situation. The hegemonic devices are there from the beginning, and they are reinforced throughout. Mary Richards is a successful single woman, but only at the expense of conforming to traditional expectations in the roles she plays for others. In addition, although Mary's friendships with women enhance her private life, the contrast between her sucess and their lack of it implies that the route to happiness is found in compliance with patriarchal norms; the resistance that Rhoda, Phyllis, and Sue Ann represent leads to dissatisfaction.

## ON READING MARY RICHARDS

Two issues growing out of this analysis deserve attention. The first, the value of recognizing strategies of hegemony in television discourse about women, is integrally related to the second, which concerns the validity of critical readings of television.

## Women, Hegemony, and Television

Feminist critics need to attend to the tension that exists between the poles of feminism and patriarchy in narratives such as *TMTMS*, as well as to how audiences might negotiate that tension. As a product of the dominant ideology, television may never be all that feminists desire, but its problems require continual redefinition. Viewing a program such as *TMTMS* with the benefit of hindsight permits such redefinition and offers possibilities for future investigation.

Such investigation likely would show that variations on the family paradigm have been used in other instances to devalue women within television programming. For example, although *Kate & Allie* has been touted as a positive portrayal of women (Alley, 1985), the fairly clear allocation of traditionally male/husband/father and female/wife/mother characteristics between its two female leads indicate elements of a patriarchal family paradigm.

Other distinct methods perform hegemonic functions similar to those explored here (for an example, see D'Acci, 1987). A recent situation comedy that has been compared to *TMTMS* is a strong candidate for this type of analysis. *Murphy Brown*, which focuses on the life of a woman who is a successful television journalist and avowed feminist, depicts the title character as embodying traditionally male characteristics; she is aggressive, competitive, and often insensitive. Moreover, her public success is counterbalanced by difficult family and romantic relationships and, in general, loneliness. It could be argued that these factors work hegemonically to contain positive evaluations of a feminist character by exploiting myths about the masculinity of feminists and their sacrifice of personal happiness.

These examples underscore the idea that television is recombinant and that strategies proven successful at defusing feminist content

in one situation are likely to be used in another. In developing a feminist critique that includes the development feminist theory for television (Press, 1989), critics must make note of such patterns.

## Criticism and Audiences

On another level, however, this reading of *TMTMS* may very well not be viewed as definitive. (See Grossberg & Treichler, 1987; Radway, 1986; and Rakow, 1986 for rejection of "preferred" reading claims.) While this essay has argued that the hegemonic patterns in *TMTMS* are both evident and troublesome, some may read *TMTMS* differently. Byars (1987, p. 294), for example, notes that a previous negative reading of *TMTMS* was countered during its presentation by an audience member who claimed that "Mary had meant a great deal to her, and to other women; she had represented for them 'independence'" and "had inspired them."

This contrast in opinions should not be surprising. It is precisely such divergent readings that ensure the success of television (Fiske, 1986). In the end, Mary is threatening to no one. She is passive, deferent, and womanly enough within her surrogate family to quiet the fears of those uneasy with women's liberation. For champions of feminism, Mary is a symbol of the possibilities for women—she is independent and still happy. This is the process through which hegemony is maintained. Enough difference is introduced to give the appearance of change, yet enough remains the same to avoid upsetting the balance within the dominant ideology. Thus, the claim is not that television "*manufactures*" ideology, but that it "*relays* and *reproduces* and *processes* and *packages* and *focuses* ideology." (Gitlin, 1982, p. 430, italics in original). However, in this processing, some "ideological seams" (Radway, 1986, p. 110) are exposed, allowing for contrasting evaluations as audiences assign "different values to different portions of the text and hence to the text itself" (Condit, 1989, p. 108). Not all viewers saw Mary

Richards as a "contained" feminist symbol, but the text of *TMTMS* offers mixed messages that limit claims for the program's progressiveness.

Although different evaluations of a program's message are possible, the hegemonic patterns isolated here are not my own creation. They exist within the *TMTMS* narrative and are available for conscious or unconscious articulation by viewers. In the 1970s, it was not necessary to watch *TMTMS* to know that the program was about a single, "liberated" woman. Nonetheless, audience research has recently promoted a methodological vision that threatens to obscure the legitimate functions performed by the type of criticism offered here. As critics we assume that we are able to see and explain what others cannot because we are trained to do so. Scholarly reading should be expected to be different from audience readings; the former must be considered and attuned to the subtleties that audience members may experience but not articulate.

Although audience research can enhance our conclusions and perhaps offer some sociological comprehension, it does not replace critical insight. To act as though it can is to erode our own credibility. Feminist critics are in a particularly precarious position with regard to this issue. Those critics with the knowledge and training to recognize and interpret patriarchal ideology in television discourse should not be silenced simply because audiences caught in cultural hegemonic patterns may not acknowledge what is happening. In that context, critics need to go beyond what audiences might tell them.

Each type of criticism offers a different type of insight. They are complementary, and each can add to a feminist critique (Rakow, 1989). The commitment to the need for real change that is part of the feminist agenda makes it imperative that we explore every reasonable path that enriches the diversity and usefulness of a feminist critique of television.

## NOTES

1. Interestingly; the proscription against incest that typifies a true father-daughter relationship is implicitly revealed in an episode late in the series in which Mary asks Lou for a date. Lou comes over to Mary's house for dinner, and both are extremely nervous and uncomfortable. They decide to end the suspense and they kiss, during which both begin to giggle. Agreeing that a dating relationship will never work, they settle down to talk about the office. Clearly, the patterns created in their father-daughter relationship prohibit romance.

2. There are a few exceptions to this general rule, and Grote (1983) cites *M*A*S*H* as an example.

3. The creators of *TMTMS* had originally conceived of Mary Richards as a divorced woman, but CBS executives vetoed the idea, explaining that viewers would not accept such a character because of Mary Tyler Moore's previous popular role as the dutiful and happy wife on *The Dick Van Dyke Show*. But "the network feared that the mass audience wouldn't accept the proposition that an attractive and competent woman on the far side of thirty had never been married" (Gitlin, 1983, p.214). These incidents show hegemonic considerations at work from the outset of the show's creation.

## REFERENCES

Alley, R. (1985). Values on view: A moral myopia? *Critical Studies in Mass Communication, 2,* 395–406.

Baehr, H., & Dyer, G. (EDS.). (1987). *Boxed in: Women and television*. New York: Pandora.

Barthes, R. (1973). *Mythologies*. London: Paladin.

Bathrick, S. (1984). *The Mary Tyler Moore Show*: Women at home and at work. In J. Feuer, P. Kerr, & T. Vahimagi (Eds.) *MTM: "Quality television"* (pp. 99–131). London: British Film Institute.

Brooks, T., & Marsh, E. (1985). *The complete directory to prime time network tv shows, 1946–present* (3d ed.). New York: Ballantine.

Byars, J. (1987). Reading feminine discourse: Prime-time television in the U.S. *Communication, 9,* 289–303.

Condit, C. (1989). The rhetorical limits of polysemy. *Critical Studies in Mass Communication, 6,* 103–122.

D'Acci, J. (1987). The case of Cagney and Lacey. In H. Baehr & G. Dyer (Eds.), *Boxed in: Women and television* (pp. 203–226). New York: Pandora.

De Lauretis, T. (1984). *Alice doesn't: Feminism, semiotics, cinema*. Bloomington: Indiana University Press.

Dervin, B. (1987). The potential contribution of feminist scholarship to the field of communication. *Journal of Communication, 37(4)*, 107–120.

Fiske, J. (1986). Television: Polysemy and popularity. *Critical Studies in Mass Communication, 3*, 391–408.

Gitlin, T. (1982). Prime time ideology: The hegemonic process in television entertainment. In H. Newcomb (Ed.), *Television: The critical view* (3d ed.) (pp. 426–454). New York: Oxford University Press.

Gitlin, T. (1983). *Inside prime time*. New York: Pantheon Books.

Grossberg, L., & Treichler, P. (1987). Intersections of power: Criticism, television, gender. *Communication, 9*, 273–287.

Grote, D. (1983). *The end of comedy: The sit-com and the comedic tradition*. Hamden, CT: Archon Books.

Hough, A. (1981). Trials and tribulations—Thirty years of sitcom. In R. Adler (Ed.), *Understanding television: Essays on television as a social and cultural force* (pp. 201–224). New York: Praeger.

Kuhn, A. (1982). *Women's pictures: Feminism and cinema*. New York: Routledge & Kegan Paul.

Meehan, D. (1983). *Ladies of the evening: Women characters of prime-time television*. Metuchen, NJ: Scarecrow Press.

Mintz, L. (1985). Situation comedy. In B. Rose (Ed.), *TV genres: A handbook and reference guide* (pp. 107–129). Westport, CT: Greenwood Press.

Modleski, T. (1982). *Loving with a vengeance: Mass-produced fantasies for women*. London: Methuen.

Mulvey, L. (1989). *Visual and other pleasures*. Bloomington: Indiana University Press.

Press, A. (1989). The ongoing feminist revolution. *Critical Studies in Mass Communication, 6*, 196–202.

Radway, J. (1984). *Reading the romance: Women, patriarchy, and popular literature*. Chapel Hill, University of North Carolina Press.

Radway, J. (1986). Identifying ideological seams: Mass culture, analytical method, and political practice. *Communication, 9*, 93–123.

Rakow, L. (1986). Feminist approaches to popular culture: Giving patriarchy its due. *Communication, 9*, 19–24.

Rakow, L. (1989). Feminist studies: The next stage. *Critical Studies in Mass Communication, 6*, 209–215.

Rich, A. (1979). *On lies, secrets, and silence: Selected prose, 1966–1978*. New York: W.W. Norton.

Rich, A. (1986). *Blood, bread, and poetry: Selected prose, 1979–1985*. New York: W.W. Norton.

Treichler, P., & Wartella, E. (1986). Interventions: Feminist theories and communication studies. *Comunication, 9*, 1–18.

Tuchman, G. (1978). The symbolic annihilation of women by the mass media. In G. Tuchman, A. K. Daniels, & J. Benét (Eds.), *Hearth and home: Images of women in the mass media* (pp. 4–38) New York: Oxford University Press.

Welter, B. (1966). The cult of true womanhood, 1820–1860. *American Quarterly, 18*, 151–174

# Introduction to Kathleen Battles and Wendy Hilton-Morrow's "Gay Characters in Conventional Spaces: *Will & Grace* and the Situation Comedy Genre"

Kathleen Battles and Wendy Hilton-Morrow were both doctoral candidates in the Department of Communications Studies at the University of Iowa when they first wrote this interesting study on cultural perceptions and how they relate to the television situation comedy genre. First presented as part of the Gay and Lesbian Alliance Against Defamation Center for the Study of Media and Society Research Initiative on *Will & Grace,* and partly funded by GLAAD, it is a work that draws on numerous theoretical paradigms including cultural studies, feminist theory, and the modern discourse entitled queer theory to examine how the contemporary high visibility of openly gay characters in popular culture does not necessarily translate into changes in the dominant norms of our society. Like the Bonnie Dow reading on *The Mary Tyler Moore Show*, it suggests that the formulaic nature of the situation comedy genre and the prevailing conventions of society towards homosexuality position *Will & Grace* as a mainstream television program that potentially re-enforces gay stereotypes.

# Gay Characters in Conventional Spaces: *Will & Grace* and the Situation Comedy Genre

When *Will & Grace* took to the airwaves in September 1998, it broke new ground, offering the first gay male lead on U.S. broadcast television. By its third season, the situation comedy was one of 22 shows that portrayed gay or lesbian characters in leading, supporting or recurring roles (Gay and Lesbian Alliance Against Defamation, 2000). Since its premiere, *Will & Grace* has won numerous awards, including a People's Choice Award as Favorite New Comedy Series, a Golden Globe nomination for Best Comedy Series, an American Comedy Award nomination for Funniest Television Series, two GLAAD (Gay and Lesbian Alliance Against Defamation) Media Awards for Outstanding TV Comedy Series and a Founders Award from the Viewers for Quality Television. And during the 52nd annual Emmy Awards, *Will & Grace* was nominated in 11 categories, taking home awards for Outstanding Comedy Series, Outstanding Supporting Actress, and Outstanding Supporting Actor.

The program follows the lives of Will Truman, a successful, attractive, Manhattan lawyer, and his best friend Grace Adler, a beautiful, self-employed, interior decorator. The two would make a perfect couple—and in fact, were college sweethearts—except for one barrier: Will is gay and Grace is straight. The two are in a constant search for lifelong mates, but the search has never turned up a relationship as special as the one that they share with each other. Their lives are complicated by two supporting characters, who are anything but typical. Karen Walker is a straight, wealthy socialite and alcoholic who works for Grace as her assistant because her life of leisure leaves her bored. Karen offers an appropriate counterpart for Will's friend, Jack. Jack is a flamboyantly gay, continually unemployed, self-described actor/dancer/choreographer.

As *Will & Grace* has found commercial success and critical acclaim, the U.S. remains embroiled in a number of struggles demonstrating the continued contentiousness of gay and lesbian issues within our heterosexist society. Three years after Congress passed the Defense of Marriage Act in 1996, the Vermont legislature passed a "civil unions" law, which legally recognized committed same-sex relationships. However, 34 states have enacted laws denying recognition of same-sex marriages in other states (George, 2001). After the Supreme Court ruled in a split 5-4 decision that the boy scouts did not have to accept gays or lesbians as employees or leaders, gay rights groups began pressuring sponsors and the government to withdraw funding from the organization. And three years after Matthew Shepherd was brutally murdered by two men solely because of his sexuality, gays and lesbians are more visible in the media than ever before (Wyatt, 2000).

Given this cultural climate it is not surprising that just five years before *Will & Grace* debuted, Fejes and Petrich (1993) predicted, "A regular network program with gay or lesbian main characters is far in the future" (p. 402).[1] At that time gay characters appeared only occasionally and generally in secondary roles. Later in the decade some were left wondering if ABC's 1998 cancellation of *Ellen*, whose character and actor simultaneous came out, would mean the death of gay characters in leading television roles (Sullivan, 1998). Instead of playing it safe after the controversies surrounding *Ellen*, NBC premiered *Will & Grace* the following fall. GLAAD applauded the show for presenting two different, yet likable, representations of gay men and for presenting their sexuality "simply as a part of who [Will and Jack] are as individuals" (1998). Other critics praised the show for dealing with gay subject matter and including explicit gay references. "[T]his was the first example of gay subject matter going totally mainstream, for there is nothing so mainstream—not Broadway, not movies, not novels—as The Box" (Holleran, 2000, p. 65).

Indeed, *Will & Grace's* appeal went beyond the small, niche gay market, attracting larger, mainstream[2] audiences. By the program's fourth week, it ranked number one in its timeslot in the highly lucrative 18–49 demographic (Jacobs, 1998). In its second season the show ranked among the 1999–2000 season's top 20 series (NBC, 2000). When *Will & Grace* went head-to-head with ABC's *Dharma & Greg*, a sitcom about a quirky heterosexual couple, the two networks found themselves competing for the same demographics and the same advertisers (Frankel, 2000). "All this mainstream success suggests that it appeals to viewers who might not ordinarily be inclined to watch a "queer" show" (Gairola, 2001). This increased visibility is, for some, a sign of society's growing acceptance of the gay community. In an issue of *Entertainment Weekly* devoted to "Gay Hollywood," Benjamin Svetkey (2000) made this equation:

> [T]oday, in 2000 A.D. (After DeGeneres), gay characters are so common on television, so unexotic, that their sexual orientation has become all but invisible to most viewers. It is, in a sense, the ultimate sign of acceptance…" (p. 26).

Implicit in these statements is that greater visibility equals greater social acceptance. However to say that *Will & Grace's* large audience, comprised of both gay and straight viewers, signals a cultural acceptance of the gay and lesbian lifestyle is premature. As Dow (2001) similarly points out in her analysis of *Ellen*, "saying the success of Ellen's initial coming out means the end of prejudice against gays and lesbians is like saying that the success of *The Cosby Show* in the 1980s signaled the end of racism" (p. 128; see also Gray, 1994; Lewis, 1991).

This paper takes a critical approach to examining portrayals of gay characters on television, rejecting the assumption that the mere representation of gay men in primetime television necessarily reflects a huge shift in societal attitudes towards gays and lesbians in America. Instead, we will argue that *Will & Grace* makes the topic of homosexuality more palatable to a large, mainstream television audience by situating it within safe and familiar popular culture conventions, particularly those of the situation comedy genre. Additionally, we will argue that by inviting viewers to read the program within familiar televisual frames, *Will & Grace* can be read as reinforcing heterosexism and, thus, can be seen as heteronormative.[3] Our paper will perform textual analysis of *Will & Grace* episodes from the 2000–2001 season to explore the liabilities of relying on familiar sitcom conventions. We will draw upon feminist and queer theory to demonstrate how the program continually positions gayness in opposition to masculinity, pairs its characters in familiar opposite-sex dyads, defuses the most outrageous characters' threats to heteronormativity, and emphasizes interpersonal relationships at the expense of gay politics.

## WILL THE TRU-MAN PLEASE STAND UP: GAYNESS AND MASCULINITY

Before *Will & Grace* first premiered, GLAAD (1998) applauded the representations of Will and his more flamboyant sidekick, Jack, as "different types of gay men—both of which are valued within the community." Given the negative stereotypes of gay men that have been a part of television since its earliest years (Fejes & Petrick, 1993), the two gay characters on *Will & Grace* can be considered progressive. However, these two characters are positioned within a narrative space that relies on familiar comedic conventions for addressing homosexuality—equating gayness with a lack of masculinity. In Hollywood, homosexuality historically has been defined in opposition to masculinity; gayness is that which is not masculine (Russo, 1985, Epstein & Friedman, 1996). Comedic conventions of film and television have historically reinforced and poked fun at this stereotype of the gay man (Fejes & Petrich, 1993: Dow, 2001). By relying on this conventional representational strategy, *Will & Grace* fails to challenge the heterosexist equation between homosexuality and that which is "not masculine," and in the process allows enough space in the narrative for viewers to read Will's character as straight. Additionally, the program does not force viewers to question heteronormative assumptions of gender inversion. Gender inversion refers to the commonly held belief that homosexuals are oppositely gendered; a gay man is considered more feminine than a straight man and vice versa with a lesbian in contrast to a straight woman (Sedgewick, 1990).

The character of Will could be considered more threatening to an ideology of heteronormativity because he offers a different model for homosexuality. Unlike his feminized counterpart, Jack, Will fits well into a mainstream model of masculinity, being handsome, muscular, and physically fit. He mirrors the image of the "young, white, Caucasian...with a well muscled, smooth body, handsome face, good education, professional job, and high income" that advertisers purport as the model to which all gay men should aspire (Fejes, 2000, p. 115). This version of gay masculinity is in no way different from the same image being sold to heterosexual men. Will provides a mainstream audience with a likable, well-assimilated gay character that is very different from the negative stereotypes of gay characters in early television. However, his character has been criticized for confining the portrayal of gay men to those who are white and upper-middle class, making his character more acceptable to a mainstream heterosexual audience at the expense of alienating a large portion of the gay community (Gairola, 2001). And while some praise Will's character as being positive and progressive, others have attacked the character for "not being gay enough" (Jacobs, 1998).

Rather than determining how "gay" Will is, a move that risks essentializing gay identity,[4] a more productive line of analysis is to consider how Will's "gayness" is defined at specific moments in the text. In this case, it is significant that whenever *Will & Grace* specifically deals with Will's sexuality the series falls back on the convention of feminizing Will. The November 23, 2000 (Greenstein & Burrows) episode provides the audience with the particulars of Will and Grace's romantic relationship in college. While Will generally fits very well into a mainstream model of masculinity, this coming-out episode defines his gayness in opposition to heterosexual masculinity. A flashback introduces the audience to Will and Grace as college students, where they are attending a "kegger" in a dorm room. The camera scans a roomful of couples making out. The camera lingers on one couple as the man, kissing the woman, tells her "I am so into you." As it pans to another couple kissing, the man also tells his girlfriend, "I am so into you." Then the camera comes to rest on Will and Grace, her sitting on his lap. He tells her, "I am so into those earrings." Immediately, Will is defined as being different from (more feminine than) his masculine heterosexual college buddies. Will and his roommate eventually meet up at the keg and the audience is again exposed to Will's more feminine concerns, asking his roommate if his "butt look[s] big in these jeans." His roommate replies, "Dude, I'm a guy. I don't know. Just get some pants that fit and leave me alone," insinuating that Will is not a real "guy."

Will is likewise effeminized in the episodes featuring his most significant romantic relationship to date, with Matt, a sportscaster. As a sports fanatic, Matt is instantly marked as more masculine than Will. For their first date, they meet at a sports bar, where the following exchange takes place (Poust, Kinally, & Burrows, 2000):

> Matt: [To bartender] Two more please. [To Will] I love sports. I always wanted to be a sportscaster. I used to hold my mother's curling iron and pretend I was Howard Cosell.

> Will: Funny. You know when I was a kid, I used to hold my mother's curling iron and pretend I was Eartha Kitt.

The marking of Will as feminine continues, as Will takes batting lessons from Grace because he believes that Matt broke up with his last boyfriend for not sharing his interest in sports. As Will discusses Grace's adventures redecorating Jack's apartment, Grace looks on in disgust as Will misses every ball pitched to him by the machine, finally blurting out in frustration, "Hit the freaking ball you damn sissy!" Then Grace proceeds to show Will how to hit the ball, doing her best imitation of macho-style ball playing, finally instructing Will to get some snacks. The next scene finds Will and Grace back at their apartment, where Will asks Grace to admire his first "sports injury," a blister on his finger. Grace congratulates him and then tells him that she hopes that he didn't mind that they had to move to the "kiddie" area. She chides him for feeling like a man when he hit the clown, to which Will sheepishly agrees.

These episodes reinforce a definition of gayness as that which is not masculine, and even present gay masculinity as a "pale imitation" of heterosexual femininity, asserting the primacy of heterosexuality (Butler, 1991). Additionally, they

preserve an essential heterosexuality within desire itself by emasculating Will in his relationship with the macho, sports-oriented Matt. Because Will is portrayed as more feminine in the episodes that focus on their relationship, the heteronormative understanding of desire—as existing between a masculine person and a feminine person—is upheld (Sedgewick, 1990). (Although, as will be discussed below, Will and Matt's relationship might be better understood as male bonding rather than actual desire.) Ironically, these episodes that demonstrate Will's gayness through gender inversion are the exceptions to how Will is generally portrayed. It is when the program must explicitly account for his homosexuality that he is defined as "not masculine."

If gayness is defined in this manner, then the usual oppositioning of Will and Jack is important. They are defined by their difference. They are contrasted by physical appearance, responsibility levels, and even the relationships that they pursue. Will is always in search of romance, desiring a man with whom he can share "His and His SUVs and 2.5 Jack Russell Terriers." Meanwhile, Jack juggles multiple boyfriends, continually flirting with nearly every man—gay or straight—with whom he comes in contact. Jack fulfills the stereotype of the flamboyant gay man and Will provides the norm of masculinity against which Jack's gayness is defined. "Even Will and his other friends poke fun at Jack's campiness, thus drawing a distinction between their 'straighter'-seeming gayness and Jack's overt 'queeniness'" (Gairola, 2001). Because the program repeatedly codes nonmasculine qualities as gay, then one must wonder about the sexual coding of masculine qualities, which is not made as clear. This allows Will's sexuality to be more ambiguous. Additionally, Will's character, because it is defined against the flamboyant gay man, becomes a safer, better-assimilated portrayal of a gay man. He fits into the new masculine, asexual images of gays in the media that "in no way challenge the heteronormativity of mainstream society" (Fejes, 2000, p. 116).

## "ROMANTIC" COMEDY?

*Will & Grace* typically pairs its characters in opposite sex dyads. It is in these heterosocial (relationships between men and women) dyads that these characters find their most successful relationships. While all four characters interact with one another, there are clear bonds along heterosocial lines. Will and Grace are oftentimes positioned as a couple and Jack and Karen usually operate as "partners in crime." These pairings are represented in the program's opening sequence in which the characters stand in a line—Will, Grace, Karen, and Jack—visually framing the dominant character interactions on the program. Will and Grace are standing closer together, as are Jack and Karen, than are Grace and Karen, emphasizing their heterosocial pairings. Will and Jack, the two gay characters, are farthest away from each other, signaling the absence of romantic tension in their relationship. Read alone, each of these relationships can be read positively as challenging typical representation of straights and gays, offering safe, caring relationships between both opposite and same sex dyads that do not lead to sex. Read against each other, however, and in terms of sitcom and popular cultural romantic conventions, these pairings can tell a different story. *Will & Grace* continually privileges heterosociality, while homosociality (relationships between same-sex individuals) constantly fails or is safeguarded within the parameters of "male bonding" rather than same-sex desire.

A staple of the situation comedy, and of mainstream television and film in general, is the search for romance, many times played out as a battle of the sexes. Scodari (1995), for example, explores the spate of romantic situation comedies of the late 1980s as an adaptation of the screwball romances of the 1930s and 40s. These situation comedies find their humor in the playful interactions within the ostensibly egalitarian relationships between men and women who are either already in romantic relationships or in search of them. Oftentimes these relationships are played out in terms of a delayed consummation plotline. Originally the term applied to classical era Hollywood films in which sex before marriage was not permitted to be portrayed, leading to films that usually centered around the male lead's desire to consummate the relationship and the female lead's desire to get married. In between, a lot of playful barbs were exchanged between the couples (Epstein & Friedman, 1996). As Scodari has argued, television sitcoms adopted this type of plot, which in the weekly series format allows for a constant replay of the delay of consummation between the lead male and female characters. In fact, many working in the television industry argue that consummation often equals the death of the series as the dominant narrative tension that keeps viewers tuning in week after week disappears (Jacobs, 1998). *Will & Grace* offers the "ultimate twist" on the delayed consummation trope, separating potential lovers by sexual orientation. Armistead Maupin, whose book-turned-miniseries *Tales of the City* featured a gay man and straight woman, acknowledges that the old obstacles of distance or class are no longer convincing to audiences: "The only thing you can come up with that keeps the lead actor and actress from doing it today is homosexuality" (quoted in Jacobs, 1998). By relying on this largely heterosexual romantic convention writers are able to tease audiences without fear of the post-consummation ratings drop. As its creators have acknowledged, *Will & Grace* likewise relies on this latest twist of the delayed consummation convention (Svetkey, 2000).

Will and Grace share an intimacy with one another that they cannot find in a sexual partner. They routinely perform roles associated with couples, particularly married heterosexual partners. They have lived together, arguing over matters of bathroom time and other mundane issues associated with marriage. In the third season premiere (Kohan, Mutchnick, & Burrows, 2000), when Will returns unexpectedly from an extended business trip overseas, he asks Grace, "Where's the love? I just flew coach." Grace jumps up into Will's arms, wrapping her legs around his waist and then hugs him from the behind. After their initial greeting Will explains to Grace why he decided to come back. "I missed you. I just felt every time you needed me I wasn't there." As the episode progresses, Will grows jealous over Grace and Jack's new-found closeness. When Grace asks Will what she can do to reassure him that she has not replaced him with Jack, he responds, "I don't know. How about something like you need me more than anyone else. There's no one who could ever take my place. And that you promise when your last breath escapes you in this earthly life it will whisper my name. [In a whisper] 'Will.' But you know, in your own words." After Grace assures Will that her affections are true, they share a kiss on the lips and an embrace.

Another episode (Barr & Burrows, 2001) deals with the provocative issue of gay marriage by having the four characters attend a commitment ceremony for their friends Joe and Larry. However, throughout the episode Will and Grace are clearly positioned as a shadow couple of Joe and Larry and it is their relationship that takes center stage. When Will and Grace meet Joe and Larry for dinner in New York, Joe looks fondly upon Will and Grace bickering over dessert, asking, "You guys are so cute together. Are we?" Then, Joe and Larry ask Will and Grace to do a reading together at their ceremony, further positioning them as a couple. As the episode progresses Grace is clearly being positioned as Will's wife, much to Will's resentment. While in the car ride on the way up to Vermont, the two continue to fight over money, prompting Karen to blurt out in frustration, "Just climb on top of each other and get it over with already!" While meant as a joke, Karen's comment highlights the way in which the tension in Will and Grace's relationship closely resembles the sexual tension and bickering between heterosexuals in other

sitcoms prior to the consummation of their relationships (e.g. Sam and Diane in *Cheers* or Rachel and Ross in *Friends*).

The two continue to bicker, until they are prompted to stand and perform their reading during the ceremony. As they recite the short poem about love, they begin to address each other, until finally they admit their love for each other and make up. On the one hand, this poem, which discusses the possession of infinite amounts of love, indicates that Will and Grace can love each other, and still have enough love for potential romantic partners. The poem also suggests that fulfillment cannot be achieved through others, or at least, need not be achieved through a romantic partner. On the one hand, Will and Grace clearly get caught up in this reading designed to commemorate a marriage. Once they finish they turn to each other and confess their love to each other, each uttering the statement "I do." When finished, the guests applaud, and Will and Grace march down the aisle as if they are, in fact, the pair getting married. It is a gentle reminder from Joe and Larry that brings Will and Grace back to their seats, but only after the same sex union ceremony has become incidental to the vows exchanged between Will and Grace. In this way the program deflects attention from the potential threat posed by portraying gay marriage to a mainstream audience by focusing on the relationship between Will and Grace, who have been coded as a couple.

By pairing Will and Grace as the central dyad in the text, the program deftly escapes having to deal in a more overt manner with same-sex attraction. While heterosocial pairings are successful, the program does not allow the same success for homosocial relationships, which are often marked by a failure to communicate and achieve intimacy. This is especially true between Jack and Will, who are the only recurring gay characters on the program, but can rarely spend meaningful time together. Whatever time they do spend together is purposively devoid of any hint of sexual intimacy or attraction between the characters. On the one hand, this can be read as a positive representation because it demonstrates that gay men can form bonds that are not based solely on sexual intimacy.[5] On the other hand, the manner in which any possible attraction between the characters is dealt with marks even the hint of same-sex intimacy as a perversion. Moreover, when considered in comparison to the romantic tension in Will and Grace's relationship, the lack of a similar tension between Jack and Will could be understood as a significant absence. As Fejes (2000) explains, "While in the past same sex desire and the males who practiced it were depicted as 'not really men' at best, and sick and depraved at worst, today representation of gay males in the media often separate same sex desire from the males who practice it, representing the latter in a positive, masculine, and upbeat manner while making the former invisible" (p. 116). While Jack and his desires are not invisible in the show, Will's frequently are; when they do appear they are safely figured within the conventions of male bonding.

Occasionally the denial of desire between Will and Jack becomes quite explicit. During a visit to Psychic Sue (Palmer & Burrow, 2000), Will is told that he already knows the man with whom he will spend the rest of his life, and that his name begins with the letter "J." In this humorous scene we see Will pondering over whom he currently knows whose name begins with the letter "J," the audience knowing, of course, that Psychic Sue is speaking of Jack, whose name she finally blurts out, much to the horror of Will. The rest of the episode focuses on Will's revulsion of the idea, which is explored through a series of humorous interludes between him and Jack, leading to a playful reenactment of a standard "honey, I'm home" scene common to the imagining of domestic sitcom life. Will arrives home and is greeted by Jack emerging from the bathroom greeting him with an ironic "Hi honey."

Will: [Clearly upset] What are you doing here?

Jack: Calm down, I was just using your tub [pause] and your ylang ylang. [Jumping towards Will] You like? You like?

Will: Why don't you leave, you leave.

Jack: Why are you so crabby? Bad day at the office?

Will: No, I just wanted to come home and not to Madame Butterfly.

Jack: [approaching Will]: Helloooo gorgeous suit. Where did we get this, huh? [He runs his fingers up Will's arm and then moves behind him, grabbing him.] Nice. The shoulders, the pecs, the pits, the waist. Woo!

Will: [Breaks away from Jack in horror and blurts out.] I AM NOT HAVING SEX WITH YOU!!

Jack: [Shocked] WHAT!

Will: I am never having sex with you. We are never having sex. Sex with you, NO!

Jack: Oh, you poor thing. That wasn't sex. Alright, how can I explain this [pauses as he moves closer to Will] When two men are in love and committed and greased up like two pigs at a county fair…

Will: NO! Psychic Sue said I'm going to spend my life with a man named Jack.

Jack: Jack who?

Will: Jack you.

Jack: Jack me?

Will: No THANKS! [Voice goes up on thanks. Looking perturbed, he moves next to Jack.] You know ordinarily I wouldn't believe all this psychic stuff, but she's been right about everything else…[pause]…What if she's right about this? [Both walk to opposite ends of the room].

Jack: Well, what if she is right [looking somewhat horrified]?

Will: I wonder what that is going to be like.

Jack: I'm gonna [stuttering slightly] have to have my own place.

Will: Sex is out of the question. I don't even like to see your head poke through your sweater.

This scene offers an extreme play on the denial of possible consummation of a relationship between same-sex friends. The scene, played ironically within the format of a sitcom marriage, with the husband coming home after a long day at work to a feminine, stay-at-home wife who is making herself presentable for her tired husband, is one that will be familiar to most situation comedy viewers. What makes it strange (and humorous) is that two men perform the role of husband and wife. The disruption caused to this domestic scene is handled with absolute denial of any same-sex affection or erotic desire, as played through a culturally-constructed revulsion against gay male sex. Will's revulsion at Jack's touch mirrors similar homophobic scenes played over and over again in films and in television. It is telling, for example, that Will's outburst of revulsion comes when Jack is grabbing him from behind, a position that suggests anal intercourse. When Grace touches Will from behind in the episode discussed above (Kohan, Mutchnick, & Burrows, 2000), it is in no way threatening. Will's outburst, in fact, amounts to what can be seen as a hysterical denial of same-sex desire. At the same time, in an ironic twist, the idea of same-sex relationships can only be imagined through the conventions of heterosexual relationships, thus underscoring that heterosexuality is at the root of all desire.[6] The most curious statement in this exchange, however, comes from Jack, who, when trying to explain

sex to Will, says that two men should be in love and committed. This is a strange comment for Jack to make, as he is frequently portrayed as having multiple sexual partners and is devoid of any desire for a long-term stable relationship. This comment, however, allows gay sex to be safely figured in conventional heterosexual terms of emotional intimacy, thus de-eroticizing the gay male sexual act. The second part of the comment, "greased up like two pigs at a county fair," simultaneously marks homosexuality as deviant. Here we have a catch-22: in a heteronormative system of gender and sex relationships, same sex desire must be denied or marked as deviant; at the same time, if it must be imagined it can only be done so through heteronormative social and cultural conventions.

After receiving much criticism for Will's apparent asexuality, the program's creators introduced a more serious love interest for Will. However, instead of allowing the audience to see the development of a sexual relationship between two male characters, the relationship is safely figured within the convention of "male bonding." Their first date takes place in a sports bar (Poust, Kinally, & Burrows, 2001). During this scene, Matt mentions that he plays weekend ball with some "buddies," a term more typically associated with heterosexual male bonding. The two play basketball together, which ends in a locker room scene during which Will finally confesses his disinterest in sports. This locker room scene is potentially threatening due to the common homophobic fear of gay men staring at straight men, and indeed the scene can be read as a direct and provocative challenge to this fear. However, this locker room scene, and one from the following episode (Kohan, Mutchnick, & Burrows, 2001), also works to safely contain any threat of desire between the two male characters by placing it within the safer sphere of heterosexual male bonding. When they embrace, it is devoid of apparent romantic affection, and their hugs frequently end with shoulder pats, or other gestures that read more like male bonding.

Relying on the convention of male bonding to frame potential male-to-male desire allows for a safe representation of homosexuality at a time when the portrayal of gay desire on broadcast television is generally accompanied by disclaimers and advertiser wariness. However, the de-eroticization or total erasure of same-sex desire in a text that does not de-eroticize or erase heterosexual desire[7] fails to challenge the homophobic sanction against same-sex desire.

Generally, *Will & Grace*'s funniest and most outrageous moments come not from the two leading characters, but from the two supporting characters, Karen and Jack. Both characters continually call into question the assumptions and beliefs of a heterosexist culture through their dialogue and actions. However, the potential social criticism offered by these characters for a mainstream audience is often contained by their position within the sitcom narrative structure. Situation comedies feature stable recurring casts of characters who rarely remember events from previous episodes, and who hardly ever achieve personal growth, instead occupying a particular slot in the sitcom narrative: father, mother, best friend, precocious child, buffoon, etc. Thus, the situation comedy relies on a set of domestic and familial-like relationships to structure the narrative slots available to characters in the program. Even when programs do not take place within a family or home, the setting still functions as a surrogate home and the characters relate to each other as part of a family (MacDonald, 1979; Newcomb, 1974). We see this in *Will & Grace* as Jack and Karen are continually infantilized, occupying the slots of children to Will and Grace's narrative slots as parents. For example, in two episodes during the 2000–2001 season, the four characters appear together in automobiles. In each case, Will and Grace sit up front, acting as de-facto parents to Jack and Karen, who sit in the back seat and remain oblivious to where they are going, concerned only with their own desires. In one episode (Rosenstock & Burrows, 2000), Will and Grace enter her office to find Karen talking dirty on the phone. When she sees

them, she says, "Crap, I gotta go. Mom and Mom are home." While each character calls into question dominant cultural ideologies regarding gender and sexuality, this is limited by their placement in the narrative.

Karen can be read as calling into question those roles generally associated with being a woman—supportive mother, friend and wife. In one episode (Palmer & Burrows, 2001), Karen's stepson, Mason, wins a spot on his school's swim team, and Jack chides Karen for not attending any of the meets. Feeling guilty, Karen attends, but with a large plastic cup full of booze in hand. She argues with the other mothers who chide her for her bad mothering skills. As Mason competes, Karen cheers him on, yelling, "Go! Go! Honey, Swim! Swim! I know you can do it. Hey! Hey, if you win, tonight I'll let you watch the Spice Channel! [To another mother] That lit a fire under the horny little monkey!" Karen even sexualizes the most basic maternal behavior when she sees it. In the November 23, 2000 (Greenstein & Burrows) episode, when the group is sitting in a bar, the camera frames a two-shot of Grace and Karen. Karen is looking across the room at someone out of the camera's frame. She pulls down her shirt to reveal her cleavage. Grace looks on horrified and asks Karen why she is doing this. Karen's childish reply is "She started it," to which Grace emphatically responds, "SHE'S NURSING!" Karen, proving her inability to recognize such maternal behavior, is left to respond, "Oh, well that explains the little bald man."

Karen also rejects the role of comforter, which again leads to the failure of any homosocial bonding. In many scenes Karen proves that she is incapable of offering real emotional comfort to any of the characters, instead she remains primarily concerned with fulfilling her own desires. Moreover, Karen challenges traditional ideologies about marriage, making it clear that her marriage is based on an exchange model. She gives her husband sex and he gives her all the money she wants. She views marriage as a contractual obligation that must be fulfilled, not as a loving relationship between two people, and thus not through the heterosexual ideology of romance. In the February 8, 2001 (Kohan, Mutchnick, & Burrows, 2001) episode, Karen and Jack go to the bank so that Karen can take out some jewels from her safe deposit box to attend a charity ball. Fondling the jewels, she says to Jack, "Look at all of these jewels. Stan has been so good to me honey. [Picking up the jewels one at a time.] On my knees in Belize. On my back in Iraq. Oh, and then there was that time in Nantucket. [She and Jack both giggle.] Oh, good times… Well, good jewels anyway."

Karen provides a delightfully funny character who rejects all traditional ideologies about what it means to be a woman—failing at even the most basic maternal level, putting herself before all others, and rejecting any notions of marriage as anything more than an exchange of sex for money. In this way, Karen could be read as challenging the dominant gender structure and sexist and heterosexist assumptions. One popular press critic calls her "the only really gay character on the sitcom" (Holleran, 2000). However, she is such an extreme character that the sheer audacity of her words and actions can safely diffuse any potential threat she may offer. Karen's comments are generally followed by audience/laugh track laughter demonstrating that she is a screwball character not to be taken seriously. Additionally, the more mainstream characters, Will and Grace, offer reactions that demonstrate how over-the-top she actually is. In the breastfeeding example offered above, Grace is horrified by Karen's behavior. After Karen's final comment about "the little bald man," Will redirects attention back to his story by beginning, "ANYWAY…," as if to completely dismiss Karen. While Karen might offer a gay sensibility for some of the program's viewers, her position within the familiar role of child or buffoon within the situation comedy narrative means that such a sensibility need not be taken seriously by the mainstream audience.

Jack's character can also be read as threatening traditional categories of gender and sexuality. He constantly objectifies other men, refusing to conform to any traditional notions of masculinity. He acknowledges that he doesn't "pay attention to the straight world," and certainly lives in a world of his own. However, Jack also is infantilized by the more stable characters. Like Karen, Jack is continually scolded by Will and Grace. The camera routinely cuts to Will and Grace for reaction shots, which typically involve a shaking of the head or rolling of the eyes to demonstrate that Jack is not to be taken seriously.

Jack's character is more complicated than this, though, because of the possibility that he can be read as camp. "This classic gay (male) strategy of subversion is camp—an ironic stance toward the straight world rooted in a gay sensibility" (Gross, 1989, p. 143). Therefore, Jack's exaggerated behavior could be read as a critique of mainstream culture. However, as John Fiske (1987) argues, jokes function to open up the meaning of a text "through a collision of discourses" (p. 87). The script of *Will & Grace* cannot control the meaning that audiences make of jokes about Jack's performances. So, while Jack is a likable character who provides an alternative to heterosexual masculinity, the polysemic nature of joking allows audiences to either laugh *with* Jack or *at* jack. In fact, this ambiguity of meaning is necessary in a primetime television text attempting to reach a large audience.[8] And because Jack's performance of gayness fits within a historical framework of media images that make homosexuality the focus of humor, his character can also be read as upholding heterosexism. When the studio audience roars as Will refers to Jack as "Mrs. Jack McFarland," the pleasure comes from an understanding of the "sissy," or the "queen." If viewers agree to position themselves in a way that recognizes these stereotypes of gay men, they get the payoff—the laugh and the pleasure it brings.

Jack and Karen provide much of the humor on *Will & Grace* and are allowed to do and say things the more palatable main characters aren't.

This is due, in large part, to their positions within the narrative structure of the sitcom. As "children" or "buffoons," Jack and Karen can say and do as they please because their positioning within the narrative structure indicates that they are not to be taken seriously.

# THE PERSONAL, NOT THE POLITICAL

Perhaps the most limiting convention of the situation comedy, and one that also makes it a safe space for the exploration of controversial topics, is the genre's emphasis on interpersonal relationships between characters rather than their relationship to the outside world. The effect of this in *Will & Grace* is to depoliticize gayness in two important ways. First, when the program explicitly deals with the question of sexuality, it falls back on the convention of treating homosexuality as a problem, especially for straight characters in the narrative. Second, the emphasis on interpersonal relationships prevents a consideration of gay politics and leads to a failure to acknowledge the social consequences of gay and lesbian persons living in our heterosexual culture. Dow (2001) recently argued that these were particular pitfalls of the way homosexuality was dealt with in *Will & Grace*'s predecessor sitcom, *Ellen*.

Stories that specifically confront the issue of homosexuality frequently do so through the common cultural convention of presenting it primarily as a problem for the heterosexual characters (Dow, 2001; Fejes & Petrick, 1993; Gross, 1989). This is the case in *Will & Grace*, where Grace is the one who must deal with the problems raised by Will's sexuality. A particularly poignant example of this comes during the coming-out episode (Greenstein & Burrows, 2000). What might have been a story exploring the range of emotions that accompany this experience, the story revolves around Grace's reaction to Will's revelation and her pain. This is

indicated right from the beginning of the episode when the four characters, out for dinner, encounter a woman at a bar upset because of relationship problems with her boyfriend. The group quickly realizes that this is because her boyfriend is gay. To help her figure this out, Will and Grace recount their own experience, which is told in a series of flashbacks to their college years, when they were dating. Feeling hopeful about their future together, Grace invites Will home for Thanksgiving, hoping that they will finally consummate their relationship. While trying to get Will to kiss her in bed, Will stalls by mistakenly proposing marriage to her, forcing himself to come out to her before she begins planning their future together. This leads to Grace's breakdown and estrangement from Will. Later in the episode, Grace learns that during the year that they didn't speak, Will slept with another woman, just to make sure that he wasn't sexually attracted to the opposite sex. Feeling hurt, she leaves, forcing Will to follow her, and to comfort her and reassure her that he loves her. Thus, the episode doesn't deal with the social consequences that Will faced by admitting his homosexuality. Instead, it frames Will's coming out as a decision for which Grace paid the consequence.

Homosexuality is likewise posed as a particular burden for Grace in the episode where Will breaks off his relationship with Matt due to Matt's refusal to come out of the closet in his workplace (Kohan, Mutchnick, & Burrows, 2001). The voice for social change in this episode is Grace's, but her voice says that social change is the personal responsibility of gays and lesbians, not of the larger society. Throughout this episode it is Grace who advises that Will end the relationship, insisting that he live an honest and open life and, by inference, insisting that all gay persons should do so. The episode begins with Will watching Matt cover a basketball game on television. When he goes down to the stadium to see Matt after the game, he meets Matt's boss. Matt introduces Will as his brother, thus indicating his desire to not reveal his sexual preference to his employers. Will is extremely angry, and when he tells Grace, she tells him to break up with him. When WIll reports his conversation to Grace, he states the following: "I just said I'm an out and proud gay man. I'm not about to go back in the closet for the sake of relationship." Grace responds with emphasis, "Oh, that is so good! And it's so right! We're here, we're queer and he getter get used to it [waving a spoon above her head]." Then Will sheepishly admits to not breaking off the relationship because Matt "said he likes me." This scene clearly indicates that Grace is more willing to stick by her guns than is Will.

Later, Will invites Grace to join him and Matt at an out-of-the-way fish restaurant in Queens where he and Matt can be safe from being recognized, and though she shows up at the restaurant, she refuses to join them, explaining that "I've thought about it and I cannot in good conscience have dinner with you two, I'm not going to be a party to your lie." While she waits for her "killer onion blossom" Will attempts to return to his dinner with Matt, but is distracted by Grace's disapproving looks. When he confronts her about it, she responds, "Look, if you're feeling guilty because you're compromising everything you believe in, that's your thing. Don't put that on me. I'm just standing here thinking about clam strips, which is moot because they're all out. Out and Proud [smug look]."

Will again attempts to return to his dinner with Matt, only this time they are interrupted by Matt's homophobic boss, Harry. Harry tells Matt that he has spent the day fighting rumors that Matt is gay, to which Matt sheepishly responds that "the idea of two guys together...creeps me out." Will boldly response, "I think two guys together is hot." Following the charade that he is Matt's brother, Will "comes out" to Matt and Harry and, addressing Matt, says "I can't go on lying. I know I said I would and I'm sorry, but I can't. The only way I know how to be in a relationship with you, [looking at Harry] *brother,* is if we are open and honest. Those are the terms. Can you accept that?" Grace applauds Will's adamant stance.

The "lesson" of this episode is that gay men should live their lives out of the closet. The "problem" is that it is his "straight" friend Grace who has to remind him of this. It is Grace—an unmarked, middle-upper-class, white, heterosexual woman—who seems to suffer the burden or consequences of Will's sexuality and his choice of disclosing it or not. Drawing on the cultural convention of treating homosexuality as a personal rather than political issue, *Will & Grace* also does not take into account the social consequences of a gay man outing himself in a potentially homophobic profession.[9] It assumes a "post-gay" rights environment in which publicly acknowledging one's homosexuality carries no social consequences and denies that this marking matters in the lives of gays and lesbians. This episode implicitly lets the audience know that Harry's homophobia is wrong, but it also suggests that Harry's views are personal, rather than cultural, while Matt's decision not to come out on the job is similarly treated as a personal failure rather than as a painful decision reflecting the realities of our heteronormative culture.

## CONCLUSION

*Will & Grace* is a potentially subversive program that portrays male homosexuality in a way that many different audiences can identify with, appreciate, and enjoy. One of the program's co-creators, David Kohan, is very open about the fact that *Will & Grace* is an attempt to reach a wide demographic and not to educate the American public about gay life:

> We never really set out to make a *gay* show...we were just trying to come up with something original, to mine a dynamic that hadn't already been mined on TV. And we came up with the idea of a gay man and his relationship with a straight woman. It was something we hadn't seen on TV

before, a fresh approach to romantic comedy. (Svetkey, 2000, p. 28)

When considered from the perspective of visibility, this "fresh approach" represents an important shift in popular culture representations of homosexuality. By placing an out gay man, who is comfortable with his sexuality, as the star of a primetime broadcast television series, *Will & Grace* presents the idea of social acceptance of gays and lesbians as a positive one. It is important to recognize that it is popular culture conventions that help make gay and lesbian characters palatable for a mainstream audience, thus creating the space for increased media visibility of gays and lesbians.

Yet visibility alone cannot serve as the framework from which to evaluate the program. As Bonnie Dow (2001) argued regarding *Ellen*, visibility on the television screen does not necessarily signal a shift in dominant social attitudes towards gays and lesbians. After all, as the program's creators and other have admitted, the pairing of a gay man and straight woman at the center of a narrative has as much to do with the exhaustion of the delayed consummation narrative on television series than with any attempts to contribute to social acceptance of gays and lesbians. It is important to remember that visibility often comes with the price of having to conform to or be made sense of within dominant cultural discourses (Dow, 2001; Sedgewick, 1990; Warner, 1993). To become visible is to enter into a dominant discourse that marks the boundaries of normalcy—which in contemporary U.S. society means hetero-normalcy. As this paper has argued, in the case of *Will & Grace*, the representation of gayness enters the realm of heteronormativity through its reliance on certain popular culture conventions that historically have reinforced, at the least, heterosexism and, at worst, homophobia. *Will & Grace* makes homosexuality safe for broadcast television audiences by framing its characters within the familiar popular culture convention that equates gayness with a lack of masculinity and through

the familiar situation comedy genre conventions of romantic comedy and delayed consummation, infantilization, and an emphasis on characters' interpersonal relationships rather than the characters' connections to the larger social world. Taken together, these conventions work to confine homosexuality within its paradoxical position in dominant heteronormative discourses; homosexuality can only be represented through heterosexist categories and language, while at the same time it is marked as a deviation from the norm.

Regardless of the positive intentions of the program's producers and actors, and regardless of viewers' capacity for multiple readings of the text, these conventions, combined with the weight of the dominant discourse of heteronormativity, set boundaries for the mainsteam representation of male homosexuality. Such conventions guide, but do not wholly determine, viewers' expectations of and experiences with popular culture texts. For the mainstream audience, *Will & Grace* offers a potential glimpse into a world with which many viewers might not have first-hand experience. For gay audiences the program offers a space for identification and self-construction. However, the conventional emphasis on interpersonal relationships and personal responsibility possibly encourages straight audiences to believe that we have entered a "post-gay" period in which the struggle for gay rights has already been won and that an individual's personal rejection of homophobic attitudes equals the improved social standing of sexual minorities. Viewers are congratulated for their acceptance of gays and lesbians, but without any real consideration of the compromised lives of gays and lesbians within our heteronormative culture. This possibility is one that media critics should be attendant to in their research on reception of television programs featuring gay and lesbian characters.

As gay characters become more common on broadcast and cable television, it will be tempting to equate this increased visibility with social acceptance and valuation of gays and lesbians.

Therefore, media critics need to continually interrogate the assumption that a quantitative increase in gay representations (increased visibility) signals a qualitative change in representational practices. Qualitative challenges to current representational conventions, which have the power to call into question normative cultural ideas, serve as a more powerful indication of and contribution to social change. Instead of looking at numbers as a sign of social progress, critics should look for ways in which gays and lesbians are represented in popular culture texts targeted to a broad audience, and how such representations conform to and challenge normative structures of our heterosexist society. As the case of *Will & Grace* suggests, the mere presence of gay characters on broadcast television, even in leading roles, does not necessarily represent a challenge to the dominant norms of U.S. culture.

## NOTES

1. For a more extensive history of the representations of gays and lesbians on television, see Dow (2001) and Fejes & Petrick (1993).

2. We use the word "mainstream" here with some caution. We understand that the proliferation of cable channels in the 1990s ushered in an age of narrowcasting, in which networks target particular demographics, especially those that are most desirable to advertisers. This shift ended the days when the majority of the U.S. population tuned into one of only three networks. NBC targets *Will & Grace* to an audience of young, educated professionals, of whom most are presumably straight. Thus, the audience for *Will & Grace* is not necessarily a large portion of the U.S. public. However, we believe that the four major networks continue to symbolically represent the "mainstream" of U.S. culture. The appearance of previously marginalized representations on broadcast television ("the big four") is considered by many to indicate movement of certain ideas into this "mainstream," as demonstrated by popular press television critics' use of the term (Gairola, 2001).

3. Heteronormativity refers to the discourses and practices by which heterosexuality is constituted as the natural and compulsory norm, against which homosexuality is defined as its binary, and hence negative, opposite (see Butler, 1991, 1993a,b; De Lauretis, 1984, 1991; Foucault, 1978; Warner 1993).

4. Feminist media scholars, embracing performative theory, have worked to move beyond analysis of stereotyped characters in narratives and models in advertising that look for distortions in representation of women. van Zoonen (1994) recognizes the problematic nature of simply arguing against stereotypes: "Before media could translate more realistic images of women, it would be necessary to define incontrovertibly what the reality about women is" (p. 31). That is to say, in rejecting an essentialist model of gender, it is an impossible task to ascertain which representations are "truer" or "more authentic" than others. This would be an equally impossible project for determining "realistic" images of lesbian, gay, bisexual or transgendered people.

5. Thank you to Bonnie Dow and the two anonymous reviewers for pointing out this reading of Will and Jack's relationship.

6. An important project for queer theorists has been a thoroughgoing critique of the ways in which heterosexual norms are used to make sense of and define gay and lesbian categories and experiences. Warner (1993) writes that a particular pitfall of theorizing queer sexuality is that the theoretical language in questions can specify sexual identities only in ways that produce the ideology of heterosexual society. Bonnie Dow (2001) writes that "the romantic narrative of autonomy and liberation that undergirds the rhetoric of *Ellen* allows it to be celebrated by gays and straights alike. For many gays, the fiction of personal authenticity and control provides psychological comfort in a deeply homophobic culture; for sympathetic straights, this narrative facilitates blindness toward the heterosexism and homophobia in which they are complicit and from which they benefit."

7. Grace talks explicitly about her sexual relationships with men, and viewers have seen her in bed with at least one of her boyfriends.

8. Norma Schulman (1995) found the success of *In Living Color* (a program produced by, written by, and primarily performed by blacks) came not simply from its camp humor about race relations in America, but from its ambiguity, which "gives it bimodal appeal—a quality deemed all important in a commercial medium for whom the aggregate minority viewing audience is insufficient in itself to garner the kind of ratings that yield substantial revenue" (p. 438).

9. Bonnie Dow convincingly argues *Ellen* used the same kinds of strategies in dealing with the possible political consequences of her "coming out." In fact, when it comes to explicitly dealing with the relationship between homosexuality and the broader political culture, *Will & Grace* clearly follows the conventions that were used in *Ellen*.

# REFERENCES

Barr, A (Writer) and Burrows, J. (Director). (2001). Coffee & commitment. [Television series episode]. In D. Kohan, M. Mutchnick, & J. Burrows (Producers), *Will & Grace*, Studio City, CA: KoMut Entertainment.

Butler, J. (1991). Imitation and gender insubordination. In D. Fuss (Ed.), *Inside/out: Lesbian theories, gay theories*. (pp. 13–31). London: Routledge

Butler, J. (1993a). *Bodies that matter: On the discursive limits of sex*. New York: Routledge.

Butler, J. (1993b). Critically queer. *GLO: A Journal of Lesbian and Gay Studies, 1*, 270–282.

de Lauretis, T. (1984). *Alice doesn't: Feminism, semiotics, cinema*. Bloomington, IN: Indiana University Press.

de Lauretis, T. (1991). Queer theory: Lesbian and gay sexualities. *Differences: A Journal of Feminist Cultural Studies, 3*(2), iii–xviii.

Dow, B. (2001). *Ellen*, television, and the politics of gay and lesbian visibility. *Critical Studies in Media Communication, 18*, 123–140.

Epstein, R., & Friedman, J. (Producers/Writers). (1996). [Videocassette]. Tri-Star Home Video.

Fejes, F. (2000). Making a gay masculinity. *Critical Studies in Media Communication, 17*, 113–116.

Fejes, F., & Petrich, K. (1993). Invisibility and heterosexism: Lesbians, gays and the media. *Critical Studies in Mass Communication, 10*, 396–422.

Fiske, J. (1987). *Television culture*. London: Methuen.

Foucault, M. (1978). *The history of sexuality: An introduction, volume 1*. New York: Random House.

Frankel, D. (2000, April 3). It's Dharma vs. Grace. *Media Week*, 6.

Gairola, R. (2000). *Will & Grace:* Watching with ambivalence. *PopMatters.com*. Retrieved August 8, 2001 from http://www.popmatters.com/tv/reviews/w/will-and-grace.html.

Gay & Lesbian Alliance Against Defamation. (1998). *Will & Grace come out on Monday*. Retrieved November 15, 2000 from http://www.glaad.org/org/publications/alerts/index.html.

Gay & Lesbian Alliance Against Defamation. (2000). *The 2000–2001 Television Season: Leading Roles from the World Wide Web*. Retrieved November 15, 2000 from http://www.glaad.org/org/projects/tv/index.html.

George, R. (2001, July 23). The 28th amendment. *National Review*, 32.

Gray, H. (1994). Television, black Americans, and the American dream. In H. Newcomb (Ed.), *Television: The critical view* (pp. 176–187). New York: Oxford.

Greenstein, J. (Writer) and Burrows, J. (Director). (2000). Lows in the mid-eighties. [Television series episode]. In D. Kohan, M. Mutchnick, & J. Burrows (Producers), *Will & Grace*, Studio City, CA: KoMut Entertainment.

Gross, L. (1989). Out of the mainstream: Sexual minorities and the mass media. In E. Seiter, et al. (Eds.), *Remote control: Television, audiences, and cultural power* (pp. 130–149). London: Routledge.

Holleran, A. (2000). The alpha queen. *Gay and Lesbian Review*, 65.

Jacobs, A. (1998, October 23). When gay men happen to straight women. *Entertainment Weekly*. Retrieved August 9, 2001 from http://www.ew.com.

Kohan, D., & Mutchnick, M. (Writers) and Burrows, J. (Director). (2000). New Will city. [Television series episode]. In D. Kohan, M. Mutchnick, & J. Burrows (Producers), *Will & Grace*, Studio City, CA: KoMut Entertainment.

Kohan, D., & Mutchnick, M. (Writers) and Burrows, J. (Director). (2001). Brothers, A Love Story. [Television series episode]. In D. Kohan, M. Mutchnick, & J. Burrows (Producers), *Will & Grace*, Studio City, CA: KoMut Entertainment.

Lewis, J. (1991). *The ideological octopus*. New York: Routledge.

MacDonald, J. F. (1979). *"Don't touch that dial!"*. Chicago: Nelson-Hall.

Newcomb, H. (1974). *TV: The most popular art*. Garden City, NJ: Anchor Press.

NBC. (2000). Will & Grace: *About the show*. Retrieved November 15, 2000 from http://affiliate.nbci.com/LMOID/bb/fd/0,946,-0-2153,00.html.

Palmer, K. (Writer) and Burrows, J. (Director). (2000). Gypsies, tramps, and weed. [Television series episode]. In D. Kohan, M. Mutchnick, & J. Burrows (Producers), *Will & Grace*, Studio City, CA: KoMut Entertainment.

Palmer, K. (Writer) and Burrows, J. (Director). (2001). Swimming pools...movie stars. [Television series episode]. In D. Kohan, M. Mutchnick, & J. Burrows (Producers), *Will & Grace*, Studio City, CA: KoMut Entertainment.

Poust, T., & Kinally, J. (Writers) and Burrows, J. (Director). (2001). Crazy in love. [Television series episode]. In D. Kohan, M. Mutchnick, & J. Burrows (Producers), *Will & Grace*, Studio City, CA: KoMut Entertainment.

Rosenstock, R. (Writer) and Burrows, J. (Director). (2000). Love plus one. [Television series episode]. In D. Kohan, M. Mutchnick, & J. Burrows (Producers), *Will & Grace*, Studio City, CA: KoMut Entertainment.

Russo, V. (1985). *The celluloid closet: Homosexuality in the movies*. New York: Harper & Row, Publishers.

Russo, V. (1996). *The celluloid closet*. [Videocassette]. Tri-Star Home Video.

Sedgwick, E. K. (1990). *Epistemology of the closet*. Berkeley, CA: University of California Press.

Schulman, N. M. (1995). Laughing across the color barrier: *In Living Color*. In G. Dines and J. Humez (Eds.), *Gender, race, and class in media: A text-reader*. Thousand Oaks, CA: Sage.

Scodari, C. (1995). Possession, attraction, and the thrill of the case: Gendered myth making in film and television comedy of the sexes. *Critical Studies in Mass Communication, 12,* 23–29.

Sullivan, R. (December 1998). Dull and duller: After *Ellen,* gay characters are still a novelty. *The Boston Phoenix*. Retrieved August 8, 2001 from http://www.bostonphoenix.com/archive/1in10/98/12/TELEVISION.html.

Svetkey, B. (2000, October 6). Is your TV set gay? *Entertainment Weekly,* 24–28.

van Zoonen, L. (1994). *Feminist media studies*. London: Sage Publications.

Warner, M. (1993). *Fear of a queer planet*. Minneapolis, MN: University of Minnesota Press.

Wyatt, D. (2000). *Gay/lesbian/bisexual television characters*. Retrieved November 15, 2000 from http://home.cc.umanitoba.ca/~wyatt/tv-characters.html.

# Introduction to Elana Levine's "Toward a Paradigm for Media Production Research: Behind the Scenes at *General Hospital*"

Elana Levine was a Ph.D. candidate in the Department of Communication Arts at the University of Wisconsin at Madison when she wrote this piece examining the dearth of media production research under the paradigm of what is commonly called cultural studies. Influenced by such scholars as Stuart Hall, Richard Johnson, and Muriel Cantor, Levine argues for the need to examine how the demands of production itself shape and control the authority and content of popular culture and especially television programming. What she presents are five provisional categories for scholarly research plus a remarkable in-depth analysis of the production process for the contemporary soap opera and the cultural implications of that procedure on the viewing audience. Important to the area of media production research, Levine's work is based on a solid academic underpinning coupled with two weeks of field service as an outside observer on the popular soap opera *General Hospital*, where she saw firsthand how these processes impact on media content.

# Toward a Paradigm for Media Production Research: Behind the Scenes at *General Hospital*

Cultural studies of media have made significant contributions to our understanding of the social and political implications of mediated representation and the contextually-dependent meanings made of media by their audience members. The study of media production, however, has received much less attention from cultural studies scholars. This gap in research is *not* intrinsic to the field's models of cultural circulation. In fact, models such as those provided by Stuart Hall (1980) and Richard Johnson (1986/87) explicitly call for attention to cultural production and for the integration of production analyses and studies of texts, audiences, and contextual influences. In this essay, I argue that cultural studies scholarship can be usefully expanded and nuanced both by taking on more production-centered research and by drawing upon the media production scholarship of those working under other theoretical and methodological perspectives (Gans, 1979; Tuchman, 1979; Cantor, 1971; Cantor & Cantor, 1992). The development of theoretically and methodologically rigorous and sophisticated approaches to production studies can offer cultural studies researchers, as well as communications scholars working within other paradigms, new insights and heretofore unrecognized connections between media production, media texts, media audiences, and the social contexts within which they circulate. To demonstrate the benefits of such a broadened strategy, I here analyze the production process of *General Hospital*, a U.S. broadcast television network daytime soap opera, and suggest ways in which production factors relate to questions about texts, audiences, and social contexts.

The cultural studies bias toward analyses of texts and audiences over production has existed to varying degrees throughout the field's studies of media. Inspired by Stuart Hall's (1980) encoding/decoding model, various cultural studies projects of the early and mid-1980s did include industrial analyses along with their presentations of audience readings. But because the most revelatory aspect of Hall's model was its recognition of contextually-influenced variability in audience decoding, much of the scholarship in its wake focused disproportionately on audiences over industries. Studies of soap operas, including those by Hobson (1982), Ang (1982), and Brown (1994), have exemplified this trend, examining such issues as the gendered address of the soap opera text, the rewards and costs of soap viewing, and the negotiations audiences make with the raced, classed, and gendered norms of both the soap world and the social world within which soap viewing occurs.

This text- and audience-centered bias has understandable origins in cultural studies history. Founded, at least in part, as a reaction against economically determinist interpretations of commercial culture, cultural studies has logically emphasized the resistive power of audience readings over the constraining forces of production. At the same time, an ongoing debate between political economy and cultural studies has

From *Critical Studies in Media Communications, Vol. 18, No. 1, March 2001* by Elana Levine. Copyright © 2001 by the National Communication Association. Reprinted by permission.

kept production-centered scholarship largely in the hands of political economists, where it serves as a reliable marker of difference from their less classically marxist cousins.[1] With production-oriented scholarship practiced for so long by those more interested in the circulation of money than the circulation of meaning, it has been difficult for cultural studies scholars to connect production practices to the questions of discourse and power (aside from economic power) that the field most frequently addresses. While cultural scholars readily admit that capital plays a chief role in commercial media production, they tend to stop their thinking there, failing to look for the roles of discourse, knowledge, and daily practice in cultural production.

In attempting to broaden the cultural studies approach to media along such lines, this essay offers a case study of soap opera production and thereby puts Richard Johnson's (1986/87) circuit of culture model into practice. Johnson's model poses a mutually influential relationship between production, texts, audiences, and contexts. To get at this relationship, he urges a two-pronged analysis of production. The examination of material means and the capitalist organization of labor are one prong, but Johnson suggests that production scholarship should also engage in exploring a range of *cultural* elements, such as rules of language and discourse and classed, raced, and gendered struggles over these rules as they occur within the production sphere (p. 55). Having advocated this two-pronged analysis of the production process itself, Johnson also suggests two means of relating production to the other spheres of cultural circulation. First, he argues for the examination of production moments as distinct and particular, as specific acts, not just general conditions. Secondly, and at first glance contradictorily, he argues for a *lack* of distinction between production, texts, and audiences. He urges, for example, careful analysis of the "productive" elements in cultural *consumption*, thereby retaining the cultural studies insistence upon active audiencehood (p. 57–58). Instead of negat-

ing his call for the distinctiveness of production, this second suggestion avoids economic determinism while remaining materially grounded in audience experience and production practice.

How the various aspects of the production process contribute to texts and shape possibilities for audience readings are the focus of the rest of this essay. I here categorize, describe, and analyze five major factors that shape a particular kind of cultural production, U.S. broadcast network television production. Even more narrowly, I examine the production of one particular television soap opera. The five categories I outline—production constraints, the production environment, production routines and practices, the production of characters and stories, and the role of the audience in production—have grown out of interviews and observations I conducted on-site at the *General Hospital* studio. I spent two weeks of August 1997 on the set, in the control booth, and around the offices of the show. I chose this particular program largely because I had spent the last sixteen years as a devoted viewer and thus had an immense backlog of information about its storylines, style, and personnel. I gained access by writing a letter to the executive producer, explaining my academic project and my interest in *General Hospital*. The coordinating producer called me months later and invited me to visit. The ease with which these arrangements were made illustrates the potential accessibility of commercial production to interested scholars. The ease with which a long-time fan was able to become a critical researcher and a critical researcher was able to turn back into a long-time (albeit somewhat more jaded) fan has helped me to analyze the similarities and differences between audience experience and the production world in ways unavailable to the more traditionally "objective" researcher. While the resulting analysis should offer useful insights to those interested in television soap opera, my aim here is also to provide a model for further research of television production practices, and possibly even for other forms of commercial culture.

## PRODUCTION CONSTRAINTS

This first area of cultural production focuses on the production history and constraints of *General Hospital* in order to better understand the way the production process is shaped by its own background. While production as a whole is seen as a limiting or constraining factor in theories of media culture, I here illustrate some of the large-scale constraints that shape not only the resultant text, but the rest of the production process, as well. While mainly economic in origin, these large-scale constraints also have cultural impact. They influence the environment within which employees work and the routines and practices they follow, as subsequent categories will demonstrate. This section focuses on the large-scale constraints of ownership structure, the program's own production history, and the status of soaps in the contemporary television industry. While constraints can be imposed by the histories and specificities of the medium, the genre, the show, and the people who create it, as well, the three constraints I touch on here were particularly salient during my research trip and seem particularly formative to *General Hospital.*

While most U.S. broadcast network television programming is produced by independent production companies that license their products to networks for a fee, *General Hospital* is wholly owned and produced by ABC/Disney itself. While all of ABC's soap operas are network-owned, they are the only one of the three major networks with that arrangement. As Joe Montrone (personal communication, August 20, 1997), ABC executive in charge of daytime production for the west coast explained, "Technically, everybody on the show is an employee of ours, whether they're contracted, daily hire, or full staff with benefits. They all get an ABC paycheck." Because of this, there is intense network involvement at every level, with ABC's west coast executive in charge of daytime programming attending weekly story meetings between the executive producer and head writers, ABC Daytime publicity handling media relations, and ABC network offices in New York holding the budgetary purse strings. As a result, when network policies forbid guns to be held directly to characters' heads or restrict the explicitness of sex scenes, the show's staff sometimes feels creatively constrained. Yet the backing of ABC and its parent company, Disney, has benefitted the show by providing a degree of financial security less likely for a soap owned by an independent production company. According to one *GH* staff member who had previously worked at a soap not owned by its network, *General Hospital* has larger budgets for sets, wardrobe, and other such necessities than does this other soap because the production company owning the other show is unwilling (or unable) to spend as much, given its smaller size.

The show's own history also affects its production, setting it apart from even the other ABC-owned soaps. The enormous success of *General Hospital* in the early 1980s not only changed the soap opera industry, but earned *GH* a certain status with its network from which it still benefits today. According to coordinating producer Marty Vagts (personal communication, August 12, 1997):

> What we heard in those days was that ABC Daytime…was dropping 67% of the network profits. Right to the bottom line. We were clearing 67%.… And the pack was led by *General Hospital.* It was a giant cash cow.… And *General Hospital* had the ability to go to the well, the network well, and say that we needed a prop budget of X number of dollars or we needed a scenery [budget] of X number of dollars and we would get it. The other shows did not have that ability.

The material benefits the show received during the 1980s continue to pay off in substantial back-stocks of wardrobe, sets, and props; in the contractually secured earnings of star performers; and in the current studio space itself, which was constructed specifically for the show in the late 1980s and is substantially larger than the studios for ABC's New York-based soaps. Such historically earned perks set *GH* apart from other soaps, allowing it an opulence that is increasingly rare in the financially strained soap industry of the 1990s and 2000s.

Soaps are no longer the "cash cows" they once were for the broadcast networks. The soap opera audience, at least as it is measured by Nielsen, has shrunk drastically since the 1980s, a change attributable to the increasingly fractured television marketplace and the growing numbers of women in the workforce. Both of these trends have eroded the industry's formerly solid base of housewife viewers and have kept the genre from attracting newer, younger audiences, who, 20 years ago, might have begun watching with their mothers or grandmothers (Parney and Mason, 2000, p. 13). Since the early 1990s, soaps have lost more than 20 million daily viewers, or about 25% of their total audience (Johnson, 1999, p. 1E; McFadden, 1999, p. D1). As a result, today's highest-rated soap hovers around a 7.2 rating while the lowest-rated ones survive on ratings in the 2.0 range. In August 1997, at the time of this study, *General Hospital* floated in the middle of this range, rating a 4.6, at least 6 to 8 million viewers less than in the early and mid-1980s. As a consequence, ABC and the other networks are making less and less money on these productions, resulting in decreased budgets for the shows. One specific result has been the virtual elimination of remote location shooting, a practice *GH* once engaged in up to seven times a year. Another has been a reduction in the show's clothing budget. According to costume designer Bob Miller (personal communication, August 20, 1997), "Our budget next year will probably be the same budget that we had in 1986. And clothing has probably tripled [in cost]."

As with any kind of constraints, the show's staff works to maintain a certain level of quality within these budgetary limits. For example, the wardrobe department sells used clothing to a specialized television and film resale shop, returning $70,000 to their budget from one year of these proceeds. Miller and co-designer Steve Howard make 3 or 4 wholesale shopping trips to New York design houses each year, purchasing high-fashion clothing a season in advance at much-reduced prices. Part of the reason they are able to do this is Miller's 10 year employment history with the show, a background that has provided him with a strong sense of the clothing many characters will need. But the wardrobe department's ability to reduce costs in this way is also assisted by the fact that, "Our gals are in a size range from 0–2 to 6 mainly" (B. Miller, personal communication, August 20, 1997). The clothing they purchase will fit, or else can be slightly altered to fit, a number of different actresses. Even the body types of performers shape the production process, their similar, extremely small, sizes allowing advance, wholesale wardrobe shopping that saves money and establishes a high-fashion, designer look.

This variety of physical and fiscal production constraints illustrates just a few of the distinctive shaping factors that media scholars might consider in analyses of television production. Though production is frequently understood as limiting or constraining texts and readings, these examples point to the constraints within such constraints. The limits of commercial culture are more complicated than simple profit motivation or the exploitation of workers. They can affect studio size and body size, the scope of the on-screen world and the scope of femininity. An understanding of such factors not only informs the interpretation of texts, but helps us to comprehend the priorities of capitalism, the imperatives of the television medium, and the reasons behind the products the medium offers. Denaturalizing the television world in these ways is the first step to not only knowing that world, but understanding the particular ways its power is shaped and its money and meanings are circulated.

# PRODUCTION ENVIRONMENT

Large-scale industrial factors, and the specific production details through which they have an impact, necessarily constrain the rest of the production process, even the environment in which ABC's employees work. Exploring this environment can uncover relevant economic determinants, such as the role of labor unions in the production process. But it can also provide insight to the cultural issues at stake within production situations. Hierarchies of gender and institutional positioning, for example, operate in *General Hospital* production and affect production routines and practices, as well as the television narrative constructed through the work process. Two aspects of the production environment that best bring to light these economically and culturally shaped processes are the overall workplace milieu and the organizational hierarchy.

Though the *General Hospital* work environment functions like any other television production in may ways, it is significantly different, as is any soap, because of the continuous, unending nature of the work. With preemptions no more than one or two times a year and production running only 2 to 3 weeks in advance of airing, the staff must produce an entire episode each day of the week. Thus, every task must be executed as efficiently as possible. The *General Hospital* studio must constantly negotiate high-level efficiency, technological intricacy, and creative selectivity. The tenuous blend of a tight production schedule and the emotionally-charged material endemic to soap operas escalates the tensions already present in any dramatic production.

These contradictory working conditions play out in the weekly production meetings, held one week in advance of the actual production. Here, issues up for discussion range from the kind of undergarments needed for a scene where a character disrobes to the maneuverability of the cameras in a new set. The meetings are a care-fully balanced combination of practical or technical details and creative speculation on character motivation and story progression. While the director, who coordinates discussion of his or her particular episode, tends to work on the side of the practical and technical, questions of character motivation inevitably intervene, such as how vitally important it is for the abandoned-at-the-altar Brenda, now in a precarious emotional state, to rid herself of all remnants of her wedding, even her dress. This character motivation then requires practical back-up, as in the decision to slightly re-design Brenda's wedding gown to cover the undergarments she will wear as she sheds the dress in her hurt and angry post-wedding scene.

These tensions and their practical repercussions continue in daily production. While the director must be concerned with technical details of camera placement, lighting, and sound, he or she is also responsible for imparting performance notes to the actors. While these duties are no different than those of any television director, the pace at which the soap opera director must work, shooting 25–30 "items," or scene segments, per day, makes concerted attention to all these factors impossible. As such, the line producer (a duty rotated among 3 of the show's producers) gives the director notes on all these aspects throughout the shoot, though she tends to comment most often on aesthetic and creative issues over technical ones. While performance notes often originate with the producer, they are usually relayed by the director or through the floor manager at the director's request. The director is also freed from attending too closely to performance because the show has an acting coach on staff who works with the actors off-set or confers with the line producer and director in the control booth.

The distinctions in duty between the director and the line producer operate as gendered distinctions as well as efficiency-motivated time-savers. While all of the *GH* line producers are women and most of the directors are men, the gendering of their duties is not determined by the workers who fill the roles. In the *GH* production world, bodily aesthetics, questions of emotion, and delicate personnel issues are distinguished from technical matters and time constraints. The socially feminized aspects of production remain the exclusive domain of the producers and other "artistic" departments, while the more masculinized aspects are less selectively assigned. While the show certainly employs technical specialists in areas such as lighting and editing, the producers can and do dictate decisions in these areas. But technical personnel, often including the directors, remain far removed from the producers' reign over the more feminized concerns. For example, when an actress known for wanting excessive rehearsal time slowed down a scene with questions about character motivation, the technical director discounted her concerns, commenting, "That's not our business; that's not what we're here for," to his cohorts in the control booth. The production staff surrounding him agreed, emphasizing their prioritization of efficiency above all else. The line producer handled the actress.

The divisions in duty and agenda are also matters of positioning within the organizational hierarchy. Because the socially feminized areas are handled by those highest in the institutional ranks, the feminine is distinguished, but not necessarily disempowered, in this production environment. The producers have authority over so many areas, and particularly more delicate ones like talent relations, because of their prominent institutional status. Gendered distinctions meet organizational ones and result in the validation of socially feminized concerns. As the exasperation with the actress' demands suggests, resistance to such concerns is also a factor, be it in the name of efficiency, technology, or masculinized disinterest (such as when crew members watched broadcast feeds of golf matches on their camera viewfinders during particularly time-consuming scenes). Certainly, such differences in duty and agenda result from the soap opera's dual imperatives of cost- and time-efficient production and emotionally intense,

time-consuming drama. But the fact that these economically motivated constraints become distinguishable elements with gendered overtones suggests that the production environment is as culturally shaped as it is economically determined.

The production environment is also shaped by those personnel less visible in the daily work process. The writing staff is one of those nearly invisible influences. During my visit, it was clear that the current head writing team was temporary, as the show worked through complicated contractual negotiations to re-hire a former, well-regarded head writer. Because the current head writers, as well as their most recent predecessors, lived in New York, and the rest of the writing team worked out of their homes, the writers held a mysterious, and somewhat revered, place within the organizational hierarchy.[2] The writers, at least according to assistant David Goldschmid (personal communication, August 11, 1997), often feel isolated from the rest of the show and are hungry for information on how their work is received in-house. The only people in-house who have contact with them are the writers' assistants, the executive producer, and the network programming executive, illustrating the physical and conceptual isolation of soap writers from the activities on the set and in the control booth.

The executive producer and the network programming executive, who hold the highest positions within the organizational hierarchy, were also physically removed from daily production. Their remove was only partial, however, as they would watch the on-set action from monitors in their offices and frequently call the line producer in the control booth with comments and suggestions. While many employees, particularly actors, claimed that executive producer Wendy Riche has an "open door" policy and that they are always welcome to speak with her about storylines and their characters, her physical door was rarely open, her physical presence rarely visible, and any physical contact with her filtered through her two protective assistants. Yet the fact that I would often be referred to her to answer my questions illustrated her controlling involvement in nearly all aspects of the work process. The isolation of Riche and the writers from the rest of production (and from me as researcher, for that matter) was telling of the institutional hierarchy and of the physical and experiential distance between high-level decision-making and daily production. Those highest in the institutional hierarchy were most removed from daily production, though they controlled it in ways unobservable to most employees.

The production environment and its complicated tensions of efficiency and creativity, hands-on labor and removed, hierarchical control, demonstrate that struggles in soap opera production occur along cultural as well as economic lines, between duties and agendas distinguished and hierarchized by gender and institutional positioning, as well as by the larger-scale constraints of ownership structure, production history, and industrial trends. All of these constraints can affect the program they're meant to produce by determining the time and attention paid to performances, the allocation of budget to salaries or equipment or production elements like sets and wardrobe, and the shifts in meaning or emphasis as the production passes through the hands of network executives, executive producer, writers, line producers, actors, and production staff and crew. The environment within which these players are positioned is crucial to an understanding of their impact upon the resulting program.

## PRODUCTION ROUTINES AND PRACTICES

While the weekly production meeting and the role of the director in daily tapings are some of the most significant routines and practices at *General Hospital*, a host of other routines and practices inform the production process. Such practices continue to speak to the cost- and time-efficiency demanded of soap operas. But they affect the program in other ways, as well, influencing the kinds of stories that get told and the paths by which those stories proceed. I discuss the practices of writing and production scheduling here to illustrate the way daily work routines negotiate textual meaning, at times fracturing it and at times fixing it. The continuity practices running throughout this daily work are the main method employed to stabilize such meaning before the program is offered up to audiences.

The vast quantity of stories and scripts required of a daily, hour-long dramatic production makes even the creative practice of writing a routinized one. Head writers plan stories that outline writers break down into daily segments and scriptwriters translate into dialogue and action. Despite this fractured system, continuity checks are built in to encourage consistency. Scriptwriters are given detailed, scene-by-scene summaries of each episode's happenings in the script outlines. Writers' meetings and producer notes help to hammer out questions about character motivation and plot convolutions. And continuity questions are asked and answered throughout each production day. Script continuity thus serves as the first line of defense against unstable meaning, against holes in the fictional world.

In addition to battling the writing system itself, continuity must fight against the idiosyncrasies of the daily scriptwriters, each of whom has his or her own character biases. As scriptwriter Elizabeth Korte (personal communication, August 18, 1997) admitted:

> I have a real affinity for dark, driven, really scarred, very screwed up characters.... However, you can't give good characters short shrift. You have to make them interesting, too...you have to try hard to guard against having every single scene be about the characters that you like.

Yet character consistency and balance does not happen just by writers trying very hard to be fair. Writers sometimes find alternative ways to write for "their" characters. As writer's assistant David Goldschmid (personal communication, August 11, 1997) explained:

> I've seen examples where certain writers of ours, they would love characters so much that they would trade scenes with other writers. [Say] you have writer A and writer B. Writer A will say, 'Oh, I'd KILL for the Jason/Robin stuff in your day.' And writer B will go, 'Well, that was kind of giving me some problems. If you do those scenes for my script, can I pick up your Kevin/Lucy scenes?'

Such internal negotiation of scenes is part of the process by which *General Hospital* writing practices work to stabilize textual meaning. Jason and Robin are identifiable characters with consistent voices because of such trades and because the layering of writers builds character and story continuity checks into the writing process.

Despite such checks, however, continuity slips inevitably occur. The writing staff must sometimes make leaps of logic to keep the plots coherent. Elizabeth Korte (personal communication, August 18, 1997), who handles script continuity as well as writing scripts, explains a slip that occurred when the character of Robin said she was leaving for Paris the next day and actually left that evening:

> There's this thing called justifying where it's like, maybe we can believe that it was so traumatic that she broke up with Jason that she left earlier. Or we do this; this is our favorite thing that we do. It's the yellow sticky. This is a willing suspension of disbelief ticket and sometimes when I'm just asking people to believe, I'm like, take

a yellow sticky. It's like, that's what you get, we're doing it, it's gotta be that way.

The willing suspension of disbelief operates as a substitute for continuity when production efficiency disallows re-writes or re-takes of problematic scenes. The writing team, along with the audience, agrees to suspend their doubts about situational particularities and even the fictional status of the world itself in favor of the character and relationship motivations that drive the narratives in the first place. In both the successes and failures of continuity within the writing process, textual meaning is fractured and fixed, disputed and conceded, all before the script is even produced.

The production schedule also opens up multiple opportunities for fractured meanings and confused plots. While the ideal situation is the full production of an entire episode in one day, this is rarely the case at *General Hospital*. Because only a limited number and configuration of sets can fit on the stage on any given day, and because the cast of approximately 35 contract players has a myriad of personal and professional scheduling conflicts, each day's production schedule is organized by grouping together related scenes, not by proceeding in a linear fashion through an episode. Coordinating producer Marty Vagts and his assistants try to schedule as much of one day's episode per shooting day as possible, but inevitably plan pre- and post-tapings of other episodes because of cast or set conflicts. The implications of this production schedule are numerous. Pre- and post-taped shows mean higher fees for the director, per Director's Guild rules. The long production days (rarely less than 10 hours) mean overtime pay for the unionized crew. Actors are rarely present en masse, instead working on set for only portions of the day. The makeup and hair room oscillates between periods of intense activity and no activity. Meanwhile, actors (and the producers who guide them) must conceptually shift their focus between scenes that are not necessarily taped in chronological order, adjusting their responses and emotional expression according to the character's place in the story, a place they have not yet worked through in their performance.

Like the writing process, the production schedule requires continuity checks to secure the potentially errant meanings it might produce. Wardrobe, hair, and makeup constantly take Polaroid photos of the actors, along with extensive notes on their appearance, so that they can replicate their looks on other shooting days which are supposed to be the same story day in the on-screen world. The production office provides an item-by-item breakdown for every shooting day, noting special props, wardrobe and makeup, or special effects and unusual technological requirements. The production continuity person then carefully tracks such details throughout the day and across days, making sure, for example, that performers carry their purses in and out of rooms and that the degree of rainfall is consistent across concurrent scenes on different sets. While such details seem trivial, they occupy an immense amount of time for many different workers on the General Hospital set and ultimately create coherent textual meaning out of a fractured work process.

While even the most effective of continuity practices can never close down the meanings that audiences might make of a given program, they do shape those potential meanings in foundational ways. The negotiations between writing practices, production scheduling, and continuity work to make the fictional world seamless and congruous. Routinized production practices allow for the routinized reliability of the soap opera's daily textual installments, where consistent character emotions, homes, and hairstyles provide justification for the on-screen world's believability, despite its extreme plots or the extraordinary attractiveness of its inhabitants. The preoccupation with details and the persistence of assembly-line routines are in some ways necessitated by the textual form, in some ways by audience expectations, and in some ways by eco-

nomic imperatives. Their effect on the text and on potential readings of it is to offer a provisional baseline of meaning upon which characters and stories are built.

# PRODUCTION OF CHARACTERS AND STORIES

The meanings audiences make of *General Hospital* proceed beyond a baseline of plot coherence and character consistency. They operate on more complex levels of story and character, as well, in both the world of production and that of audience consumption. The ways that characters and stories, in all their ideological intricacy, are produced involves nearly all *GH* employees to some extent. Most salient, however, are the writers, actors, and production departments that bring the characters to life and the stories to fruition. Each contributes to the characters and stories, bringing together layers of narrative significance that can be decoded in a range of ways, depending on which layers are deemed significant in any given moment of reception.

Since soap opera characters are first created through writing, the way that writers conceive of characters is an influential aspect of their generation. Scriptwriter Elizabeth Korte (personal communication, August 18, 1997) described her characters as living beings, "[Sonny] loved Brenda, but she was horrible for him. And he honored Lily but did not love her.... She was in every way the perfect wife for him. He wasn't unstable around her.... She was like human lithium. She calmed him down." But Korte also conceived of her characters as archetypes, explaining how this particular love triangle was a retelling of such classic stories as *The Godfather* and *Gone With the Wind*:

> Scarlett O'Hara, that's Brenda, is sure she's in love with Ashley Wilkes. Which, I know Sonny doesn't seem like Ashley, but if you really take a step

back from it, he is, he's a person who lives according to this archaic code.... He's gonna be a gentleman, he's gonna be a mobster, even if the world he was raised to be in is no longer there.

Characters like Sonny and Brenda are constructed, then, not just in the minds of their creators, but through cultural constructions of tragic sagas and tortured romance. While the textual analyst or the lay audience member might make such connections by watching the program, the fact that the program's writers also view their characters in these ways suggests that similar meaning-making processes occur during stages of production, reception, and perhaps even critical analysis. The originary location of the intertextual connection between Sonny and Brenda, Ashley and Scarlett, is insignificant. What does matter is that cultural archetypes consciously operate within production decisions about characters, that production processes are invested in and influenced by the surrounding culture.

Industry practice also involves itself with the surrounding culture in actors' conceptions of their characters. The fact that actors tend to discuss their characters as living beings, often as beings with experiences parallel to their own, is a telling reminder of the fluidity between lived experience and cultural production. Twenty year cast member Jackie Zeman (personal communication, August 14, 1997) collapsed her own life, her conception of her audience's lives, and her character's life when commenting on audience reaction to her character, Bobbie:

> The first half of your life is one way and you finally hit 40 and now what becomes normal to you was never normal; it's a big deal. And so just having a husband and a child and a house and a home and a job and a family and a husband that's not fooling around or lying or drinking or taking drugs or doing any bad things, this is like, oh my God, I made it.

Zeman expressed pride in her own family life elsewhere in this discussion, assumed a similar interest in family experience for her audience, and applied both to her understanding of Bobbie's life and the audience's response to it. Such belief in the authenticity of the character's tribulations helps many of the show's actors to sustain their characters for years on end. According to *GH* acting coach John Homa, (personal communication, August 20, 1997) one of the primary difficulties of acting is that, "You as an actor must suspend your disbelief. You've got to quit bitchin' and moanin' about this being real or not real and just make it work." Much like the suspension of disbelief that the writers employ to make sometimes far-fetched events cohere, so too do soap actors suspend their disbelief, justify actions through reference to character motivation, and call upon their own knowledge of human relationships to make sense of narrative events.

But neither writers nor actors solely determine the construction of characters and stories. The various production departments—Set design & decoration, Makeup & Hair, Wardrobe, and Lighting, for instance—also produce characters and stories. For example, Sonny and Brenda's last romantic dinner before their wedding (a wedding the production staff knew would never take place) was a long and drawn out series of "items" because of the intense attention to detail during them. Not only were the actors dressed in formal-wear and elaborately coiffed, but senior supervising producer Julie Carruthers halted taping while Makeup matched Sonny's facial bruise to its previous incarnation and Props arranged the candles and table settings to look opulent, but not cluttered. Pink gels and screens were placed on the lights and the studio air conditioning was turned off because it kept putting out the candles around the set. When discussing the following day why the previous one had run so late, Carruthers (remarks made on set, August 21, 1997) explained how important it was to take the extra time to relight and perfect the romantic scene because, "It was their dance..." Her justification for the extra work demonstrates how production details not only support, but help to construct, narrative significance. Because this scene was lit a certain way, because special care was taken with makeup and wardrobe, because the staff used valuable production time to perfect one scene of many scheduled for that day, this scene became more important to everyone in the studio. It also became more distinctive within the flow of its episode, since it would look different than most other scenes. Because it featured the couples final romantic moments before Sonny's last minute decision to run away by himself to save Brenda's life, it merited this extra time and attention. The meaning of the scene was constructed through writing and performance, but also through production details. This major story and character moment was constructed as a moment about romance and poignancy (as opposed to, say, sex and excitement) because of these details.

While the production of characters and stories seems more obviously meaning-laden than other aspects of production, exploring the ways in which character and story construction *generate* meaning and significance can help to demystify the creative process. This demystification can then help to expose cultural products and their messages as constructed as opposed to real or natural. Studying the production of Sonny and Brenda's final moments in this way can allow media scholars to point out how culturally constructed ideals of love and romance are perpetuated, in this case through intertextual associations, careful attention to visual details, and extended preparation time. To understand the way characters and stories are specifically created is to understand how cultural images and narratives hold and, more significantly, execute their power.

## THE AUDIENCE IN PRODUCTION

Lurking throughout all aspects of production is the audience, the industry's conception of the audience, the processes of audience decoding that both precede and follow any given *General Hospital* production day, and the actual audience around whom so much scholarship has centered. Though the audience figures implicitly into many aspects of production, such as in continuity efforts to stabilize textual meaning, the audience can also play an explicit role at certain moments. One such moment is the handling of audience response by the production team. Another way in which audiencehood figures into production evokes Richard Johnson's (1986/87) perspective on the lack of distinction between production, text, and audience. Processes of audience meaning-making, such as speculating about future storylines and tracking character knowledge of potentially explosive information, also occur during the production process, and suggest new ways of thinking about production itself. Finally, the meeting of production, audience, and critical research, as discussed here in my relationship to *General Hospital*, can offer new insights to the role of the audience—and the media scholar—in cultural production.

The way *General Hospital* handles its audience response is telling of the limited presence of actual audience members in the production process. The show's production team fits audience responses into an established system that allows for efficient categorization and acknowledgment. When fan mail arrives at the show, those letters addressed to actors are tallied and sent unopened to the actors themselves. Those letters addressed to the writers go to one of the writer's assistants, who reads them and summarizes their responses in a monthly report that includes selected quotes from letters encapsulating what many people are saying. A large chunk of the mail is addressed to the producers or to the show itself. This mail is opened and tallied by the student interns, who register whether the response is negative (if the writer says he or she will stop watching the show), positive (even if they have specific criticisms, as long as they don't threaten to stop watching), or requires a response (to which the interns send one of a series of form letters). The writers' mail report and all the numerical tallies go to the assistant to the executive producer, who compiles them into a monthly report for the producers, head writers, and network executives. The interns are additionally responsible for summarizing the phone messages left daily on a viewer response voice-mail box. The assistant to the executive producer types and distributes these summaries to the producers and head writers. Lastly, the network sends regular summaries and choice selections from postings in the ABC Daytime Online bulletin boards about the shows. The network also conducts viewer focus groups a few times a year to get additional audience feedback.

While the system in place to handle audience response is thorough and efficient, it does not really account for most viewers' perspectives, as the letters must be neatly classified into positive or negative categories and the actual words of audience members are only rarely seen by anyone higher in the chain of command that a writer's assistant. Additionally, the writing and production schedule requires storylines to be mapped out several months in advance, so viewer responses to just-aired episodes can have little direct or immediate impact. Still, the network and the producers are interested enough in audience response that they have, on rare occasion, adjusted storylines accordingly. Predictably, the more established actors were less invested in audience response than were the newer performers and the producers were more interested in viewer feedback than were other employees. Overall, the specific opinions and perspectives of audience members were valued less than their general responsiveness. For example, the production staff appreciated the fan war being waged between those viewers wanting Brenda to be paired with Sonny versus those wanting her paired with Jax more for its vociferousness than for the specific opinions offered on the dysfunction or strength of the relationships.

But audiencehood played another, less expected, role in production, when meaning-making processes usually associated with reception were enacted by production personnel. Crew members would discuss storylines, expressing disgust with devious characters or adoration for blossoming romances as would any other viewer, despite the fact that actors were playing out those storylines in front of their very eyes. The writing staff spoke as passionately about characters and their motivations as do soap fans chatting with their peers on the Internet. As Elizabeth Korte (personal communication, August 18, 1997) in script continuity explained, her job requires her to keep track of the different characters' points of view, to know what they've done, seen, or said previously. It has been well-documented in studies such as Brown's (1994) and Allen's (1985) that audience members engage in the same kind of tracking, eagerly awaiting the revelation of some vital piece of information a character does not yet know.

The fact that show employees frequently have as little information about future storylines as do audiences assists in this sort of audience-like speculation. In one between-takes conversation between actresses, for example, the two women debated who would turn out to be the father of Carly's baby. Like any audience members uninformed about future storyline, they weighed the ramifications of A. J. being the father instead of Tony. (Their consensus: It would most likely be A. J. because of all the future storylines with his family it would open up.) While a plethora of storylines serves production interests, it also serves audience interests, and rumination about storyline possibilities is a common feature of audience discourse on soaps (Hobson, 1982; Ang, 1982). The actresses' lack of power to control the parentage of Carly's baby, given their position within the *General Hospital* institutional hierarchy, makes their speculation and prediction more like audience activity than like producer machination. While such audience activity can be understood as "producerly" for its actions upon the text, such production activity can be understood as "audience-like" for its refusal to accept textual meaning as pre-determined.

The third role of the audience in production is more accurately that of the audience in the *study* of production. If media scholars hope to research Johnson's circuit of culture (1986/87), we need to make room for ourselves within that circuit. Particularly if we choose to engage in on-site production research, media scholars should consider the role of the researcher in relation to production (much as cultural scholars have done in considering the role of the researcher in relation to audiences under study). When the media researcher is also an audience member (as most are likely to be, whether as fan or as critic), audiencehood enters into production through an otherwise non-existent channel. During my trip to *GH*, I functioned as researcher by interviewing people, sitting in on meetings, observing my surroundings, and taking notes. But I was also an audience member, coming close to tears while watching the taping of a goodbye scene between Sonny and his father and momentarily thrilling at sitting at the bar of Luke's blues club. I'm less certain about how my presence affected the production process itself, though having a stranger sitting in the corner of the control booth or jotting on a notepad on set each day may have subtly shifted the work process.

My interpretations of the processes I observed have also undoubtedly been shaped by my long-time viewership. For example, I easily chatted with cast members in their dressing rooms due, at least in part, to my intense familiarity with their on-screen selves. Though I knew I was a stranger to them, they felt like old friends to me. Instead of challenging my researcher's professionalism or blocking my objectivity, my audiencehood provided me with a perspective on the production process potentially more valuable than that of a disinterested observer. My view of the production process was the audience view as well as the researcher's view. Since audiencehood has been historically privileged within cultural studies of media, exploring the role of the audience in production, even literally *within* the production environment as a researcher/audience member, helps to keep production scholarship from losing sight of the other spheres of cultural circulation. Analyzing the distinctiveness of production, both economically and culturally, while continuing to explore the continuities among production, texts, audiences, and social contexts, can keep cultural studies true to its theoretical models while moving the field beyond its text- and audience-centered focus.

## CONCLUSION

These five categories for analyzing the television production process suggest one of many potential templates for organizing industry-centered scholarship. Certainly other forms of television programming, other television systems, other media, and other temporal and spatial contexts could lead to other categorizations. Neither the categories nor their implications can serve as universal truths about all cultural production or all U.S. broadcast network television production or even all soap opera production. Hopefully, however, they demonstrate the significance of production-centered scholarship to a broad understanding of the entire cultural circulation process.

Putting Johnson's model of cultural circulation into practice involves recognizing that production contains both economic and cultural elements, that it is both a distinctive process and a process intertwined with other spheres of cultural circulation. Conducting analyses of cultural production along these lines, as well as drawing upon the production scholarship executed by political economists, mass communications analysts, and sociologists, can help cultural studies scholarship gain a fuller picture of the intricacies of cultural circulation. In addition, those scholars working in paradigms other than cultural studies might find new insights to the production processes they are already investigating. As a range of media communication scholars have realized and continue to realize, production-centered research can demonstrate the links between commercial media's capitalist base and their ideological messages. In addition, delineating specific production practices can alert media activists to vulnerable points at which to intervene and can assist scholars in unmasking the constructed naturalness of media images. If media researchers seek to understand the paths through which media products come to exist, if they seek to understand the constraints that shape the products available to us, then this sort of rigorous, layered attention to production processes is vital.

## NOTES

1.  The 1995 *Critical Studies in Mass Communication* colloquy on the debate between political economy and cultural studies exemplifies this trend.

2.  The scattering of soap opera writers outside the confines of the studio and even the city of production challenges traditional notions of authorship, even of television authorship, which is acknowledged to be less univocal than most. The work processes of writers, so vital to soap opera production and yet so removed from the production space, are significant elements of the production process that deserve further exploration and analysis.

## REFERENCES

Allen, R. (1985). *Speaking of soap operas*. Chapel Hill and London: The University of North Carolina Press.

Ang, I. (1982). *Watching Dallas: Soap opera and the melodramatic imagination*. (D. Couling, Trans.). London and New York: Methuen.

Brown, M. E. (1994). *Soap opera and women's talk: The pleasures of resistance*. Thousand Oaks, California: Sage Publications.

Cantor, M. (1971). *The Hollywood TV producer: His work and his audience*. New Brunswick: Transaction Books.

Cantor, M. and Cantor, J. (1992). *Prime Time Television: Content and Control*, 2nd Edition. Newbury Park, CA: Sage.

Colloquy. (1995). *Critical studies in mass communication*, 12, 60–100.

Gans, H. (1979). *Deciding What's News*. New York: Random House.

Hall, S. (1980). Encoding/decoding. In S. Hall, D. Hobson, A. Lowe, P. Willis (Eds.), *Culture, media, language: Working papers in cultural studies 1972–1979* (pp. 128–138). London: Hutchinson.

Hobson, D. (1982). *Crossroads: The drama of a soap opera*. London: Methuen.

Johnson, K. V. (1999). Soaps in a lather. *USA Today*, 2 July, 1E.

Johnson, R. (1986/87). What is cultural studies anyway? *Social text*, 16, 33–80.

McFadden, K. (1999). Another era leaves *Another World* kaput. *The Seattle Times*, 24 June, D1.

Parney, L. and Mason, M. S. (2000). Selling soaps. *The Christian Science Monitor*, 7 July, 13.

Tuchman, G. (1979). *Making News*. New York: Free Press.

# Introduction to Sarah R. Stein's "Legitimating TV Journalism in *60 Minutes*: The Ramifications of Subordinating the Visual to the Primacy of the Word"

Sarah Stein is an Assistant Professor in the Department of Communications at North Carolina State University and a documentary filmmaker. In her examination of *60 Minutes*, she casts her eye on a wide range of subjects, from problems associated with the "myth of objectivity" to a short history of television news documentaries. Central to her work is an understanding of how formulaic elements and cultural stereotypes impact on the content of news magazine programs and how the use of the dramatic is often used to conceal the ties between modern television documentaries and the governmental/corporate systems that produce those stories. A primary means of blurring the lines between fact versus fiction, according to Stein, is showcased in three signature examples from *60 Minutes* that demonstrate the struggle between the visual and the verbal to express ideological meaning.

# Legitimating TV Journalism in *60 Minutes*: The Ramifications of Subordinating the Visual to the Primacy of the Word

When CBS refused in 1995 to air a *60 Minutes* interview with a former tobacco executive who claimed the tobacco industry had long known of nicotine's addictive properties, newspaper stories and editorials associated that refusal with a climate increasingly hostile to investigative reporting. Stories in *The New York Times* and *The Washington Post* labeled the CBS retreat a capitulation to corporate pressures, pointing to the imminent sale of CBS to Westinghouse Electric Corporation (Kurtz, 1995a, 1995b; Glaberson, 1995). While the *60 Minutes* episode subsequently aired, it was only broadcast after most of the details had become public knowledge.

The perception that the major news media engaged in self-censorship in relation to the tobacco industry had been fueled earlier that year by ABC's settlement with and public apology to Philip Morris Co. and R. J. Reynolds Co. ABC had settled in the face of a $10.5 billion lawsuit over a *Day One* newsmagazine story that claimed those companies had knowingly "spiked" nicotine levels; the segment's reporter and producer, however, refused to sign the settlement papers (Kurtz, 1995b). The facts learned since have borne out ABC's story.

Subsequently, *60 Minutes* found itself again on the receiving end of negative media attention. A feature film, *The Insider* (1999), has been released; it dramatizes the events leading up to CBS's 1995 suppression of the interview of the tobacco executive, Jeffrey Wigand, and the personal cost of his decision to become a whistle-blower. The film portrays Wigand and Lowell Bergman, the *60 Minutes* segment producer, in a relatively favorable light. However, Don Hewitt, *60 Minutes'* executive producer, and Mike Wallace, the most renowned of what CBS refers to as the show's "hard-hitting investigative" correspondents, are seen acquiescing, at least initially, to corporate pressures. *The New York Times* and *The Washington Post* among others devoted attention to Wallace's outraged reaction to his portrayal in the fictional film:

> Mr. Wallace whipped off a series of letters to Mr. Mann [the film's director] protesting the characterization and other issues in the script…. His letters ranged from thanking Mr. Mann for addressing his concerns to railing about the unfairness of being depicted as a "soulless and cowardly laggard who lost his moral compass until Lowell [Bergman, the producer] set me back on the straight path."

> In a telephone interview, Mr. Wallace said: "If this is entertainment, why does he use my name and have words come out of my mouth that I never would have said? There was never any doubt in anyone's mind at CBS on where I stood on this. And to be portrayed as having lost my moral compass, caved in. To whom? For what?

From *Critical Studies in Media Communications, Vol. 18, No. 3, September 2001* by Sarah R. Stein. Copyright © 2001 by the National Communication Association. Reprinted by permission.

This is important to me, or I wouldn't go on like this." (Applebome, 1999, p. E1).

"Moral compass" is a fitting metaphoric juxtaposition to the clicking stopwatch that has been the dynamic symbol of *60 Minutes* for more than thirty years. Both the compass and the stopwatch refer to a particular perspective—a view of a world that is mechanistic, that yields directly to rational inquiry, and one in which hidden truths like just below the surface awaiting exposure. Moreover, this positivist perspective supports the *60 Minutes* team's belief in objectivity and enables them to confidently occupy the high moral ground—the true north of Wallace's fiercely guarded and much lamented moral compass.

Yet, this modernist sensibility reflects unrecognized ideological connotations. Among them is a belief in objectivity achieved through control of words. Closely allied is a fairly straightforward view of good and evil—where both reside in individuals, not systems, and where evil can be located and vanquished through proper investigative journalism. As in so much of our news media, the personification of systemic and institutional inequities have resulted in analyses that have targeted individuals rather than real examination of structural inequities in social, political and cultural realms.

The invisibility of these ideological lenses allows the makes of *60 Minutes* to be confident in occupying the irreproachable ground of objective journalism, while obscuring how supportive the show can be of American liberal-capitalism's ideological interests. The obscuring power of this ideology is particularly visible in Wallace's outrage over the accusations *The Insider* levels. His attempt to translate the film's depiction of *60 Minutes'* capitulation into an ad hominem attack deflects a systematic inquiry into the nature of *60 Minutes* as an institutional cash cow for CBS and its corporate owners and the implications of the news magazine format itself as "documentary lite." The film's portrayal of the chilling effect of corporate

ownership of media institutions is reframed by Wallace as an attack on the individual, a rhetorical sleight-of-hand that exactly mirrors the journalistic and narrative practices of *60 Minutes* itself.

It is precisely these practices that I propose to investigate in this article. In doing so I will examine how belief in and adherence to the objectivity of print culture in the midst of an escalating visual culture is interwoven with the more obvious political implications of these practices. I contend that the television news magazine genre carries with in an implicit bias that began in an earlier stage of television's dissemination when TV journalism sought to be legitimized, using standards of objectivity handed down from newspapers and magazines. I argue that this was accomplished by valorizing the rhetorical power of the spoken word and effectively ignoring that visual images carry independent persuasive power—persuasive power, moreover, that could often contradict the verbal and escape the containment of the objective word.

The tension produced by this attempt to contain meaning of the visual is addressed by Roland Barthes in his 1977 work, *Image–Music–Text*. His examination of press photographs is useful in illuminating the way visual communication is treated by *60 Minutes'* producers and correspondents. Barthes looks at the captioned photographs of newspapers and identifies two different structures of transmitted information: the one, linguistic, and the other visual, or imagistic. The photograph in this medium professes to be a "mechanical analogue of reality.... Of all the structures of information, the photograph appears as the only one that is exclusively constituted and occupied by a 'denoted' message" (18). As Barthes notes, the photograph's denotative status and the completeness of its analogy, "in short, its 'objectivity'," (19) lends itself to the naturalized state of ideological common-sense he critiques in his 1972 work, *Mythologies*.

When coupled with the "reality" claims of news programming in general and the news magazines in particular, the visual image taken as a transparent window into unsullied fact plays a powerful role in shaping our cultural and social perceptions. In support of this contention, I closely examine several episodes of *60 Minutes* programming, paying particular attention to verbal and visual juxtapositions in which the visual imagery and editing choices subvert the stated intentions of the verbal elements. My aim is twofold: first, to contribute to critical rhetorical analyses that seek to comprehend the impact of the visual in verbal or print-oriented contexts; and second, to uncover some of the program's ideological underpinnings by casting light on the particular version of reality it constructs, and the beliefs, attitudes and values it shapes. I will first look briefly at the background of *60 Minutes*, and then trace the rise of the television news magazine out of the tradition of cinematic and televisual documentaries. I then examine closely the formal conventions and the verbal and visual rhetorical strategies employed in the construction of several *60 Minutes* episodes. In addition, I explore the construction of the relationship between the viewer and the reporter as presented in the news magazines' brand of journalism, in an attempt to gain some understanding of its place and impact in popular culture.

## BACKGROUND OF *60 MINUTES*

*60 Minutes* is in its thirty-second year of broadcasting, television's oldest and most successful news magazine. It is the most lucrative and the most popular network show in television history, setting a record of twenty-two consecutive seasons in the top ten Nielsen ratings, and the only broadcast program to finish the season in three different decades as number one. *60 Minutes* has won every television journalism award numerous times and spawned numerous clones on CBS (including the recent *60 Minutes II*) and other networks. The show averaged nineteen million viewers in the 1998–1999 season, a significant number in the current age of diminished

major network audience viewers.[1] In broadcast TV's heyday, the show averaged 32 million viewers (Campbell, 1993).

Mike Wallace's name and those of the other correspondents have popularly come to be associated with hidden cameras and the ambush of bad guys. Watching the show has taken on an aura of a cultural tradition through which television is valorized as a medium of depth. In turn, for at least one hour a week, television loses its reputation of shallow ephemerality.

In 1968 when *60 Minutes* was created and first broadcast, high culture versus low had critically defined parameters. The television medium was clearly low-brow. The medium of television was the escapist entertainment wasteland, a degraded realm, and a purveyor of pictures that serious journalism had to define itself against. The term "magazine" was affixed to "news" to indicate the longer coverage of feature stories over ordinary newscasts. At the same time it contained the visual territory in a manner that paralleled picture magazines: images were made meaningful only by affixing verbal explanations to them (captions in magazines translated in television terms into voiceover narration). Images were simply illustrations of the meaning and depth contained in the verbal text with no independent persuasive agency of their own that might subvert the written/spoken word. Such blindness to visual communication leads to a kind of ideological delusion by which correspondents such as those on *60 Minutes* could genuinely consider themselves free to operate, if they so desired, in opposition to the interests of their corporate owners.

*60 Minutes* represents itself as a tireless champion of the individual and the enemy of the bureaucratic or corporate tyranny. Its early muckraking stance, however, has been frequently compromised in recent years as the show itself has taken on an aura as impervious as the institutions it challenges. Many segments expose the show's location within a political landscape that protects institutions and subverts individuals, especially those representing groups threatening to liberal-capitalist power structures. In addition, the insistently ahistorical and decontextualized nature of the show's narratives undermines its stated aim to inform its audience and thus empower it to take an active role in addressing the injustices portrayed.

The 25th anniversary of the show in 1993 found the self-promotion and self-celebration of the *60 Minutes* team at an all-time high.[2] The occasion was marked by much of the popular media. Phil Donahue devoted the entire hour of his talk show exclusively to *60 Minutes'* twenty-five years of broadcasting. The show's creator, Don Hewitt, and the correspondents were treated as celebrity superstars in their own right. The analyses that follow the brief documentary film history below take a close look at three segments from *60 Minutes* broadcasts in that period, as well as some comments lifted from the *Donahue* celebration.

## BACKGROUND OF THE TELEVISION DOCUMENTARY

The televisual documentary grew out of and in response to the cinematic documentary films of the 1930s. In its diverse non-broadcast history, the documentary film often served as a vehicle for a strongly argued protest against social injustice. Many of these films were attempts to portray social ills and inequalities for a wide audience. In *Film on the Left*, William Alexander (1981) quotes Paul Strand, one of the producers of *Native Land* (1942). Strand argued for the necessity of a partisan stand on the parts of artists and audiences "in the interests of peace, human progress, and the eradication of human misery and cruelty, and towards the unity of all people" (p. 238). Although some of these films were produced for the government as propaganda for New Deal programs (for example, *The Plow That Broke the Plains, The River*), others were produced independently of any governmental or corporate funding to avoid compromising the producers' aesthetic and political goals. Alexan-

der remarks that many of these films "remind us of something potential in ourselves" (238) and "raise in us our own latent heroism" (294).

The early 1960s saw the rise to prominence of the broadcast network documentary as hundreds of documentary programs were produced and televised. The television networks in the early 1960s developed a format known as the "journalistic" documentary, with a clear mandate to depart from the partisan stand of the earlier film documentary.[3] In contrast, the televised documentary was to be a professional, objective inquiry, a "mirror-like" reflection of social reality. Nevertheless, the television documentary's goals were to serve as a clarion call to citizens, to encourage a wider sense of accountability and responsibility for those living within and beyond one's immediate community. William Bluem (1975), who wrote about the television news documentary in 1965, argued that meaning was embedded in social facts, and that the function of the news documentary was to assemble those facts (pp. 90–91). The resulting assemblage would enable the viewing audience to make rational choices and take socially conscious action. Documentary expertise was seen to play a significant role in the practice of democracy. One of the most powerful and enduring documentaries that followed in the tradition of social commitment is *Harvest of Shame* (1960), with Edward R. Murrow as the reporter/narrator.

By the end of the 1960s, however, the enthusiasm on the part of television executives for documentary films had peaked, and the political fallout from the films' muckraking tendencies was being felt as several industries considered lawsuits in protest. In 1968, CBS premiered *60 Minutes*, a hour-long "news magazine." Don Hewitt (1985), the show's creator and executive producer, was interested in "a new type of personal journalism.... *CBS Reports, NBC White Papers,* and *ABC Closeups* seemed to me to be the voice of the corporation, and I didn't believe people were any more interested in hearing from a corporation than they were in watching a document" (p. 29). In the startup period of *60*

*Minutes*, during Frank Stanton's presidency of CBS, the possibility might have existed that a marginal news program could operate in some minor ways independently of the corporate voice. That period, however, is long over and yet *60 Minutes'* correspondents continue to present themselves as maverick reporters, independent and capable of countering the aims of the multinational corporations of which CBS is a part.

Hewitt (1985) valorized the narrative form for imparting news by highlighting the personal story over the general issues involved, a tendency reflected in television news in general. The convention of the impartial, professional journalist employing a scientific, objective methodology to uncover issues of public interest was now joined to narrative reconstructions of experience featuring dramatic characters. *60 Minutes'* inception coincided with the height of prime-time entertainment's popularity and rode that crest by presenting a variety of short, entertaining segments populated by clearly defined good guys and bad guys to displace the greater ambiguities of the long-form documentary.

## THE NEWS MAGAZINE FORMAT

The news magazine utilizes several formulaic elements that serve to position both the correspondents and the viewer in particular ways. In virtually every program we are presented with stories that feature a dramatic urgency, a "you're not going to believe this" sense of outrage, one that finds justification in seeking out and turning over rocks to reveal the maggots lying beneath.

In his extensive work on the news and journalistic procedures, Edward Jay Epstein (1975) describes this construction as "highly simplified melodrama, built around conflict, and illustrated with visual action" (p. 204). Michael Stern (1990) points out that when the rhetoric of unmasking scandal is used as the subject of news shows, it simultaneously masks the interests of the dominant economic and political institutions:

> the assumption that underlies the very possibility of scandal is that ordinary economic and political activity is "normal," unproblematic, unworthy of attention. This assumption inhibits, if it does not altogether repress, awareness that this 'order' is both suspect and open to change (p. 70).

Before looking more closely at several recent *60 Minutes* episodes, I will take a brief look at some of the influences on journalists and story selections in general, as well as some of the visual and verbal rhetorical strategies employed in *60 Minutes*.

In his work on television news documentaries, Hal Himmelstein (1994) emphasizes the liberal capitalist perspectives of news organizations and their corporate parents that impact on television news; the personal biases of individual journalists, who frequently come from backgrounds of privilege in terms of education and class; and the culturally dominant ideological frameworks that select and shape what is reported.[4] Central to television journalism, as can be seen in *60 Minutes*, is the myth of individualism. Richard Campbell (1991) observes that *60 Minutes* is designed to maintain and reinforce mythic ideals held dear by Middle America, "a mythology that celebrates the dignity of the *self* in the face of bullying bureaucracy and sinister *others*" (p. 137). The personae of the reporters themselves are embodiments of this mythology. They are the journalist-heroes, portrayed as rugged, intrepid individuals, valiantly confronting danger and deception, and presenting solutions, or at the least interpretations, that simulate closure. In keeping with the celebrity status that attends these reporters, the *60 Minutes* correspondents are on-camera far more than any of the subjects of their stories (Campbell, 1993). What remains resolutely *behind* the public eye are that they are of an elite class, are highly paid employees of a transnational conglomerate, and are served by scores of staff members who actually produce and construct each story.

The news magazines promote the myth of the individual through their selection of stories that feature individuals as criminals and/or as victims of faceless institutions and heartless bureaucracy. Institutions themselves are addressed generally in terms of individuals, and the social and ideological contextualization of individual problems through an understanding of organizational and corporate power structures is avoided.

As Campbell (1991) observes, the reporters in *60 Minutes* straddle and mediate the conflict at hand, with middle class moral values and attitudes regarding such issues as security, democracy, and justice embedded in the mediation. The reporter as mediator is reinforced stylistically by visual framing through camera composition. Joshua Meyrowitz (1986) uses the term "paraproxemics" for the perception of the interpersonal distance between the on-screen subject and the viewer, as well as spatial relationships among people and objects within the image.

Echoing this idea, Campbell (1991) notes that shots of reporters are generally framed wider, and thus at a greater distance, than the frequent closeup framing of the subject. The extreme closeup framing of the subject, he suggests, conveys the sense of the subject being out of control of his or her environment and, consequently, his or her narrative. I would also point out that the framing of a face with the top of the head and the chin cut off is a visualization of the intimidating intrusion of the camera into that person's physical and psychic space, and thus reinforces the sense that the reporter as the seeker of truth—who controls the camera— holds the power.

On the other hand, the medium shot, from the chest up, places the reporters in a metaphoric middle ground, from which they have access to an overarching perspective, and complete control over their environment. They are reinforced in their posture of non-partisan objectivity and are thus able to mediate narrative tension.

Campbell (1987) analyzes *60 Minutes* in terms of narrative and metaphor, with narratives constructed around conceptual formulas that present reporters in three main roles: as detective, as analyst/therapist, and as tourist. Thus, the reporters are inserted as fictionalized characters in the storytelling frame. The detective persona relies heavily on the rationality of the "scientific mind" that is used to "solve" the mystery or crime. All three of the reporter personae share what can be considered the central conflict of most *60 Minutes* segments: the individual versus the institution (p. 328).

*60 Minutes* was the first news magazine and has become the standard for its imitators on CBS and the other networks. At the time of *60 Minutes'* twenty-fifth anniversary, the news magazines included *Day One* (ABC), *Dateline NBC*, *NOW* (NBC), *Prime-Time Live* (ABC), *20/20* (ABC), *Eye to Eye* (CBS), and *Front Page* (FOX). Bottom-line cost control came to dictate network programming and the networks discovered the financial benefits of producing these relatively inexpensive shows at far less than the cost of acquiring Hollywood-produced "entertainment" productions.

The other news magazines adopted the *60 Minutes* format in virtually every detail. They utilized the same visual rhetoric of tight camera framing of subjects and the medium shot of the correspondents, and again also gave more screen time to the reporters than the subjects. The only differentiation they made from each other and *60 Minutes* was in choosing ever more highly sensationalistic, tabloid-style stories.

The most frequent lead subject of all the news magazines is violence and crime. The gamut runs from one pole, with *60 Minutes'* carefully cultivated aura of respectability and traditional journalism, to the other extreme, with the now defunct *Front Page's* MTV-style editing, computer graphics, and stories such as one on homosexual sex clubs where unsafe sex is practiced, enticingly shot with upper bodies blurred and bare legs visible. On the 1993 *Donahue* show celebrating *60 Minutes'* twenty-fifth year anniversary, Hewitt expressed disgust with the computerized special effects and graphics used on other news shows, once more rendering opaque the artifice of *60 Minutes'* "objective" camera and editorial style. His remarks dismissed the impact of the visual, as he sought to distinguish the "transparent" images of his show from the visual gimmicks of other news magazines.

While *60 Minutes* claims to present a reasoned discourse that persuades by the power of its rational disclosure, it is the ethos of its reporters that is clearly relied upon to persuade viewers of the show's veracity. Style and personality predominate. The reportorial tone is one of intimate direct address, the effect of which Horton and Wohl (1956) describe in their work on "para-social relationships." It also constructs a sense of a reporter-viewer partnership, one whose common sense and rationality are a match for any attempts to conceal the truth or meaning of a situation. We are presented with correspondents whose rational, skeptical, unpretentious, and indefatigable zest for setting straight the convoluted byways of modern civilization can be counted on without question. These are reporters who will ask the tough, probing questions that get to the bottom of things, apparently letting no one off the hook. The journalist as victor over evasive or arrogant figures recurs so frequently it can be viewed at least in part as the audience's vicarious opportunity to bring the powerful low and to believe, as expressed in *TV Guide*'s tribute to *60 Minutes*, there is "someone with a little clout...watching out for us" (Coffey, 1993, p. 26).

Robert Stam (1983) notes the correlation of the direct address of the newscaster with power and with fiction. The privilege of the voice on the airwaves implies immense power in political, narrational and discursive terms. The fiction lies in

the appearance of an unmediated relationship between the correspondent and the viewer:

> It is framed, in other words, as a simulation of face-to-face, two-person communication; the newscaster singlehandedly imitates the characteristic rhythms of dialogue. The "communication" is unilateral, not a reciprocal exchange between two transmitter-receivers but rather a powerful transmitter enjoying direct access to millions of subjects (p. 38).

## FICTIVE PERSONA: THE REPORTERS AS PERSONALITIES

The week leading up to a specially produced two-hour show by *60 Minutes* on the occasion of its twenty-fifth anniversary was filled with media hype for the special and the series itself: there were newspaper and magazine articles, as well as interview on other networks. Television moved into an excess of its usual self-referential and self-cannibalizing functions. John Chancellor conducted an interview with Mike Wallace and Don Hewitt on CNN's *Larry King Live*, and Phil Donahue invited the entire cast onto *Donahue* (NBC) for the full hour devoted exclusively to *60 Minutes*. Both shows aired days before *60 Minutes'* November 7, 1993 anniversary show, with considerable air time plugging the show and the coffee table book published celebrating the *60 Minutes'* anniversary.

The anniversary special further blurred the lines between journalist and television personality. Mini-vignettes featured footage and personal details from the reporters' private lives, helping to construct a mythic appeal that far exceeds the role of the journalist as a source of social facts. Mike Wallace is portrayed as the incorruptible and indefatigable White Knight, willing and able to charge into the fray on our behalf. To further the fictive nature of the intimate relationship we as viewers have with Wallace, the anniversary special revealed that Wallace lost a son thirty years ago. At the time, he made a pledge to quit his lucrative work in commercials and, as he told it, "quit all the things I was not proud of and see if I can't go back to work in news, doing something that is useful. And if I have to take a big cut in salary, fine. But I'm going to do something that would make Peter proud."

The 'something' Wallace chose was *60 Minutes*. Charles Kuralt, hosting the anniversary special, called Wallace the "national district attorney," who asked tough questions and utilized hidden cameras and ambush interviews to expose wrongdoers. But, to render him even more the mythic, paternal hero and consequently even less subject to criticism, Kuralt informs us that "to those who know him best, Mike Wallace has a reputation for kindness and generosity when others are suffering." This narration is read over footage of Wallace at the Vietnam Memorial, ending with a close-up shot of a tear rolling down Wallace's cheek.

The illusory relationship fostered between the viewer and the news celebrity, such as Mike Wallace, is a product of the pseudo-intimacy of television's mode of address. This "fictive We" that establishes an emotionally charged "us" and "them" situation has political consequences:

> Television news, then, claims to speak for us, and often does, but just as often it deprives us of the right to speak by deluding us into thinking that its discourse is our own. Often it gives us the illusion of social harmony, the ersatz communication of a global village which is overwhelmingly white, male and corporate (Stam, p. 39).

The *60 Minutes* cast have become revered as the elder statesmen of broadcasting. They exude a sense of wealth, success, privilege, and paternalistic, corporate power. The sense that *60 Minutes* is the gold standard leaves them with little restraint on their product. The correspondents have become reified, and as evidenced by the letters from viewers, regarded primarily as inviolate and incorruptible. The hundreds of letters they receive each week from viewers suggesting scandals *60 Minutes* should investigate cast the correspondents in the role of much-needed vigilantes, the true champions of justice, especially in the face of continual revelations of police and congressional corruption that are featured on these programs and in the news in general.

The textual analyses below offer a close examination of the way in which the spoken words, written and recorded by the *60 Minutes* correspondents and lifted from the filmed interviews of the subjects, are juxtaposed with the visual images of the broadcast. In doing so, I aim to illuminate how the visual can and does skew the spoken word, in ways that give *60 Minutes* more power and sometimes less power. I argue that the attempt to subordinate the communicative and persuasive function of the visual in order to legitimate the journalistic status of the news magazine is in service of powerful hegemonic functions.

## TEXTUAL ANALYSIS

Don Hewitt is quoted in *TV Guide* as saying, "In television, you can't edit something till you hear it…I rarely look at the pictures when I'm editing a piece. I just listen" (Coffey, p. 20). The implication that the pictures do not carry the same weight as the spoken word is misleading. In *60 Minutes* stories, Hewitt and his staff may well write the narration first and then edit the pictures to fit the words in terms of content and speech rhythms. But the power of words in conjunction with images is in the spin each gives to the other, which can critically skew the meaning, or seeming neutrality, those words previously conveyed on paper.

In the section that follows I examine in close detail three episodes of *60 Minutes* that aired around the time of the 1993 twenty-fifth anniversary. This event celebrated a show whose style (along with its stars) had been able to mature into a formula successfully and firmly entrenched in viewers' expectations. The episodes I examine were aired in proximity to the anniversary (two within a couple of months, a third the previous fall); this gave me the benefit of media coverage of the show's creators and executive producers reflecting on the production of the show and the decision-making factors behind it. I chose the episodes primarily because their story structures and mode of execution offered the critic clear examples of the ways in which visual images can subvert stated intentions as evidenced by audio narration or can underscore political biases and ideological subtexts not overtly acknowledged by the show's producers and correspondents. These episodes fit into familiar modes of the program's story types: an investigative piece geared to sound the alarm of a threat to American security, another that purports to address an ongoing social affliction, and finally a "soft news" piece that functions in a normative mode, dictating far more overtly "sensible" attitudes and behavior. In keeping with Campbell's taxonomy of reportorial personae, these three stories also invoke *60 Minutes* correspondents as detective, analyst, and as tourist. In the first episode examined, the correspondent as detective is featured and we can witness in it vivid instances of some of the consequences of a hegemonic perspective that subordinates the visual to the word.

## Episode 1: "How Did He Get Here?"

In late August of 1993, *60 Minutes* ran a story titled "How Did He Get Here?"[5] Lesley Stahl, the correspondent, was seated in front of the customary photographic blowup, on this occasion featuring Sheik Abdul Rachman, the blind Muslim cleric accused of inciting the World Trade Center bombing. Stahl's report began with filmed scenes of the Sheik and his followers behind bars, while Stahl in voiceover recounted the Sheik's past involvement with terrorist operations in Egypt and the elliptical route by which he was able to enter the United States on a tourist visa.

As is often the case with *60 Minutes*, however, the opening was not what the actual report was about. The story in this case was about the ability of immigrants without proper credentials to gain entry into the U.S. by requesting political asylum. The remainder of the report took place in New York's JFK airport, with Stahl interviewing an official with the federal immigration agency and filming scenes of several men arriving and asking for asylum. An interview with a man from a private organization called FAIR, the Federation for American Immigration Reform, was intercut throughout these scenes. Stahl questions the Immigration and Naturalization Service official as to the number of foreigners arriving illegally daily. She expresses astonishment on hearing that fifty "inadmissibles" a day are not in fact put back on the plane and sent home: "They come in under false pretenses but can seek asylum here anyway. It doesn't matter." Stahl shakes her head, registering disapproval. "No wonder people do this. They can still get in."

As Stahl speaks, we see two young Pakistani men being interviewed by Customs officials, and then handcuffed. Throughout the scenes in which we see these men, no explanation is given to them regarding the filming, and they appear visibly agitated. Stahl determines that they have come in with counterfeit passports. The camera cuts to Stahl asking Stein, the head of FAIR, how many immigrants he would judge to be legitimately escaping persecution in their countries. Stein answers, "One to two percent," and proceeds to express his contempt for the government: "The U.S. government is like the Keystone Kops. One agency doesn't talk to another—it's a comedy of errors." He then voices his worry that many of these illegal immigrants come here to wage violence. When asked by Stahl how often that happens, Stein replies "a lot" and then relates the story of one Egyptian terrorist, seen now in photographs, who gained entry and then assassinated a CIA agent. It is significant to note here that the photographs of the assassin related in the story are imagistically twins to the opening footage of the Sheik, first seen in huge blowup behind Stahl in the customary *60 Minutes* open. Thus, the opening footage, in fact unrelated to the present story, is subtly interwoven into the body of the episode and through association with the two men waiting in handcuffs at the airport.

Back at the airport, one of the Pakistani asylum seekers nervously stands by as the cameras follow him, the Customs officials interrogate him, and Stahl asks him pointed questions in English, a language he does not speak. The Pakistani in fact exhibits all the generic visual conventions we as television viewers have been trained to associate with the role of the 'villainous Arab' in second-rate drama—the shifting eyes, sweating brow, stealthy glances;[6] these happen also to be the way many people would look in this man's circumstances, compounded by a camera following his every move. Stahl, in narration over the shots of the illegal immigrants, tells the viewer that the immigration official was not allowed to voice an opinion on current policy, but his aide had confided the frustration they felt that "no one could tell if these people were murderers, terrorists, or had AIDS, they just have to let them in."

The Pakistani seen throughout this scene is released when no evidence to refute his claim of political abuse can be found by the Customs interrogation; he leaves with an asylum hearing date set for ten days hence. The camera follows him from behind as he walks with his luggage through the lobby, out the door and across the street until he is lost from sight. Over this long shot, Stahl speaks:

> As we watched that young Pakistani, probably confused, probably terrified, as he walked out into New York, we wondered, "Are you good, are you bad,

are you really fleeing persecution, are you a terrorist, or are you a good son here to help your family?" The way things work out, it appears not to matter who you are. To walk freely into the United States and then stay as long as you want, it only matters that you get here.

The blatant xenophobia and thinly veiled racism expressed throughout this report found its most virulent expression here, in this last voice-over. The image of this young man occurs most often with the incessantly repeated word "terrorist." The construction of this report repudiates Hewitt's contention that only the words count. Beginning with the opening footage of the Sheik, "a villain we can all hate" (Stahl on-camera lead-in), the constant juxtaposition of the sweating, frightened faces of the asylum seekers with the discussions of the terrorist acts of people like the Sheik and the reiteration of the "illegal" status of these foreigners effectively created the impression that *these* men must be terrorists, too, and that through some outrageous oversight in misguided democratic policy the U.S. government regularly welcomes terrorists into our country. This brand of reporting could be considered more of the making of lynch mobs than thoughtful and rational consideration of an issue as complex as immigration and political asylum. It should be noted as well that the majority of terrorist deaths on U.S. soil in which innocent civilians were killed en masse, were committed by white Americans who look like the mythic "boy next door." Of equal significance is the questionable utilization of an "authority"— the spokesman for FAIR—whose opinions went unchallenged and whose political agenda and organizational backing was never revealed in the course of the segment. A subsequent editorial in *The New York Times* identified FAIR as an organization that gets support from the Pioneer Fund, a New York Foundation that also supports research seeking to prove that blacks and Latinos are inherently inferior (Lewis, 1994).

In a time when shows such as the news magazine *Dateline* attempts to distinguish itself by allowing its viewers to register their opinions about the scandal just served up to them, and when factions extol the virtues of electronic voting, these quick impression images can be immensely powerful. As paranoia toward foreigners and hostility toward immigrants from Third World countries runs very high (all the asylum seekers in the piece were people of color), visualizations in news stories that match precisely the stereotypes of maniacal Middle Easterners recreated in Hollywood action films may be highly influential. The visual rhetoric of the intrusive camera style that marked this production gives license to a climate of disrespect and puts the viewer in the position of judge and jury. Not acknowledged within this show is the fact that immigrants in every historical period have been greeted by hostility, especially during times of greater economic distress. Neither were there images of the adverse conditions many people flee. A much needed explanation of the difference between the *illegal* status of the asylum seekers and a *criminal* status was also omitted. Indeed, the visual historical contextualization provided was that of the convicted Sheik and his adherents behind bars at the beginning of the episode. As a visual narrative, it was constructed to arouse outrage against an evil villain defined by the performative conventions familiar to popular cultural genres. In this case, it constituted an ideological manipulation whose subtextual objective was apparently the mobilization of public opinion against political asylum seekers and immigration by "undesirable" racial and national groups in general. Indeed, Stahl, in her on-camera close, announced, "After our story, President Clinton proposed a series of reforms, including one that would allow immediate deportation of those people whose claims for asylum appear clearly fraudulent."

## Episode 2: "Acceptable Risks"

The presence of a genre-specific *visual* contextualization and the absence of an appropriate historical contextualization are again evident in "Acceptable Risks," a report featuring Ed Bradley.[7] The segment deals with AIDS treatments, and the social ramifications of the FDA's policies on distribution of experimental drugs. The report foregrounds the show's customary stance of support for the underdog and the lone rebel, while a close analysis finds that another institution—this time the FDA—has been strangely rehabilitated in the process.

"Acceptable Risks" begins with the standard formula of selecting individual narratives instead of presenting the overarching themes involved. In this case, two AIDS activists, Jim Korty and Martin Delaney, are to be the focus. Korty has been manufacturing drugs for AIDS treatment and selling them illegally through 'underground' buyers' clubs. The drugs are ones that the FDA has withheld for years from release pending the results of testing. Korty is filmed at work in his laboratory, an antiseptic and professional-looking small space—very much a one-man operation.

The correspondent Ed Bradley begins by asking Korty if he would agree with the government and pharmaceutical companies that say what he is doing is dangerous. Korty does agree, with a caveat:

> But not as dangerous as the sure death sentence for people who can't get the drugs they need. Whatever the side effects of this might be, the side effects of dying are a little more concrete. So I'm willing to do this for that very reason.

Bradley interviews a representative of the FDA, who says that the FDA is aware of the underground's existence and has kept hands off. He states his sympathy with people who are dying and willing to try any possible treatment, but expresses the concern that dying people can easily be exploited. Bradley counters by pointing out that these aren't "snake oil peddlers," that in fact they are making drugs available through the underground that the government is already testing.

At this point in the segment we are in one of the standard *60 Minutes* formulas in which an institution, the FDA, is portrayed as stuck in a bureaucratic mire, isolated from any intersecting interests, and a clear-sighted maverick individual has taken matters into his own hands for the public good.

The scene cuts to a buyers club where medicine is being purchased. Bradley's narration is heard in voice-over: "In fact, the underground has put pressure on the system to make experimental drugs more widely available before they're approved. A bad batch of Jim Korty's DDC illustrates the point." The last line of narration falls over a closeup of tablets, and we cut to David Kessler, the FDA commissioner, in an on-camera interview:

> [Kessler]: We became aware that some of the buyers' clubs were selling a super potent form of DDC. We couldn't turn our backs. We insisted they stop selling it. But on the same day we did that, we called the drug manufacturer to make sure we could make the drug available *legitimately* [spoken with emphasis] to patients. That's what we want to achieve.
>
> [Bradley]: So what did you do, send the police out there, agents?
>
> [Kessler]: When you're dealing with people who are dying, with people who are doing things out of desperation, I'm not going to go in and show my badge.

The above exchange signals the slant the piece is about to take. What's at stake here seems to be a matter of *who* is going to manufacture and sell the drugs. The term "legitimately," which is intended to conjure up proper supervision and necessary control over quality, is also resonant with control over profits. Bradley ignores a significant contradiction at this juncture in

Kessler's narrative: at the moment when the FDA wanted to stop the buyers clubs from selling DDC, remarkably enough a pharmaceutical company was able and ready to supply it, although it had been withheld from the market until then. The homosexual community in particular has expressed its view that corporate, profit-making issues like behind AIDS research. But instead of picking up on this issue, Bradley steers the story in a direction that allows Kessler to present himself, the embodiment of the FDA, as an official moved to act in a caring fashion because of the plight of dying people.

Commissioner Kessler is filmed throughout the segment in a book-lined office, a warm, non-institutional environment, very much supportive of the humanist frame being constructed for him verbally. Employing the rhetorical visual strategies mentioned earlier by Campbell, subjects are generally represented by camera framing that is much closer than the images of the correspondent. In "Acceptable Risks," however, the medium shot symbolic of rational authority is reserved not only for the *60 Minutes* correspondent, Bradley, but also for David Kessler. Thus, the Commissioner is visually extricated from "subject" status into "authority" status on a plane parallel to the correspondent, leaving Jim Korty to be filmed in the extreme close-ups used most often for those called on trial by *60 Minutes*.

> [The FDA commissioner, Kessler, reappears on-camera]: There's no question that we've learned a lot from the activists. We've learned we have to be accountable. What we've seen is a dramatic change in the last couple of years. [Beginning to speak more heatedly]: Look where we started off. I mean, the activists were out there scaling this building. Really, burning us in effigy. Now they're sitting at the advisory committees, knowing, uh, bringing in an awful lot of expertise, scientific expertise.

The implication in Kessler's statement, un-challenged by Bradley, is that when the "ac-tivists" finally started acting in a civilized, rational manner, they were brought into advisory posi-tions. Scenes of Dr. Anthony Fauci, the National Institute of Health's director of AIDS research, meeting in San Francisco with Martin Delaney and other underground activists accompany a statement from Bradley that it has been because of Delaney's "persistent and reasoned appeals" over a seven-year period that "those powerful fig-ures have started to listen." Kessler's statement, unchallenged by Bradley, entirely obfuscates the history, in the beginning years of the spread of HIV, of the Reagan administration's complete in-accessibility to homosexuals. It was in response to that institutionalized indifference that gay ac-tivists organized into groups like the Gay Men's Health Crisis and ACT-UP in order to force their concerns into public consciousness and to pres-sure the government into listening to them at all.

Back in the lab, Korty is again at his station. Bradley's narration informs us that Korty is no longer making DDC but is developing other al-ternative treatments. The camera cuts to Korty, still working, in an extreme closeup of his face, a low angle shot from the side and slightly dis-torted by a wide-angle lens. Bradley is off screen and behind him, so that Korty's eyes shift fre-quently to the side as he answers Bradley's ques-tion. This camera framing is similar to that used in popular entertainment portrayals of the "mad scientist":

> [Bradley]: Do you think the FDA has changed enough?
>
> [Korty]: Nope. But that's like turning a great ocean liner. You're not going to turn it on a dime like a speedboat. It's going to take a while for this great ship of state to come around.
>
> [Cut to Kessler on-camera for the last statement of the segment, speaking very sincerely and with great empha-sis]: The riskiest thing we can do when

it comes to AIDS is to be unwilling to take any risks.

The institution of the FDA has been fully re-habilitated, and in *60 Minutes'* terms is now on the side of the "good guys." It is now FDA's stated position to be an advocate for risk-taking, and the two individual activists have been effective-ly marginalized once again. Kessler's statement, because it follows Korty's without mediation by Bradley, becomes the answer to what is thus re-framed as Korty's cynicism and, ultimately, mis-guided radicalism.

Visually, except for the one scene shot in wide angle of men seated around a conference table, the camera frames lone individuals. The shot, counter-shot formula of the interviewee and reaction shot of the correspondent is re-served for David Kessler and Bradley. Bradley never appears on camera with Korty in his lab, even further isolating him as the lunatic fringe. The word "homosexual" is never used in this re-port. Gay Men's Health Crisis and ACT-UP are never named; the "activists" seem to be reduced to Korty and Delaney. The fact that the govern-ment refused to fund serious research on AIDS until it started to show up in the heterosexual population has been bitterly documented by ho-mosexuals.[8] The critical role that civil disobedi-ence played in this drama is suppressed and condemned in Kessler's recital, with the full sup-port of Bradley and *60 Minutes*. From the stated mission of *60 Minutes,* it would have seemed the perfect opportunity to champion a devas-tatingly victimized group of individuals against the indifference and self-interest of powerful in-stitutions, but the viewer is left with the reverse case.

## Episode 3: "Don't Leave Home"

The rhetorical power of the juxtaposition of words and images to present a strong class bias is revealed in "Don't Leave Home," a story by Morley Safer on the tourist industry.[9] This report represents the kind of story that so often blurs the lines between news and polemic, between the reporter of factual events and the slant of the privileged voice with the power to select what will be reported as "news." Safer introduces this segment with, "Tourism is creating its own abomination. The world has too much money, and believe it or not, the world is too peaceful to stop it."

We are then treated to a travelogue of Safer's "too peaceful" world, in which the great cultural attractions of Europe are depicted overrun with tourists. The images throughout this report are of hordes of people, the camera always positioned to accentuate the numbers: shots from ground level at vast numbers of legs and feet passing by, shots from within crowds, shots from hotel balconies at a sea of umbrellas or a forest of tents, and the like.

The narration that accompanies these images is delivered in a tone often adopted by Safer, a cross between irony and contempt, with the contempt winning out by the end of the story. What the piece tells us is that the poorer classes want to see and experience what has always been the exclusive province of the rich:

[Over shots of small tents and vans, many with laundry strung on make-shift lines]: In summer, the Bois de Boulogne, Paris' marvelous urban forest, looks like a displaced person's camp. And it is in a way. Eastern Europe sends out its tired and poor [this over shots of people using public wash basins at a campsite], tourists who spend only pennies on the local economy [over a shot of a couple carrying loaves of bread], but add by the hundreds of thousands to the competition to glimpse something important [over a shot of a crowded tour bus].

Safer takes us to Thailand, France, Italy, and England. Over shots of a crowded street in an English village he tells us, "Hordes laid waste to this pretty provincial town. Where there was

once a baker, a butcher, a candlestick maker, is now a junk bazaar. Another bastion fallen to the cheap and ugly" [over a couple licking ice cream cones, the man with a spot of ice cream evident on his beard].

As shots continue of people parading by, many with backpacks, all clearly tourist class and under, a musical track of Noel Coward's song "The Wrong People" is heard, with the lyrics, "Why do the wrong people travel, and the right people stay back home?" followed by Safer's narration:

Somehow the most decent people, away from home, become the most monstrous intruders.... Mr. Coward was having a bit of fun at the expense of the economy classes. But the fact is, regardless of class, we all become the wrong people [these last words fall over a shot of an obese woman and man stuffing food into their mouths in a doorway].

The spoken word in this last piece strikes the populist chord *60 Minutes* purports to champion, yet here is a prime example of the visual belying the verbal. While Safer mouths the words "regardless of class," the image escapes the "objectivity" and balance of the verbal and clearly portrays its class bias. The man and woman gorging on food in the doorway are unmistakably representative of Mr. Coward's peripatetic "wrong people;" the right people who presumably pollute less because they spend much more than "pennies in the local economy" are safely hidden from the camera's eye, perhaps by the sheltering walls of first-class restaurants.

The piece ends with Safer announcing that the "biggest blows are yet to come." The shots cut to streams of Chinese people, over which we are told that right now only a tiny fraction of humanity owns a passport and the means to travel: "What happens when another billion people get the urge? We know how to liquidate each other. DO we have the brains to put up with each other? No—so stay home." *60 Minutes* again stays true to the customary convention of using only shots of huge numbers of Chinese, all moving together. IT has become so much the genre marker of the anonymous Asian, one wonders if television producers fear the viewer would fail to even visually register a *single* Chinese person. Safer's implication is that these boorish "hordes" travel only because they have been sold on it as the thing to do, visually supported by the lemming-like quality of the pictorial representation. Safer could have asked what it is both in contemporary existence and perhaps in the human spirit that turns people into pilgrims. Patrick Wright (1985), looking at cultural traditions in England, comments on the popularity of touring to see historical remains:

> [I]t would take massive arrogance to argue that people do this only because as tourists they are under the false spell of the past as fetishized bits and pieces…. for all the manipulation, the sense of the "unique" in modernity cannot be written off as merely elitist. At the vernacular level, the "unique" gains in importance and meaning with the rationalization and disenchantment of everyday life (pp. 79–80).

What we are presented with ultimately is an objectivist argument in service of classist ideologies and cultural capital. The Noel Coward song, allegedly used only for ironic effect, meets no contradiction in the verbal or visual text. As would be expected by critics of mainstream media, there is no discussion of the increasing homogenization and commodification by Western consumer culture of all parts of the world, and its contribution to the hunger people may feel to experience something authentic, something created or revered for reasons other than its monetary value. Nor is there any effort made to portray the kinds of working and living conditions that would make people put up with the discomforts represented in this piece in order to

spend a few days in a place that is beautiful, or historically resonant, or stimulating.

Safer's narration tells us that "we all become the wrong people" when we travel, but there are *no* shots of the expensive vehicles, hotels, and opulently clothed people that would serve as evidence that Safer considers the wealthy as undeserving of travel as the "poor and tired" he depicts. It is reasonable to assume as well that most people do not have country estates of the likes of Safer's (glimpsed fleetingly and voyeuristically in the two-hour anniversary special) that might make staying home more attractive.

This episode entertains issues that speak to a pro-environmental and anti-materialistic stance of crucial importance to an over-populated world developed often blindly to the interdependence of life on the planet, and it can be interpreted as such. But in Safer's critique, the selection and juxtaposition of the visual implicates only the individual tourist marked by the conventional codes of the lower socio-economic classes. Moreover, as is typical for a *60 Minutes* piece, there is no attempt to explore the dependence on tourism for the future existence of many historically significant, but dying, towns; nor is there any effort to widen the focus into the travel industry per se. The pollution and erosion of many areas is a grave problem, but organizations that attempt to transform tourism into a force to save the natural world rather than destroy it, are ignored entirely. Finally, beyond its mean-spirited condemnation, there is no thoughtful or useful investigation of how to preserve the favored places of the earth and the inspiring artifacts of human creation without shutting them off from the many who need them.

It may seem at first reading that the segments analyzed here are unusual for *60 Minutes*, and yet I found many more segments than I have space for here that reveal, on close analysis, similar political biases, and consistent visual formulas that can be easily "read" by the frequent and infrequent viewer alike. There are stories on *60 Minutes* that do uncover real injustices, and by power of the reputation and popularity of the program, affect the events at hand in ways that are needed. The problem is that they are always limited to the individual case at hand—the corruption of a particular homeless shelter operator, for example, rather than the institutionalized social and economic factors in the creation of homelessness per se, which must be addressed if any larger change is to come about. In this way, as well, the news magazine ensures its own continuance: the guarantee of an endless source of dramatic stories upon which to draw.

## CONCLUSIONS

Critical approaches to television and popular culture have developed considerably since the days when the *60 Minutes* correspondents first took on the mantel of the aesthetic and ideology of print journalism. Visual communication has also received greater and more sophisticated attention. Yet the *60 Minutes* correspondents and producers' conceptions of image/text relations and of themselves as ethical gladiators have not progressed accordingly. This can be seen most vividly in the news stories involving Mike Wallace with which this article began. Wallace counts on the ethos he has established in the minds of millions of viewers; the attack he perceives as leveled at him personally threatens an erosion of trust in him as an ethical professional. Within that frame, there is no room for Wallace to comprehend the possibility of criticism of the larger ideological context of which he is a part.

However, as my examination of the three selected stories has shown, the visual not only cannot be contained, it is often used in an unacknowledged fashion to promote hegemonic messages. In constructing themselves as reliable and objective correspondents, the *60 Minutes* team in effect calls on the classic appeals of logos (rational argument) and ethos (character and fundamental values). In doing so they do not account for the excess of meaning

in the visual that the verbal text fails to contain. Not only does this provide a strong and unrecognized appeal to pathos (feelings not subject to rational argument) beyond the control of the producers and correspondents of *60 Minutes*, this appeal is, as Barthes suggests, strongly ideological. The gap between these appeals needs to be examined by analyzing the visual/verbal interface. Where Barthes provides a frame in his discussion of the static image, Campbell provides a starting point with his important analysis of the "middle ground," the space around the reporters' bodies in interviews. But this is only a beginning; there needs to be a fully developed rhetoric of visual argumentation. I have attempted through the analyses in this essay to add to the visual vocabulary and techniques of deciphering such a rhetoric, so essential for navigating the emerging world of visual communication we inhabit. In turn, this can provide a way to pry open the ideological grip of the visual to examination.

The ubiquitous ticking stopwatch at the open and close of every segment of *60 Minutes* serves as a resonant symbol for the constraints placed upon the content in *60 Minutes* by its format and its framing (and fraying) symbols. Besides making visual the title of the show, the stopwatch with its greatly amplified ticking acts metaphorically to establish a sense of urgency, of precision, of scientific objectivity. The symbol of the watch conjures up an image of a mechanistic, orderly universe, subject to rules and understanding guided by conceptualizations grounded in linear causality. In a mechanistic reality, parts can break and be "fixed." The urgency of the passing time justifies the reduction of complex, intersecting social and moral issues to the good and the bad, resolvable by exposing the 'problem' through commonsensical, rational discourse. In a culture that celebrates ever-faster ways of communicating ever more information, the ticking watch insists that we move on, that there is no time to linger over that last disturbing scandal because other outrages are waiting, demanding attention.

The news magazine format of *60 Minutes* and its clones resolve this dilemma for us by presenting their material in a form and at a pace that makes simply tuning in all we *can* do. The *60 Minutes* format assures us that we are attending to those dimensions of life whose continued exposure will keep the fabric of social order from shredding entirely, the stability of the form makes an implicit claim that it does so. In fact, Don Hewitt is quoted in a 1989 interview as saying, "very few things in America look the same way they did when you were a kid. The stores look different, the gas stations look different, everything looks different. *60 Minutes* looks the same. There was some talk…about we ought to change it…I said, 'No!'" (quoted in Campbell, 1993, p. 28).

Millions of viewers check in every Sunday night to a world that still plays by the rules: where the journalist-heroes are still smarter than the bad guys, and the old certainties of rationality and predictability still prevail. The world according to *60 Minutes* stays manageable through reasoned discourse by paternal figures of power and privilege. The anxieties that arise in the face of a world in which the rules seem to be changing by the minute, are laid to rest, at least while that clock keeps ticking. However, the images of incurable viruses, of alien intruders on American shores, and myriad other images incommensurate with a world subject to rational repair, slip through the grasp of the written and spoken word to construct their own reality. Wallace's distress over his lost compass points as much to his anchoring belief in his power to control meaning through the word, as it does to any true containment *60 Minutes* can achieve.

## NOTES

1. CBS Web site on *60 Minutes*: http://db.cbs.com/ prd1/now/template.display?p_story=62387#top

2. The show was titled *25 Years: 60 Minutes* and aired on Sunday, November 7, 1993 for two hours beginning at the show's regularly scheduled time.

3. Interview with Albert Wasserman in Alan Rosenthal (Ed.), (1980).

4. For further analyses of this kind see also Tuchman, G. (1978). *Making news: A study in the construction of reality*. New York: The Free Press; Epstein, E. J. (1973). *News from nowhere*. New York: Random House; and Williams, R. (1974). *Television: Technology and cultural form*. New York: Schocken Books, pp. 44-54.

5. This episode ran August 22, 1993, and was produced by Rome Hartman.

6. Edward Said (1979) is one source that discusses the production and use of such stereotypes.

7. This segment aired in the fall of 1992.

8. See, among others, Randy Shilts (1987).

9. This report aired August 29, 1993, and was produced by John Tiffin.

## REFERENCES

Alexander, W. (1981). Film on the left: American documentary film from 1931 to 1942. Princeton, NJ: Princeton University Press.

Applebome, P. (1999, July 13). The stopwatch keeps ticking in a squabble over ego and truth; Film drama shines a harsh light on *60 Minutes* and CBS. *The New York Times*, E1.

Barthes, R. (1977). *Image-Music-Text*. (Stephen Heath, Trans.). New York: Hill and Wang.

Barthes, R. (1972). *Mythologies*. New York: Hill and Wang.

Bluem, A. W. (1975). Documentary in American television: Form, function, method. New York: Hastings House.

Campbell, R. (1987). Securing the middle ground: Reporter formulas in *60 Minutes*. *Critical Studies in Mass Communication* 4(4), 325-350.

Campbell, R. (1991). *60 Minutes and the news*. Urbana: University of Illinois Press.

Campbell, R. (1993, September/October). Don Hewitt's durable hour. *Columbia Journalism Review, 32*, 25-28.

Coffey, F. (1993, October 31–November 6). Inside *60 Minutes. TV Guide*, 18–26.

Epstein, E. J. (1975). *Between fact and fiction*. New York: Vantage Books.

Glaberson, W. (1995, November 17). *60 Minutes* case part of a trend of corporate pressure, some analysts say. *The New York Times*, B14.

Kurtz, H. (1995a, November 10). *60 Minutes* kills piece on tobacco industry; CBS fears lawsuit, cites ABC settlement. *The Washington Post*, A03.

Kurtz, H. (1995b, August 23). Long-term effect of ABC settlement concerns critics. *The Washington Post*, A04.

Hewitt, D. (1985). *Minute by minute.* New York: Random House.

Himmelstein, H. (1994). Television news and the television documentary. In *Television myth and the American mind*. (2nd ed., pp. 247–286). Westport, CT: Praeger.

Horton, D. and Wohl, R. R. (1956). Mass communication and para-social interaction. *Psychiatry 19,* 210–221.

Lewis, A. (1994, January 14). The politics of nativism. [Op ed page]. *The New York Times*, A26.

Mann, M. (1999). *The Insider.*

Meyrowitz, J. (1986). Television and interpersonal behavior: codes of reception and response. In G. Gumpert & R. Cathcart (Eds.), *Intermedia: Interpersonal communication in a media world* (pp. 253–272). New York: Oxford University Press.

Said, E. (1979). *Orientalism*. New York: Vintage Books.

Shilts, R. (1987). *And the band played on: Politics, people, and the AIDS epidemic.* New York: St. Martin's Press.

Stam, R. (1983). Television news and its spectators. In E. Ann Kaplan (Ed.), *Regarding television* (pp. 23–43). University Publications of America.

Stern, M. (1990). Making culture into nature. In A. Kuhn (Ed.), *Alien Zone.* (pp. 66–72). London: Verso.

Wasserman, A. (1980). Interview. In Rosenthal, A. (Ed.) *The documentary conscience: A casebook in film making* (pp. 90–103). Berkeley: University of California Press.

Wright, P. (1985). *On Living in an Old Country*. London: Verso.